THE ROLES OF PUBLIC OPINION RESEARCH IN CANADIAN GOVERNMENT

It is a common assumption that governments use public opinion research primarily to help them make decisions about major policy issues. However, how valid is this assumption? In *The Roles of Public Opinion Research in Canadian Government*, Christopher Page presents a major scholarly investigation into the uses and effectiveness of polls and focus groups.

Focusing on public opinion on policy rather than on public support for political parties, Page explores the relationships between government officials and pollsters, and the contributions of public opinion research to the policy process. Three high-profile policies are considered in depth: the patriation of the Constitution and the establishment of the Charter of Rights and Freedoms by the Trudeau government, the introduction of the Goods and Services Tax by the Mulroney government, and the controversial strengthening of gun control by the Chrétien government.

The Roles of Public Opinion Research in Canadian Government demonstrates that opinion research has a greater variety of roles than is often recognized, and that, despite conventional wisdom, its foremost impact is to help governments determine how to communicate with citizens. It is an essential contribution to the study of Canadian politics, filling a major gap in the scholarship.

CHRISTOPHER PAGE is an instructor in the Department of Political Science at Carleton University.

IPAC — The Institute of Public Administration of Canada

IAPC — L'Institut d'administration publique du Canada

The Institute of Public Administration of Canada Series in Public Management and Governance

Editor: Donald Savoie

This series is sponsored by the Institute of Public Administration of Canada as part of its commitment to encourage research on issues in Canadian public administration, public sector management, and public policy. It also seeks to foster wider knowledge and understanding among practitioners, academics, and the general public.

Networks of Knowledge: Collaborative Innovation in International Learning, Janice Stein, Richard Stren, Joy Fitzgibbon, and Melissa Maclean

The National Research Council in the Innovative Policy Era: Changing Hierarchies, Networks, and Markets, G. Bruce Doern and Richard Levesque

Beyond Service: State Workers, Public Policy, and the Prospects for Democratic Administration, Greg McElligott

A Law unto Itself: How the Ontario Municipal Board Has Developed and Applied Land Use Planning Policy, John G. Chipman

Health Care, Entitlement, and Citizenship, Candace Redden

Between Colliding Worlds: The Ambiguous Existence of Government Agencies for Aboriginal and Women's Policy, Jonathan Malloy

The Politics of Public Management: The HRDC Audit of Grants and Contributions, David A. Good

Dream No Little Dreams: A Biography of the Douglas Government of Saskatchewan, 1944–1961, Albert W. Johnson

Governing Education, Ben Levin

Executive Styles in Canada: Cabinet Structures and Leadership Practices in Canadian Government, edited by Luc Bernier, Keith Brownsey, and Michael Howlett

The Roles of Public Opinion Research in Canadian Government, Christopher Page

CHRISTOPHER PAGE

The Roles of Public Opinion Research in Canadian Government

IPAC
The Institute of
Public Administration of Canada

IAPC
L'Institut d'administration
publique du Canada

UNIVERSITY OF TORONTO PRESS
Toronto Buffalo London

© University of Toronto Press Incorporated 2006
Toronto Buffalo London
Printed in Canada

ISBN-13: 978-0-8020-9039-3 (cloth)
ISBN-10: 0-8020-9039-7 (cloth)

ISBN-13: 978-8020-9377-6 (paper)
ISBN-10: 0-8020-9377-9 (paper)

Printed on acid-free paper

Library and Archives Canada Cataloguing in Publication

Page, Christopher, 1963–
  Roles of public opinion research in Canadian government /
  Christopher Page.

  ISBN-13: 978-0-8020-9039-3 (bound)
  ISBN-10: 0-8020-9039-7 (bound)
  ISBN-13: 978-0-8020-9377-6 (pbk.)
  ISBN-10: 0-8020-9377-9 (pbk.)

  1. Political planning – Canada.   2. Public opinion – Canada.   3. Federal
  government – Canada – Public opinion.   4. Canada – Politics and
  government.   I. Title.

  JL86.P64P33 2006   320.6'0971   C2005-906420-X

University of Toronto Press acknowledges the financial assistance to
its publishing program of the Canada Council for the Arts and the
Ontario Arts Council.

University of Toronto Press acknowledges the financial support for
its publishing activities of the Government of Canada through the
Book Publishing Industry Development Program (BPIDP).

Contents

Acknowledgments   vii

Introduction   3

1 Public Opinion and Polling   10

2 Public Opinion and Policy-making   19

3 The Practice and Framework of Opinion Research for
   Government in Canada   34

4 An Overview of the Uses of Opinion Research in the
   Policy Process   53

5 Opinion Research and Government Communications   66

6 Opinion Research and Constitutional Renewal, 1980–1   80

7 Opinion Research and the Goods and Services Tax   104

8 Opinion Research and Gun Control   131

9 Constraints on the Use of Opinion Research in Government   159

10 Conclusion   184

Appendix 1 Federal Government Poll on the Constitution   197
Appendices 2.1–2.4 Polling on the Goods and Services Tax   200
Appendices 3.1–3.2 Polling on Gun Control   204
Appendix 4 Selected Interview Sources   207
Notes   211
Index   249

Acknowledgments

This study began as a doctoral dissertation at Queen's University, supported in part by funding from Queen's University and the Ontario Graduate Scholarship program. I am very grateful to the Institute of Public Administration of Canada for its financial sponsorship of the book and to Donald Savoie as editor of the IPAC series. I would also like to express thanks to the staff at the University of Toronto Press, particularly Virgil Duff for his initial interest in the project and his advice and support as it progressed.

I wrote the thesis under the supervision of George Perlin. It benefited a great deal from his guidance and, more generally, I very much appreciated his ability to get to the heart of what is interesting and important in political science. During the course of the research and writing of the thesis and the manuscript, I received advice, comments, or assistance from many people, including Keith Banting, C.E.S. Franks, Kevin Gaudet, Richard Jenkins, Lawrence LeDuc, Allan McCutcheon, John McLean, Matthew Mendelsohn, Helen Moroz, Tom O'Donnell, Daniel Robinson, Jonathan Rose, Filippo Sabetti, and Linda White. Additionally, the anonymous reviewers for the University of Toronto Press made thoughtful observations on the manuscript. Of course, I remain responsible for any errors or omissions.

The study could not have been completed without the cooperation and assistance of ninety-five current and former politicians, political aides, journalists, public servants, and pollsters, who generously shared insights and information with me in interviews. Several provided me with printed information or participated in follow-up interviews. While many of them must remain anonymous, a partial list of interviewees appears in Appendix 4. As well, I would like to thank the staff of the

National Archives of Canada for helping me obtain access to records of the Canadian Unity Information Office, and staff at the Department of Finance who supplied useful documents. I also appreciate the help of Lynn Austin, who prepared the index, and Bob Burge, of the Queen's University Centre for the Study of Democracy, who kindly provided me with access to public opinion data (from what is now called the Canadian Opinion Research Archive).

Finally, thanks are due to Michelle Gouchie for her companionship and her ongoing assistance and support with the project. This book is dedicated to her.

THE ROLES OF PUBLIC OPINION RESEARCH IN
CANADIAN GOVERNMENT

Introduction

After Iain Angus learned in 1992 that Brian Mulroney's federal government had spent $700,000 on public opinion polls to find out what Canadians thought about the First Gulf War, he called this use of taxpayers' money 'obscene.' The New Democrat member of Parliament went on to charge that 'decisions to send Canadian men and women to war should not be made on the basis of polls.'[1] Angus implied that the polling influenced the government's policy, but this was simply an assumption with little evidence to justify it.

Public opinion polling has become an entrenched feature of modern politics. Even casual consumers of the news regularly encounter snapshots of citizens' attitudes on the issues of the day. Indeed, although the results were not reported, the polling on the Gulf War made it onto the front page of the *Globe and Mail*. Less visibly, political parties and interest groups employ polling to help guide their activities and strategies. Governments, too, commission polls – such as the ones that provoked Iain Angus.

While the role of polls in election campaigns is fairly well understood, journalists and political scientists know far less about what government officials do with the results and how they play a role in the policy-making process. Observers frequently assume that if elected officials and public servants are consulting polls, the information must be helping to guide decisions about policy: polling informs politicians about citizens' preferences and can therefore help them design popular policies. However, no matter who is making the claim – a journalist, a pollster, a political scientist, a politician of any stripe, or someone else – it is rare to see the subject examined systematically.

In recent years, Canada's federal government has spent over

$20 million annually on public opinion research. This is enough to purchase more than five hundred polls and focus group studies (each of these consists of a series of moderated small-group discussions). The research illuminates Canadians' opinions on major issues as varied as defence, national unity, taxes, gun control, the environment, language rights, and immigration. On top of this research, government officials learn about what citizens are thinking from polls sponsored by parties and interest groups, and they monitor polling that appears in the mass media as well as syndicated reports produced by polling firms.

All this opinion research is important in its own right for informing governments about the public's views. It is also important because it relates to a fundamental question about democracy: what sort of connection exists between the preferences of citizens and the decisions made by governments?[2] Many people believe that decisions by a democratic government should take into account the wishes of the public, although few outside the polling business actually advocate politicians using polls for this purpose. Several political scientists have investigated how closely public opinion and government policy are linked, and while there is no consensus, they have produced some evidence of a modest relationship. The explanations for this, however, remain uncertain. For example, it is quite possible that interest groups, or informal contacts between citizens and government officials, cause governments to act in a way that is consistent with public opinion. Polling has the potential to make governments more responsive to citizens' wishes; however, it is much less clear that this actually occurs in practice.

Early advocates of opinion research anticipated that polling could promote 'government by the people' – that is, increased responsiveness to citizens.[3] Some modern pollsters agree that polling can be used in this way.[4] This book looks beyond these hopes and expectations to consider how polling and focus groups are actually used in government. Examining Canada's federal government, I argue that while opinion research sometimes promotes responsiveness, it actually has greater influence on other aspects of policy-making such as agenda-setting, and its foremost use is to help governments communicate with citizens to promote support, understanding, compliance, and legitimacy.

Not only is this significant because it casts light on a neglected topic and suggests that polling contributes less to a relationship between policy and opinion than is often assumed, but this book also covers relatively uncharted territory in other respects. While most research on public opinion polling focuses exclusively on the United States, this book is about Canada. Moreover, it pulls back the curtain that often shrouds the policy process, and specifically it recognizes the importance of government communication with citizens. As well, while most authors who look at opinion research stress polling, this book recognizes that focus groups also assume a prominent role in providing information about public opinion. Finally, the existing literature emphasizes politicians; this book also explores how unelected public servants use opinion research.

Communication in Government

Most descriptions and models of policy-making stress the processes of determining and executing policy, and they acknowledge external influences on governments such as interest groups, as well as the roles of the cabinet ministers and public servants. However, they commonly neglect the communication of policies by governments.

On occasion, officials cite polls publicly to demonstrate that citizens support their policies. Much more frequently, opinion research is used to inform governments' communications strategy and tactics, which often resemble the marketing of products and services to consumers.

Communication with the public can occur throughout the process of policy-making, and for some policies it may be ongoing. Although it is rarely stated explicitly, many criticisms of opinion research reflect concerns about their contribution to the communication of policy. As Irving Crespi explains, 'one of the most important applications of polls has not been to find out what the public thinks in order to serve it better but, instead, to win elections and to influence public thinking on important issues.'[5] Although the fears may be excessive, some critics of polling even use terms such as 'manipulation' in this context.[6]

Governments communicate with the public in many ways, including speeches, media interviews, news releases, brochures, advertising, and internet sites. This often takes place as part of an effort to mobilize public support for – or contain opposition to – a policy before, during, or after its adoption. This can be quite systematic and deliberate. For example, focus groups conducted by consultant Stan Greenberg influenced President Bill Clinton's public speeches in 1993–4. Rival pollster Frank Luntz said, 'Greenberg literally pulls the words out of the mouths of ordinary Americans and puts them in the mouth of the president. The result is Clinton speaks like real Americans speak.'[7]

Examining Government Polling

When trying to understand the roles of opinion research in government, there is a shortage of literature, a problem which is especially acute in Canada. While newspaper reports were of some value, it was necessary for this study to rely mainly on primary sources. First, printed reports of opinion research for government provided some useful information. Second, archival records helped to illustrate how the federal government used focus groups and polling in 1980 and 1981. Third, and most importantly, I interviewed ninety-five current and former pollsters, journalists, public servants, politicians, and partisan officials with experience in government.[8] Where the term 'officials' is used, it includes politicians, political aides, and public servants who served in government during at least part of the period under consideration.[9]

The Case Studies

Case studies aid in understanding the role of public opinion in the policy process because they can show how officials use opinion research and suggest what sort of causal relationship might exist between public opinion and public policy.[10] The cases examined here are the patriation of the constitution and the introduction of the Charter of Rights and Freedoms by the Trudeau government in the early 1980s; the establishment of the Goods and Services Tax (GST) by the Mulroney government in the late 1980s and early 1990s; and the strengthening of gun control by the Chrétien government in the 1990s.

These issues each have origins in the 1930s or earlier; have featured conflicts between the federal and provincial governments; have inspired intense, emotional expressions of opinion; and have possessed continued relevance after the decisions and time periods examined here. With the legitimacy of government actions at issue in each case, they caused potential or actual stresses on the political system.

Patriation capped a series of attempts to end formal British control of Canada's constitution. The first ministers' deal that achieved patriation also established the Charter of Rights and Freedoms, which expanded the role of courts in governing and thereby substantially affected a wide range of policies, with decisions that reflected and nourished controversies on issues such as abortion, gay and lesbian rights, euthanasia, and language law. The agreement on patriation and the Charter did not receive assent from the Quebec government, so it stirred sovereigntist sentiments, and subsequently fuelled two controversial and unsuccessful attempts to amend the constitution – the Meech Lake and Charlottetown Accords. The latter was the subject of a national referendum in 1992, and the Reform Party's opposition contributed to its successes in the 1993 election. Under the Liberals, the federal government continued to make national unity a priority, particularly in the aftermath of the referendum Quebec held on sovereignty in 1995.

Efforts to replace the old Manufacturers' Sales Tax with a more efficient alternative also had a long history, starting by 1927. Motivations behind the GST connect to two leading contemporary concerns: globalization and its implications for Canadian competitiveness, and the need for government revenue in the context of increasing anxiety about the country's deficit and debt. The profile of tax issues rose in the 1980s and they have continued to attract attention; the GST, which took effect in 1991, was extremely unpopular with the public and helped to bring down the Conservatives in the 1993 election, and the Liberal government of Jean Chrétien was haunted afterwards by its campaign promise to kill the tax. Indeed, a senior cabinet minister, Sheila Copps, had to resign her seat and contest a by-election because the government failed to find a satisfactory way of keeping its election promise. Ultimately an agreement was reached with three Atlantic provinces to harmonize the GST with provincial sales taxes, and attempts to extend this arrangement to other provinces may be seen in the future.

Attempts to control firearms also stretch back a long time, and the Liberals' bill of 1995 was partly a response to Canadians' growing fears about violent crime. Implementation of gun control has proven extremely difficult and controversial. Target dates for licensing and registration requirements to commence were postponed several times. Moreover, the policy has attracted almost continuous criticisms of the principle and the process. Opponents have complained about the spiralling costs – highlighted by the auditor general's annual report in 2002 – and some gun users refused to comply with the new regulations.

In many ways, these three cases are diverse. They cover three different governments, and they include a symbolic issue, an economic issue, and a 'social issue.' They therefore enable us to examine different roles of public opinion. In constitutional politics, public support for government proposals increases their legitimacy, and this in turn can affect negotiations between federal and provincial governments when they seek to reach agreements. The GST case represents an example of government acting decisively in the face of hostile public opinion, which contrasts with much conventional wisdom. It also illustrates the potential contribution of opinion research to policy details. Finally, with firearms control, polling showed that the vigorous opposition to the policy from gun users' groups was at odds with the less strongly held but supportive views of the majority of the public. This evidence of the popularity of gun control did not affect the government's decision to strengthen firearms control but opinion research played several roles after the policy was in place.

The impact of public opinion is likely to be greatest on high-profile issues.[11] This is because politicians are more likely to respond to public opinion if they believe people are paying attention, and because it may affect their government's popularity and therefore electoral prospects. All three of these issues were salient enough for public opinion to potentially affect decisions. Yet, in each case, opinion research played a greater role after governments had committed themselves to a position, particularly contributing to communications strategy and tactics.

Looking Ahead

The book is divided into ten chapters. Chapter 1 examines the concept of public opinion from a variety of angles and describes its measurement through polling and focus groups. Chapter 2 discusses what existing sources reveal about opinion research and policy-making in Canada and the United States. This includes exploring the extent to which governments' policies are consistent with public opinion and the role of polling in the Clinton presidency.

The next three chapters consider the impact of opinion research on the policy process in Canada, especially the effects of the research on the content and the communication of policy. Accordingly, chapter 3 describes and analyses the framework and practice of government opinion research, examining the sources of opinion research and the work that is conducted for government, as well as asking which personnel and departments are most involved. Chapter 4 identifies the roles opinion research assume at different stages of the policy process: agenda-setting, the development of policy options, the selection of policy, implementation, and evaluation. Chapter 5 systematically explores how the research contributes to the communication of policy.

To investigate these topics in detail, chapters 6 to 8 present case studies on the renewal of the constitution, the development of the GST, and the strengthening of gun control. These chapters look in detail at

how governments used opinion research as they developed and implemented their policies. Following the case studies, chapter 9 explores
some factors affecting how opinion research is used in government.
These include pollsters' challenges dealing with issues such as questionnaire design, the characteristics of public opinion, the effects of
Access to Information law, and decisions about sampling. This and the
concluding chapter help to explain why the foremost impact of opinion
research in government is not on the content of policy but on how it is
communicated to citizens. The conclusion also briefly considers how
the uses of polling and focus groups affect the health and performance
of governments.

1 Public Opinion and Polling

The Potential for Using Opinion Polls in Governing

Ever since scientific opinion polling was launched in the 1930s, observers have believed that this mechanism for learning about the public's attitudes could transform representative democracy. Troubled by the unrepresentativeness of interest groups and the limitations of elections as expressions of public preferences, and with a confidence in the basic wisdom of citizens, the early pollster George Gallup viewed polls as 'sampling referendums' that would inform politicians about public attitudes and make their decisions about public policy more responsive to the opinions of Americans. In *The Pulse of Democracy*, published in 1940, Gallup and Saul Rae enthusiastically described polling as 'a new instrument which may help to bridge the gap between the people and those who are responsible for making decisions in their name.'[1] They anticipated that elected officials, rather than public servants, would refer to polling results that appeared in the media, and that this would influence their decisions. Gallup and Rae's book failed to consider the prospect that governments would commission their own research. Other early pollsters shared their hopes about the potential of polling. For instance, Archibald Crossley wrote: 'Scientific polling makes it possible within two or three days at moderate expense for the entire nation to work hand-in-hand with its legislative representatives, on laws which affect our daily lives. Here is the long-sought key to "Government *by* the people."'[2] While Gallup directed most of his attention to the United States, he and others believed that opinion research could also promote responsiveness in Canada.[3]

It is clear why polling was expected to contribute to responsiveness:

it informs leaders about citizens' preferences on policy issues, and elected officials generally prefer to take actions that are popular with those they represent. As John Brehm remarks, 'political folklore' often suggests 'politicians whipsawing to whatever trend emerges from poll results,' although he wisely remarks that reality is more complicated.[4] American political scientists who address the topic often stay close to the folklore. For example, exploratory works by John Geer and Benjamin Ginsberg assert, but do not demonstrate, that elected officials use polls to help determine the content of their policies.[5]

Canadian political scientists make similar assumptions about polling and decisions about policies. For instance, during a five-page discussion of opinion polls – which turns out to be one of the most thorough treatments of public opinion in any Canadian politics textbook – Rand Dyck claims that contemporary governments seem 'reluctant to make any decision until it can be based on a poll.' He acknowledges, however, that polls do not always provide clear guidance and that governments sometimes act contrary to public opinion.[6] Ian Greene and his colleagues express a comparable perspective in a volume on courts: 'Elected members do not have the luxury of straying very far from public opinion polls, even if they would like to, because of the simple truth that politicians generally want to get reelected.'[7] In the same vein, Arthur Siegel notes that the federal government initiated an average of sixteen polls each month in the early 1990s and comments that 'the proliferation of polling as an instrument for devising government policy raises questions about the nature of Canada's leadership.'[8] Siegel assumes that government-commissioned polling helps determine the substance of policy without considering other roles it could play in the policy process.

Journalists join political scientists in their perception that polling guides decisions governments make about policy. For instance, Jeffrey Simpson complains that 'pollsters have actually made many politicians the prisoners of public opinion,'[9] and Claire Hoy objects that polls 'dictate ... exactly which course to steer, not necessarily because it's the right one, or even the best one, but because more poll respondents picked that course as their favourite.'[10] An even more telling example is Robert Lewis's assertion in 1980 that 'through bouts of temporary paralysis or chronic stumbling, Liberals routinely turn to ... Martin Goldfarb or Gallup of Toronto to lead the way ahead. Surveys have figured in every major Trudeau decision, from price and wage controls and abolition of capital punishment to the defeat of the Crosbie budget and Trudeau's renunciation of his retirement vows in 1979.'[11] Although the journalists are typically more critical than political scientists, they are no more likely to offer evidence to support their claims.

While the perception that opinion research affects policy-making is widespread, there are conflicting views about whether this is desirable. The use of polls in government attracts praise at times, but more often faces criticism.

The case for using polling in policy-making has a populist ring. Proponents of polls view them as meaningful measures of public opinion, and they generally favour government consultation, responsiveness to citizens' preferences, and delegate notions of representation.[12] For pollster Michael Adams, public opinion should figure in decision-making and polls provide suitable information.[13] Although Martin Goldfarb, another pollster, believes polling complicates politicians' jobs by revealing conflicts between their instincts and public opinion, he insists that it helps them 'make wise decisions.'[14] Adams and Goldfarb implicitly echo Gallup, and a recent book by Frank Newport, the editor-in-chief for the Gallup Poll in the United States, explicitly presents an argument which the pioneer pollster would have applauded.[15]

Opponents of using polls in policy-making see matters quite differently. They are often sceptical about the ability of citizens to form meaningful opinions, and they argue that polls measure those opinions poorly and undermine the capacity of elected representatives to act as trustees.[16] This perspective is reflected in Jeffrey Simpson's judgment that many officials have become 'prisoners of public opinion.' Even more extreme is this assertion from Stephen Quilliam: 'As they are currently used by government agencies and politicians, polls remove any principle, direction or philosophy required to guide a country.'[17]

A similar argument is developed by Larry Sabato, who contends that polls exert a powerful but dangerous effect on modern politics. The process starts with election campaigns, in which candidates can become 'slaves to polls'; then, once elected, they continue to behave the same way. Sabato also claims that politicians acted more courageously in the years before polling, contending that, 'As a sad consequence [of poll-induced caution], the trustee officeholder may be nearing extinction, while the pure delegate – little more than a humanoid Qube system – multiplies and flourishes.'[18] His comments illustrate that the perception that polls turn politicians into delegates is not simply the romantic dream of early pollsters.

While the majority of observers stress the influence of public opinion on policy-makers' decisions, a minority criticize opinion research for the opposite reason: they believe that policy-makers use it to shape or lead public opinion. Led by Benjamin Ginsberg,[19] these critics argue that polls have not, overall, promoted responsiveness. On the contrary, they believe that polls help governments 'regulate' public opinion. They provide political leaders with information which they use to lead or even manipulate public opinion, and to guide the presentation of policies in a way that will promote their legitimacy and acceptance by the public.[20] This sceptical perspective signals that opinion research can affect the ways governments communicate with the public in order to promote their policies and programs.

The view that polling substantially influences what governments do is widespread, although there is disagreement about how it does this. While Gallup and Rae and some contemporary pollsters think opinion research increases governments' responsiveness, other authors agree about the effect but view this as undesirable. Still others believe that polls serve as a tool politicians use to lead and manipulate the public.

The Importance of Public Support in a Political System

We can step away temporarily from this discussion of polls to consider how David Easton's analysis of political systems helps to establish a general context for this book. Easton explores how a political system deals with stresses from the political 'environment' that affect its existence or ability to make authoritative decisions. He describes how a political system's inputs and outputs are connected in a 'feedback loop' within which government officials make policy decisions, citizens respond with demands and support, their reactions are transmitted to the officials, and in turn the officials respond by altering their policies.[21] A political system must distribute values and resources and 'induce most members to accept these allocations as binding.' As well, it seeks to protect itself from stresses that might weaken its legitimacy.[22] Applying Easton's framework, Richard Johnston investigates the significance of public support for the Canadian government and political system at a highly general level. While Johnston does not focus on governments' responsiveness to the public's preferences on specific policies or the uses of opinion polling by governments, he concludes that public support is important for the health of the political system but more dependent on the actions of political leaders than Easton suggests.[23] Easton and Johnston both highlight the importance of public support – understood broadly as support for the regime – as a consideration in explaining actions of governments. Specific government actions, if sufficiently unpopular, have the potential to undermine this support.

The specific input examined in this book is public opinion as expressed through polls and focus groups, and the relevant outputs are communications and policy-making activities by governments (we look at how opinion research may affect different phases in the policy-making process that leads to decisions). Although citizens are sometimes asked for responses prior to governments producing outputs, the specific responses of the public are measured most thoroughly by opinion research studies, which are often initiated by government officials.

Public opinion research assumes two roles in the feedback loop. First, as a mechanism for expressing what Easton called demands and support, it can inform government officials about citizens' opinions and reactions to policies and thereby influence decisions about how resources are allocated.[24] That is, opinion research can help governments make popular decisions, or avoid unpopular decisions, or adjust policies, and these actions would contribute to ensuring and maintaining their legitimacy. Second, opinion research can help to guide activities by governments which aim to promote the acceptance and legitimacy of their policies. While Easton is more interested in how governments adjust policies in response to feedback from society, this book also addresses the more significant impact of opinion research: how governments communicate with citizens to try to affect what they think, without necessarily taking substantive actions to alter policies. If successful, these efforts can maintain and build public support for a government and its policies.

Two Forms of Public Opinion

While the concept of public opinion is typically linked to opinion polls, there are many definitions. One reasonable definition is 'the opinions that government officials take into account when making policy.'[25] For V.O. Key, this means that the influence of public opinion is primarily felt through 'opinion dikes,' which establish boundaries separating a broad range of acceptable policies from alternatives which are unacceptable to a large proportion of the population. Governments have substantial discretion to act within these dikes.[26] In another view, held by Robert Erikson and his colleagues, governments often react more directly to the public's overall 'mood,' which can lean towards either liberalism or conservatism.[27] Still others claim, as we saw earlier in this chapter, that government officials determine many of their policies in response to the preferences of the public on specific issues.

In any case, these opinions are not exclusively expressed through polls. In fact, much consideration of public opinion is *not* restricted to polling, or 'passive' expressions of public opinion. Rather, it also deals with voluntary, or 'active' signals of opinion, as gauged through means such as activities of interest groups, petitions, the mass media (including phone-in radio and television programs and letters published in newspapers), contacts at public meetings, and letters, e-mail messages, and telephone calls to government officials. These involve behaviour rather than merely expressions of attitudes. The distinction between active and passive public opinion is significant for an examination of the roles of polling in government.[28]

Active expressions of opinion come from people who take the initiative to express their views. They are comparatively well-informed, engaged in political issues, and tend to have above-average levels of education and income. Moreover, incentives to organize and express opinion actively vary widely. Generally they are strongest for narrow, intense interests rather than those with more diffuse and mildly-held support. Consequently, on most issues, the citizens who register their opinions in this way comprise a small minority of the general population and their attitudes do not necessarily reflect the public as a whole. Despite this, however, politicians frequently pay more attention to active expressions of opinion than they do to polls. This is partly because these opinions are more 'vivid and emotion laden' than opinion polls, and they tend to be better remembered and therefore may influence the political calculations of decision-makers.[29] In addition, strongly held opinions are more likely to be decisive in citizens' voting decisions.

Polling, in contrast to active expressions of opinion, measures 'passive' public opinion. Because they seek to obtain representative samples of the population, most polls, in principle, give every adult citizen an equal chance of being interviewed and count all their preferences equally, rather than according greater weight to active expressions of opinion. This point, which is central to Gallup and Rae's democratic claims for polling, means that people who lack strong opinions are included in a way that they are not, say, if elected officials rely on active public opinion. As Ian McKinnon, a former pollster, points out, 'No one ... writes a letter to their member of Parliament to say "I'm deeply torn by the issue of abortion."' But polls include people who hold ambivalent views and others without strongly-held opinions, and this representativeness supports the claim that polling can serve as a sampling referendum. In fact, some observers believe the representative character of polls is a reason why officials should pay more attention to them than other expressions of public attitudes.[30] In addition, passive public opinion differs from active forms because it measures immediate responses to pollsters' questions, without the filtering or refining that takes place during public debate.

How public opinion is understood is important because the extent and nature of a government's responsiveness are central for democracy. J. Roland Pennock argues that 'a democratic government should respond to, reflect and give expression to, the will of the people. How else can democracy ... be "rule by the people?"'[31] However, he identifies several difficulties in applying this. The concept of 'the will of the people' is imprecise, and often it is divided, in favour of conflicting policy proposals, prone to change, or hard to determine.

A further problem concerns the intensity of citizens' preferences: 'how should it [a responsive government] respond to a situation in which 35 percent of the electorate strongly favor a certain proposal, 55 percent mildly oppose it, and the remaining 10 percent are indifferent?'[32] Gallup and Rae, along with other proponents of polling, think responsiveness means that governments act in accordance with the views of the majority, with all adult citizens' views weighted equally, and they believe polling can promote this. Ginsberg, however, believes that intensity of opinion – expressions of active public opinion – should receive priority, and this partly explains why he is critical of polling. No easy resolution of this question is possible.

In any case, the fact that polling is conducted for governments does not prove that it affects the content of their policies. Active public opinion appears at several points in this book, but the primary interest is passive public opinion, gauged through polls and focus groups.

Measuring Passive Public Opinion: Polls and Focus Groups

'Scientific' polls, often referred to as quantitative research, are the most visible form of opinion research, measuring behaviour, knowledge, and attitudes. They are conducted using questionnaires which are drafted by researchers with input from their clients. Some cover a specific topic for a single client and others investigate multiple topics for several clients in an omnibus survey. Most questionnaires take roughly twenty to thirty minutes to complete.

National polls in Canada typically involve telephone interviews with one thousand to fifteen hundred respondents. Lay people often wonder how interviews with a tiny fraction of the population can produce results that reflect an entire country. Useful analogies that justify the practice are that a spoonful of soup is considered representative of the whole pot and a blood test relies on a sample of just a few drops.[33] What is crucial is that, in general, pollsters try to ensure that each person in the population has an equal chance of being interviewed. If the respondents are chosen randomly or near-randomly, samples of eight hundred to twelve hundred produce a margin of error of roughly 3 per cent, nineteen times out of twenty.[34] This is adequately representative of a population for practical purposes, although users sometimes generalize carelessly about sub-samples such as age groups or residents of a specific region.

Probably the most significant change in opinion research in the past two decades has been the growing use of mechanisms other than sample surveys. Indeed, a pollster comments that qualitative research is now almost as important as quantitative research.[35] In 2002–3, 50 per cent of the federal government's opinion research projects were quantitative, while 38 per cent were qualitative, and the remainder were mixed.[36]

These might involve a small number of in-person interviews, or asking participants to watch a videotape and adjust a dial to indicate their reactions, but by far the most prominent kind of qualitative research is focus groups. In this case, researchers recruit a series of groups of about eight to twelve people each, usually paying them to participate. Typically, these groups are established in a minimum of two and a maximum of six different communities, and federal government contracts normally include separate groups of English- and French-speakers. Researchers frequently select participants according to their attitudes or demographic characteristics. A moderator leads an open-ended discussion and probes opinions and attitudes for about two hours. Researchers and clients can observe the proceedings from behind one-way glass.

Because focus groups' samples are small and unrepresentative, the findings do not readily allow generalizations and do not resemble referendum results, as polls arguably do. They therefore are more difficult to interpret than polling and lack its democratic potential.

Despite their problems, focus groups possess several advantages. They are faster and cheaper to conduct than polls. More importantly, proponents of focus groups believe that they allow attitudes to be examined in greater depth than in conventional surveys, and in a more flexible fashion. This applies particularly when researchers wish to generate or explore ideas which may be employed to communicate policy and to help develop questionnaires for quantitative research. Focus groups help to identify salient issues, show how citizens conceptualize them, and suggest what connections they see between them,[37] rather than simply how they respond to questions written by a polling firm.

While quantitative research helps to describe public opinion, qualitative research helps explain opinions or anticipate how they might change.[38] As a pollster explains, 'quantitative research is very good at answering the question "what?," while qualitative research is very good at answering the question "why?"'[39] Also, unlike polls conducted by telephone, participants in focus groups can view materials such as videotapes and drafts of forms, brochures, advertisements, and health warnings on cigarette packages.

Focus groups are not easily characterized as either active or passive public opinion. They resemble active public opinion in that participants are often screened and therefore not representative of the public as a whole. However, they are predominantly passive because the participants are not self-selected and often they are not more knowledgeable or engaged in an issue than other citizens. It follows that focus groups should be considered a modified form of passive public opinion.

Whatever the drawbacks and merits of focus groups, they are widely used. While polls with representative samples are most important to this study, and were the tool that inspired Gallup's democratic ideas, it is also necessary to consider focus groups; quantitative and qualitative research are so intertwined, and so often used in conjunction on the same policy area or research project, that it is difficult to discuss one with a pollster for long without talking about the other. In this book, therefore, the term opinion research normally refers to both polls and focus groups.

This chapter has explored some ideas about public opinion, connections between citizens' attitudes and the state, and the measurement of opinion. From here we can turn in the next chapter to a closer examination of the relationship between public opinion and public policy.

2 Public Opinion and Policy-making

Implications of the Relationship between Public Opinion and Public Policy

What is known and understood about the relationship between public opinion and public policy? Joel Brooks outlines three competing models to describe this relationship in liberal democratic countries such as the United States and Canada.[1] The first, 'democratic linkage,' sees public opinion as relatively immune from elite leadership and as a significant influence on public policy. This model is closest to the implicit or explicit assumptions of most North American political scientists.[2] Consistent with this, Robert A. Bernstein argues that the view that citizens shape the behaviour of their elected representatives is widespread in the literature on the American Congress 'because democrats desperately want the myth to be true.'[3] The second model, 'democratic frustration,' suggests that public opinion is frequently at odds with public policy.[4] The state is viewed as relatively autonomous from society. The third model, 'counterfeit consensus,' like democratic linkage, holds that opinion and policy are correlated, but explains that this is the result of elite manipulation and agenda-setting. In this view, public opinion is not autonomous; rather, elites lead, shape, and perhaps manipulate it.[5]

Although Brooks assigns various authors to the categories, it is useful to think of each of his models partially applying to a political system, with variation according to the time and issue. Brooks does not specifically mention the impact of polling, but his concepts can be easily adapted. Democratic linkage should result if politicians use polls as early pollsters anticipated. The democratic frustration model applies when opinion and policy are inconsistent, implying that polls have little influence. The counterfeit consensus model reminds us that causality in the opinion-policy relationship is a complex matter, and it is consistent with governments using polling for communicating with and influencing the public. While democratic linkage may have the largest following, there is no consensus in political science about which model is most accurate in the United States or elsewhere.

Most sources on public opinion refer to surveys, but they do so to analyse aspects of public opinion rather than the effects of polls in the political arena. This is true of American research and also of the less extensive Canadian literature. Those academic sources which explicitly address the roles of opinion research are primarily concerned with polls in news stories (mainly horse-race polls gauging support for parties and leaders), or strategy and tactics in election campaigns.[6] Similarly, the published work of pollsters analyses data far more often than it explains how they are used in the political arena.[7] This leaves three groups of sources which are worth examining in order to come to grips with the existing state of knowledge about the impact of opinion research on policy. The first group employs quantitative approaches to investigate the nature and extent of consistency between public opinion and public policy, the second sheds light on the uses of polls by American presidents, and the third consists of academic and journalistic sources that provide scattered pieces of evidence about governments' issues of polling in Canada.

Are Public Policies Consistent with Public Opinion?

The study of opinion-policy relationships at the level of nationwide policy seems to offer some help in examining some questions that are important for understanding how representative democracy works, and in particular the role of polling. How closely are governments' policies consistent with the attitudes of the public? Whether or not they are consistent, what factors might explain the connection? And what contribution, if any, does polling make? The literature examined in this section uses opinion research for analysis rather than directly exploring its impact on the policy process, and most of it focuses on the United States.[8]

A useful review article by Paul Burstein examines thirty sources, mostly quantitative studies dealing with the United States, which investigate some aspect of the relationship between public opinion and public policy. He extracts fifty-two separate findings from these sources, with a measurable relationship between public opinion and public policy in three-quarters of them. In many of these cases the impact has 'substantial policy importance.' Burstein notes, however, that these studies typically provide imprecise descriptions of their findings and their significance, and that many of these sources do not make explicit claims of causal relationships between public preferences and government decisions.[9] Burstein's efforts provide important evidence that public opinion correlates with, and probably exerts influence on, public policy. However, he warns, the existing literature probably overstates the impact of opinion on policy.[10] Moreover, they only partially describe the strength of the relationship and the mechanisms by which opinion affects policy, and they certainly do not enable us to distinguish the impact of opinion polling from other expressions of public opinion.

Some specific studies are especially relevant in the present context because they use polls on policy preferences, rather than other measures of public opinion such as citizens' overall 'mood.' For example, Joel Brooks measures consistency between public opinion as measured by Gallup polls with actual government policy between 1965 and 1975 as assessed by academic experts. Surprisingly, he finds consistency between opinion and policy in only 39 per cent of the ninety-five Canadian cases, and he reports very similar levels for Great Britain and the United States. Referring to his typology of opinion-policy linkages, Brooks naturally concludes that his research supports the democratic frustration model.[11]

Alan Monroe follows a similar approach, examining the relationship between mass opinion and public policy for 248 cases in the United States between 1960 and 1974.[12] While observing that a sizable minority of public policies are inconsistent with public preferences, he concludes that about two-thirds of the policies in his sample are congruent with public opinion. In a follow-up study for 1980–93, however, he finds only 55 per cent of 566 cases showing correlation between opinion and policy.[13] Later analysis suggests that this level of consistency persisted during the 1990s.[14] To explain why consistency is not higher, Monroe stresses the large number of issues governments are expected to address, and he suggests that politicians' inclinations to act in line with public preferences are sometimes insufficient to overcome characteristics of American political institutions.[15] Unfortunately, Monroe does not cite Brooks's research and it remains uncertain why their conclusions conflict.

Focusing on Canada, and following a methodology comparable to that of Brooks and Monroe, François Pétry examines 221 policies in Canada between 1968 and 1993. He concludes that 'public opinion and public policy are consistent about 60 percent of the time' – somewhat lower than he believes research shows for the United States.[16] In a separate study covering 1994–2000, Pétry finds policy outcomes consistent with majority opinion in just 49 per cent of cases.[17] However, he says that analysis of factors affecting correspondence between opinion and policy is beyond the scope of his research. His earlier findings differ from those of Brooks, Pétry suggests, because he includes 'retrospective survey items' and studies a different time period.

While authors such as Monroe and Pétry describe the extent to which public opinion and public policy are consistent, other researchers contribute more to an understanding of what sort of causal relationship may exist between opinion and policy. Benjamin Page and Robert Shapiro examine changes in American opinions and policies between 1935 and 1979.[18] They focus on 231 cases where both opinion and policy changed over time, finding that they were consistent in 66 per cent of cases. Looking at the timing of changes, they find that opinion shifted before policy in two-thirds of these cases – evidence of a causal relationship between opinion and policy and specifically of government responsiveness to changes in the public's preferences.

Further light is shed on this by other authors who have examined variation over time in public preferences for government spending in specific policy areas. For instance, Thomas Hartley and Bruce Russett investigated public attitudes on military spending as measured through polls between 1965 and 1990, and compared these data with actual spending patterns. Their research supports the hypothesis that public opinion influenced American military spending. They indicate, however, that the national deficit and the pressure exerted by Soviet military expenditures were at least as influential.[19] Although his methodology differs somewhat, Christopher Wlezien conducted a similar analysis for 1973–91, also finding that military spending increases tend to directly follow public preferences: 'When the public wants more spending, the Congress provides more spending,' and when the public prefers less, Congress tends to reduce appropriations.[20]

Even if this finding is accepted, it demonstrates the impact of public opinion on governments in just one policy area. Although polls are used in these studies to measure public opinion, the researchers are not claiming that they are necessarily causing the changes in policy; active public opinion, or the actual effects of spending, for instance, may be responsible. Moreover, the salience of defence spending in the United States means that the relationship in this field could be unlike other policies.[21] A recent study by Stuart Soroka and Christopher Wlezien examined the relationship between Canadians' preferences for increasing or decreasing expenditures in several policy areas and actual spending by governments.[22] Their research suggests that governments in Canada are less responsive to public opinion than in the United States or Great Britain. Although further research in this area is needed, the study offers evidence that Canadian experience can be quite distinctive.

Studying the Opinion-Policy Relationship

Joel Brooks finds a negative relationship between public opinion and policy, whereas most other researchers indicate a modest correspondence, although this is clearer and better demonstrated in the United States than Canada. The substantial degree of inconsistency calls into question the assumptions of many observers that policy-makers are significantly influenced by citizens' preferences. But the evidence of some correlation might hint that public opinion – with polls raising its profile – often drives public policy.

This would be a hasty conclusion, however. Many factors other than polls help to explain the consistency between opinion and policy – to the extent it exists – and the causal relationships between the two are extremely difficult to identify and untangle.[23]

First, a mild positive relationship between opinion and policy could easily occur, even if public opinion has no effect at all. Agreement between citizens and their representatives does not prove that either group influences the other. It could simply reflect the fact that a politician who comes from a given area is likely to share some values with other citizens from the same area.[24]

Second, some agreement between opinion and policy is not necessarily due to opinion influencing policy. Rather, as suggested by the counterfeit consensus model that Brooks describes, some correlation can be accounted for by policy, or by politicians' leadership, which in turn generates opinion change. This may be because a policy gradually becomes accepted, or because a government deliberately attempts to alter public opinion.[25]

Third, relevant polls are not always available, and when they are, their signals are not necessarily influential. Besides polls, other inputs influence officials, such as interest groups, the mass media, members of the attentive public, civil servants, other officials, and outside experts. At times these inputs are consistent with mass opinion, and frequently they exert more impact on decisions.[26] Officials' instincts about citizens' preferences and their interpretations of election results can also contribute to linkage.

Clearly much remains to be learned about the relationship between public opinion and public policy and what is known applies mainly to the United States. Still, the available sources indicate, overall, that modest consistency exists between policy and opinion; that policy change sometimes precedes opinion change; and that observed correspondence between opinion and policy – and evidence that governments are sometimes responsive to citizens' preferences – are almost certainly due to many factors. Although there is reason to doubt that polling has a substantial impact across a wide range of policies, the possibility remains that it could play an important part in government officials' decisions about specific policies. In the end, at least from this body of literature, it is difficult to say much with confidence about the role of opinion research in policy decisions.

Polling and the Presidency

More has been written about Bill Clinton's uses of polls than about this aspect of any previous presidency. The existing literature suggests that modern presidents have used polling mainly for communication,[27] and it has been argued that Ronald Reagan's presidency of 1981–9 was a big step in the 'use of polling to move and not follow public opinion.'[28] The sources on Clinton's presidency reveal uses of polling in policy decisions as well as communication.

The scale and impact of Clinton's use of opinion research was unprecedented. In 1993, for instance, his administration spent $1.99 million on opinion research – roughly nine times the amount George Bush Sr. spent in 1989 and 1990 together.[29] Clinton also had more contact with pollsters than his predecessors. During 1993–4, pollster Stan Greenberg held weekly private meetings with Clinton and participated in regular meetings of the president's closest advisers. Just as professional hockey teams with losing records change their coaches, Clinton responded to the Republicans' success in the 1994 mid-term elections by firing his consultant: Greenberg was replaced by Dick Morris, who contracted the actual polling to Mark Penn and Doug Schoen. Even more than Greenberg, Morris enjoyed frequent private contacts with

Clinton in 1995 and 1996, at first very secretly. Morris continued to advise Clinton, secretly once again but less frequently, after the consultant was forced to step down from his key role following revelations of a sex scandal in August, 1996. Penn then became the main White House pollster and attended weekly meetings with Clinton and other senior officials, influencing strategy as well as policy.

Morris's memoir reveals how he made heavy use of polling to advise Clinton.[30] While some have challenged this account, others accept that its thrust is largely correct.[31] Most significantly, three former White House insiders, none of them allies of Morris, corroborate the view that Morris had a substantial impact on Clinton's thinking and decision-making, and indicate that the consultant drew on polls to influence not just communications but also policy. For example, Harold Ickes confirmed in 1999 that Morris and his polling contributed significantly to Clinton's policy decisions.[32] As well, George Stephanopoulos noticed an 'unfamiliar frequency' when Clinton spoke; he later recognized that this resulted from Morris's influence. He comments that 'from December 1994 through August 1996 ... no single person more influenced the president of the United States than Dick Morris.' He also recalls Morris referring to a small computer containing poll data as his 'prayer book.'[33] Similarly, Robert Reich wondered why Clinton favoured a balanced budget proposal despite the views of his economic advisers. Gradually he became aware of the influence of Morris and his polling. He wrote in his diary: 'He [Clinton] doesn't want to listen to any of us who are now sitting with him around this table ... Regardless of what any of us tells him, [Clinton] is still gravitating to another spot, a black hole whose pull is overwhelming ... The black hole is Dick Morris.'[34] The agreement among Ickes, Stephanopoulos, and Reich is striking.

As president, Clinton acted *against* majority opinion on issues such as free trade with Mexico, sending troops to Haiti and Bosnia, school prayer, and affirmative action. Indeed, a memo by Morris identified areas where the president had acted at odds with public opinion, for potential use to rebut anticipated charges that he governed by polls.[35] As well, the views of the majority did not necessarily prevail as Gallup and Rae expected. For example, although three-fifths of Americans favoured the distribution of contraceptives in high schools, Morris says he advised Clinton that it would be too 'risky' to adopt the controversial proposal without at least 70 per cent support.[36]

At other times, polls influenced Clinton's policy as Gallup and Rae had hoped, and this impact peaked in 1995–6 as Clinton positioned himself for re-election in November 1996. For instance, polls affected details of Clinton's health care proposals, such as plans for employers to purchase their employees' insurance rather than relying on a new tax, and the president's support for malpractice reform.[37] As well, polling contributed to Clinton's advocacy of a smoking ban in federal buildings and his opposition to insurance companies using genetic screening.[38] Moreover, Morris says, polling showed that citizens would respond more favourably to increasing the minimum wage than to reducing a gasoline tax. With these data in hand, he advised Clinton to only agree to the tax cut if Congress also raised the minimum wage.

An unusually clear illustration of the influence of polls on policy deliberations was Morris's effort to gauge support for Labour Secretary Robert Reich's policy ideas, including his proposals on promoting re-training rather than layoffs.[39] According to Reich, Morris told him, 'I've tested your ideas. One worked, two didn't.' Later Morris spoke to Reich about his polling on the latter's proposal to use tax incentives to promote corporate responsibility for business. It was not sufficiently popular with swing voters, Morris said: 'So in the end it doesn't work. I won't be forwarding it to Clinton.' Reich reflected unhappily on Morris's influence: 'There used to be a policy-making process in the White House. It wasn't perfect by any means, but at least options were weighed. [Clinton] received our various judgements about what was good for the nation. Now we have Morris and his polls.' The point that opinion research affected policy content as well as communications is unmistakable.

Polling contributed to the development of Clinton's strategy of 'triangulation,' which in turn had policy implications. Triangulation meant distinguishing Clinton's policies from traditional Democratic and Republican positions, and synthesizing them on issues such as abortion, welfare, government regulation, crime, and the deficit. Polling showing public support for positions that are neither liberal or conservative shaped the triangulation strategy.[40] Morris discovered that more voters were interested in 'values issues,' such as television violence, fathers' child support payments, teenage smoking, and schools' responses to changing technology than economic ones, and Clinton enjoyed less support among those interested in the former type than the latter. The consultant therefore advised the president to stress values issues as the 1996 election approached. The creation of policy proposals, the selection of issues addressed, and how they were communicated were intertwined.

Morris seemed willing to poll on almost any subject. Absurdly, he polled about what kind of vacation was appropriate for the Clinton family; thinking of the president's image, he recommended a camping trip. Moreover, shortly after allegations of a sexual relationship between the president and White House intern Monica Lewinsky surfaced in January 1998, Clinton hinted to Morris that the reports contained some truth. In response, the consultant quietly took a survey to try to anticipate public reactions to a hypothetical confession by the president. Contrary to Morris's expectations, the poll signalled that the public would not be forgiving, and he reported accordingly to Clinton.[41] As Stephanopoulos cynically recounts the episode, 'the president chose to follow the pattern of his past. He called Dick Morris. Dick took a poll. The poll said lie. It was out of Clinton's hands.'[42] Although not a public policy matter, the story underlines Morris's and Clinton's readiness to use polling.

While Morris unquestionably influenced communications by the Clinton White House, he, and to a lesser extent Greenberg and Penn, drew on polling to give Clinton policy advice in a fashion roughly consistent with Gallup and Rae's hopes. Clinton respected, and sometimes followed, the recommendations. The communications and policy-related uses were more extensive than in any previous administration. The most noticeable difference appears to be the greater impact of opinion research on the content of his policy.

Some recent studies have examined the impact of polls on American government using qualitative approaches, often referring to archival material. The source which most thoroughly addresses the impact of polling on governing is *Politicians Don't Pander*, by Lawrence Jacobs and Robert Shapiro. They devote most of their attention to the struggle over health care between the Clinton White House and the congressional Republicans in 1993–6.[43] Jacobs and Shapiro acknowledge that opinion research affected certain policy decisions by Clinton, including the details of welfare reform in 1996.[44] However, drawing mainly on interviews and internal White House documents, they conclude that while elected officials – that is, Clinton and the Republicans in Congress – used opinion research to monitor public opinion, this was for communications more than guidance on policy content. Arguing that responsiveness to mass public opinion has declined since the 1970s, they believe that 'politicians try to have it both ways – to pursue their policy goals and make their positions electorally attractive,'[45] with opinion research contributing more to the latter goal. They indicate that officials tend to be sceptical of the utility of opinion research, committed to certain policy goals, and overconfident of their capacity to change public opinion.

The book stresses that opinion research contributes to communications: specifically, it describes how politicians use 'crafted talk' to try to shift public opinion. Moreover, Jacobs and Shapiro note that the congressional Republicans were often more responsive to the views of party supporters and activists than the electorate as a whole. They lament these developments, and wish that opinion research was employed more to promote genuine responsiveness to mass opinion by elected officials. This, they argue, would make government more legitimate and democratic.[46]

Jacobs and Shapiro highlight the selection of language and arguments for public statements by politicians. Valuable as this is, the emphasis comes at some cost, leading the authors to downplay the role of opinion research in other aspects of communications, such as the selection of target audiences and the measurement of public knowledge and awareness. Moreover, advertising receives little attention, and the book has nothing to say about the use of opinion research by the bureaucracy, whether for communications, or for implementation or evaluation of policy. Nevertheless, Jacobs and Shapiro demonstrate effectively that opinion research exerts a limited impact on policy content and a greater influence on the communication of policy.

However, the authors' emphasis on health care creates a picture which actually understates the impact of opinion research for the Clinton White House on other issues. In particular, the usually meticulous authors provide a rather selective and unnuanced reading of Morris's memoir. They emphasize points where Morris stresses the use of opinion research for communications, but neglect his descriptions of the impact of polling on policy content, most notably the triangulation strategy.[47] Moreover, they do not cite authors such as Reich and Stephanopoulos who corroborate the thrust of Morris's claims about the role of polling. In short, while *Politicians Don't Pander* poses and addresses many important questions, it is too much of a case study of how elected officials approached the health care issue to provide a thorough account of the impact of opinion polling on the Clinton presidency.

Still, the general argument that opinion research influences government communications more than decisions about policy content remains valid and important. While this view contrasts with some earlier research, it is supported by three recent studies that each examine several presidencies. Robert Eisinger argues that presidents since Franklin Roosevelt have referred to opinion polls to gain autonomy from other sources of information about public opinion, particularly Congress. Although it is not the primary focus of his work, he stresses the uses of polling for public relations purposes rather than policy development and in this respect his research supports the emphasis on crafted talk in *Politicians Don't Pander*.[48] Consistent with this, Diane Heith's book on polling by administrations from Nixon to Clinton does not unearth much evidence of opinion research influencing policy decisions. She affirms Jacobs and Shapiro's view that public opinion research contributes to the development of 'crafted talk,' reporting that 'during campaigns, and in the White House, polls highlight which issues to stress and not the particular policy stand to adopt.'[49] Similarly, in his study of the Truman, Johnson, and Carter administrations, Michael Towle indicates that 'the people's voice was most easily heard when it was already supportive of the presidential administration,' but also that polling did not prevent each of these presidents from losing touch with public opinion. Indeed, he argues that 'the need for and attention to public support has interfered with the ability of the modern presidency to be responsive to the public.'[50] These authors strengthen the case that the foremost effect of government public opinion research is on communications rather than policy content.

Polling and the Policy Process in Canada

In general, what is true of opinion research in the United States might be expected to apply to Canada. Beyond the indications that policy in Canada may be more frequently out of step with opinion than in the United States, however, several differences between the countries deserve noting. First, compared with the U.S. Congress, the Canadian Parliament has substantially less ability to influence the executive. Second, the existence of strong party discipline in Canada's House of Commons may reduce the likelihood of responsiveness from elected officials. Third, the quantity and sophistication of polling are greater in the United States. Finally, Canadian officials have found it harder to keep government polling secret than their American counterparts, mainly because the former use public rather than party funds to a far greater extent and therefore polling for Canadian governments is subject to Access to Information legislation.

Observers in the United States and Canada make similar assumptions about the impact of polls on government, yet the topic has not received a great deal of systematic study. The particularly low profile of this subject in Canada is evident from a glance at a recent review of Canadian research on public opinion; this review does not even mention the possible impact of public opinion on policy.[51] Although some attempts have been made to evaluate polling in government, often the subject merely receives a paragraph or two in sources with other purposes. Still, there is scattered information about the role of opinion research in the policy process in Canada.

The existing literature establishes that polling for the Canadian government originated during the Second World War. John Grierson, as manager of the Wartime Information Board, consulted publicly available Gallup polls.[52] He then persuaded Prime Minister Mackenzie King that the board should initiate regular opinion polling. From 1943 to 1945 sixty-nine government polls investigated topics such as the morale of the public; attitudes towards rationing, living costs, and Canada's involvement in the war; and expectations about the postwar economy. Grierson reported some of the results to King and his cabinet and his memos cited polls when offering advice to the prime minister. Gary Evans states that King sometimes accepted the recommendations,[53] which suggests that polls may have influenced policy at times. A finding that people with lower incomes and education, younger people, and women were relatively poorly informed was cited as a reason for increasing the propaganda to promote the war effort. Polling also showed the potential of posters and films to reach younger and less literate Canadians. This presaged more recent discoveries of low levels of public knowledge and the use of the findings to justify advertising campaigns.

The surveys helped the government communicate to Canadians about the war effort, not just by measuring support and but also by helping to build and maintain it. Grierson viewed the polling as listening to Canadians as well as talking to them, although others might view the data as a less benign contributor to the production of government propaganda. Indeed, Daniel Robinson explains that this 'polling was not designed to secure opinions about how best to organize wartime economic and social mobilization and then implement the most popular ones ... But polling did provide a versatile and powerful quantitative technique for determining effective promotional strategies for predetermined policies.'[54] The early polling, then, did not drive decisions but helped the government communicate to Canadians about its policies. This fore-shadows more recent uses of polls by governments.

A brief discussion of survey research in Canadian government comes from a 1969 article by Fred Schindeler and C. Michael Lanphier.[55] They welcomed the growth in the use of polls in government, and particularly in policy formulation, thinking this would promote participatory democracy by increasing policy-makers' knowledge of public attitudes. The authors argued that greater use of social science research could have contained the problems associated with biculturalism and bilingualism policies in the 1960s. What they actually found was less encouraging, however. Their examination of twenty-seven specific surveys commissioned by the federal government found only a handful with national samples, and their questions were too vague to be useful in policy formulation. The others sampled specific groups or geographic areas, researching questions such as the willingness of federal public servants to learn French. The article is a snapshot of polling at the time. It is dated as the volume of government polling has increased, decision-makers have considerably greater access to polls with national samples, and polls have contributed little to the development of participatory democracy. Nor is the article alert to the uses of polls for communications.

Also in 1969, in an article dealing broadly with democracy and civil liberties, Peter Russell advocated the use of polls in policy decisions. He did not urge officials to follow polls blindly but considered them 'a counter-weight to the unbalanced character of the influences to which government is subject through parliamentary and pressure-group activity.' Russell expressed concerns about the unrepresentative character of both Parliament and interest groups, and argued that those who lack political efficacy are underrepresented in the political system.[56] Like Schindeler and Lanphier, but unlike most other Canadian political scientists, Russell explicitly recognizes the democratic potential of polling, by presenting an argument roughly resembling Gallup and Rae's and Goldfarb's. While this is not the primary use of opinion research and it is important to keep in mind the use of non-representative samples, Russell's view of the representative character of polling remains relevant today.

Colin Campbell and George J. Szablowski examine the relative importance of various inputs into the policy process in the 1970s. They asked central agency officials about the importance of various ways of learning about the public's views. The media, businesspeople, provincial government officials, friends and acquaintances, political leaders, and even union leaders were all mentioned more often than opinion polls, which were referred to by just 22 per cent of their respondents.[57] A contemporary version of this study might yield different results, of course, but the low importance of polling is striking.

It has also been suggested that polling has undermined the traditional role of members of Parliament in representing and communicating attitudes of the general public. For example, Roger Gibbins describes this as a 'challenge that public opinion polls pose for parliamentary institutions ... Polls seem to offer an alternative means of expression, one that is much more precise as well as being free of the excessive partisanship that can cloud the articulation of the public voice in legislative assemblies.'[58] It continues to be the case that cabinet ministers often learn about citizens' attitudes from polls rather than backbench MPs.

When asked, however, the majority of politicians tend to downplay and even criticize the use of polls in government.[59] While prime minister, Pierre Trudeau claimed, 'Quite frankly, I do not give a damn about the polls. I do not take polls.'[60] On the specific question of whether polls influence the content of policy decisions, this is denied by Liberal adviser Keith Davey. He says polls did not induce the Trudeau government to change any of its policies.[61]

While this contention has not been thoroughly investigated in Canada, observers have asserted that sometimes polling assists with various policy decisions. One example is the Conservative government's decision to reduce the number of military helicopters purchased in 1993.[62] It is also claimed that polls affected the British Columbia NDP government's health care policies and budgets in the early 1990s.[63] Similarly, Frank Graves, the president of Ekos, has said that polling showing public support for medical research contributed to an increase in funding for the Canadian Institutes for Health Research.[64] As well, political scientist Guy Lachapelle maintains that polls did not determine policy content in the Parti Québécois government of 1976–85 – with one exception, the decision to build a roof on the Olympic Stadium in Montreal.[65]

There is also limited documentation that opinion research affects how governments communicate with citizens. Polls become most prominent in the policy process, according to Ronald Drews, when policymakers are concerned about public consent.[66] Although Goldfarb was involved in communications strategy for policies such as the '6 and 5' wage controls in the early 1980s, apparently his polls had little impact on the substance of such policies.[67] The federal government has surveyed Quebeckers about sovereignty and assessed the persuasiveness of various federalist arguments.[68] Alasdair Roberts and Jonathan Rose report that opinion research influenced the government's communications campaign to promote the GST, including the perceived need for such a campaign and the style of advertising (information-oriented rather than a 'hard sell'). This research included comparisons of public reactions to various possible arguments in favour of the tax.[69] These examples draw attention the role of opinion research in publicizing and promoting policies.

Although it is limited and unsystematic, what is established about the role of opinion research in Canadian government comes more from journalists than political scientists. There are examples of polls apparently influencing policy content, usually modestly rather than dramatically. But polls play other roles, most notably affecting the communication of policy. The signs that opinion research influences communications more than policy content have not been absorbed: observers of Canadian governments typically ignore the subject or simply assume that because polling is conducted, it shapes the content of policy.

Conclusion

Despite the scholarly attention to public opinion in the United States and to public policy both there and in Canada, and even though governments in both countries began using polls more than six decades ago, there is surprisingly little systematic knowledge about how opinion research is used by governments. Moreover, focus groups are frequently overlooked. There is some evidence that public opinion and public policy are mildly correlated in the United States, yet the nature of this relationship and the specific impact of opinion research on governments remain uncertain. Recent American sources can be tapped to show that the effect of opinion research on how governments communicate to citizens is greater than its influence on policy content, even in the Clinton administration. In addition, limited information and analysis exist about the uses of opinion research in Canada. The remainder of this book attempts to help close this gap.

3 The Practice and Framework of Opinion Research for Government in Canada

In order to understand the role of polls and focus groups in Canadian government, it is necessary to examine the context in which they are conducted and used. What kinds of opinion research – and how much – do pollsters conduct for government? What are the other sources of polls for government? How are contracts to conduct opinion research awarded? Which departments spend most on opinion research? What kinds of relationships do polling firms have with their clients in government?

Pollsters and Their Policy-Related Work

The federal government's communications policy defines opinion research in a far-reaching fashion:

> the planned gathering, by or for a government institution, of opinions, attitudes, perceptions, judgments, feelings, ideas, reactions or views that are intended to be used for any government purpose, whether that information is collected from persons (including employees of government institutions), businesses, institutions or other entities, through quantitative or qualitative methods, irrespective of size or cost of those methods.

The policy then goes on to explain that this includes – but is not restricted to – 'policy research'; 'market research'; 'communications research, including advertising research'; 'program evaluation'; 'quality of service and client satisfaction studies'; 'omnibus surveys (placement of one or more questions)'; and 'syndicated studies.' The definition concludes by broadening itself further, adding that 'the definition applies to components of other initiatives, such as communication strategies, product development and program evaluation.'[1] The resulting picture of the opinion research field is far more diverse than the one Gallup and Rae wrote about in 1940. It includes qualitative research, studies of sub-samples of the population, and research for a range of purposes which differ from the policy-oriented questionnaires of the entire adult population stressed by Gallup and Rae.

The quantity and scope of opinion research initiated by governments is important to establish in order to appreciate its potential influence on policy-making. However, this is a difficult task. First, accounting and classification practices sometimes obscure the amount of opinion research conducted for governments. For instance, one list of public opinion surveys released by the federal government included a study of 'the management implications of factors affecting trail choice in Jasper National Park,'[2] which is far removed from what is usually understood as opinion research. Second, some results and recommendations of pollsters are not reported in writing and only expressed orally. While sometimes this is simply because time is short, in other instances officials do not want a written record that may become public – a consequence of the Access to Information Act. Third, despite this legislation and recent improvements in the willingness of governments to make reports of opinion research available, officials sometimes resist releasing information. For instance, while minister of finance, Paul Martin sought legal advice when he tried to prevent the release of polling conducted for his department on the Goods and Services Tax, but he was ultimately unsuccessful in his efforts.[3]

Still, no one seriously denies that the cost and volume of opinion research undertaken by the federal government is substantial. For instance, in 1987 Helen Moroz drew on her interviews with pollsters and government officials to present estimates for annual expenditures ranging from $5 to $25 million, with one outlying figure of $100 million. Claire Hoy reported that 799 'confidential polls' were conducted for the government between 1984 and 1987, estimating the total cost at $64 million. Besides these figures, Kirk Lapointe estimated the government's polling costs at $25 million annually, excluding research for the Privy Council Office (PCO) and Prime Minister's Office (PMO).[4]

For more recent years, a clearer picture emerges. A Liberal cabinet minister, David Dingwall, indicated that the Brian Mulroney-Kim Campbell government spent at least $16 million on polling in a two-year period, although other observers suggested an actual figure around $32 million.[5] More recently, the Reform Party used an Access to Information request to produce annual amounts of $7.2 million on opinion research for the 1994–5 fiscal year, $9.2 million for 1995–6, and $11.8 million for 1996–7.[6] Since then, the government has stated that its expenditures on custom opinion research rose to $15.8 million in 1999–2000, $16.8 million in 2000–1, and $22.2 million in 2001–2; they fell slightly to $20.6 million in 2002–3. This last amount paid for 576 separate opinion research projects.[7]

This research work is contracted to private firms. Although many polling contracts have traditionally been directed to favoured companies – Goldfarb for the Trudeau Liberals and Decima for the Mulroney Conservatives – the Chrétien government divided the contracts more evenly among many firms after promising a change in practices along these lines in May 1994.[8] The standing offer procedures, discussed later in this chapter, were the catalyst for spreading out the contracts.

The Reform Party's analysis of government opinion research in the three fiscal years from 1994 to 1997 showed how the $28.3 million spent on contracts was divided.[9] The business was divided among 180 firms; 57 per cent of the contracts were awarded to eleven firms. The companies winning the most contracts were Ekos (11 per cent), Coopers and Lybrand (9 per cent), Angus Reid Group (now known as Ipsos-Reid, 8 per cent), Pollara (formerly called Insight, 5 per cent), Environics (4 per cent), COMPAS (4 per cent), and Sage (4 per cent). Createc+, Price Waterhouse, and Earnscliffe Strategy Group were further down the list. The presence on the list of companies known for accountancy and management consulting, such as Coopers and Lybrand and Price Waterhouse, highlights the breadth of what is classified as opinion research.[10] Pollara, the pollster for the Liberal party under Jean Chrétien, comes in fourth place on this list, so it was not benefitting from patronage the way some might have expected. The rankings do not necessarily reflect the firms' influence in government; for instance, Earnscliffe was generally regarded as high in that respect because of its relationship with the Finance Department under Paul Martin. Generally, the same firms that poll for the federal government also serve provincial governments, and most occasionally work at the municipal level.

Alternatives to Government-Commissioned Polling

Government contracts comprise a minority of the business of most major opinion research firms; the bulk of their work is public affairs and market research for private-sector clients. Ekos is an exception (Ekos pollster Andrew Sullivan estimates 65 per cent of the firm's work is for the federal government). For companies such as Pollara during the Chrétien era, and even Goldfarb during the Trudeau years, government contracts accounted for less than one-tenth of their billings.[11] In addition to government-commissioned work, four other categories of opinion research assume a role in the policy process: polls conducted for interest groups; polls commissioned for media organizations; syndicated or periodical surveys sold to clients in the public and private sectors; and polls taken for political parties. These are nearly all polls; very little relevant qualitative opinion research comes from any of these alternative sources. Considerable attention is paid to opinion research from all sources, says a civil servant: 'We consume it.' The internet has made some of the results more accessible. The polls with significance for the policy process are those investigating attitudes about policy, rather than parties and politicians. While government-commissioned research is stressed in this study, these other sources of data should not be neglected.

Polls for Interest Groups

Many interest groups and organizations, from businesses to unions to citizens' organizations, use polling to monitor the political landscape, gauge the views of their constituencies, assist with strategic planning, and help prepare communications plans.[12w] Less frequently, but of greater importance for this study, polls are conducted for interest groups and individual companies which then present the results to officials privately or release them publicly. In the latter case, the results are announced – often selectively – in news releases and advertising to influence public opinion and to show that the positions of the organization are in line with the views of the general public. For instance, late in 2001, hoping to encourage the federal government to allow Air Canada to launch a new discount air service, the airline released a poll by Ipsos-Reid that indicated that Canadians would welcome the initiative.[13] Similarly, in 2002, Greenpeace commissioned Decima to survey Canadians about the Kyoto Protocol for reducing greenhouse gases; the environmental group was no doubt pleased to announce that 78 per cent of respondents favoured the agreement.[14]

When interest groups privately present opinion research to government officials, the impact is normally limited because bias is expected. Former PMO official Hugh Segal makes this point emphatically: 'If the bankers' association brought in a piece of research that said Canadians don't care about [proposed bank] mergers ... if I was a deputy minister of Finance, I'd say, "That's fine, I'll sort it out myself." So I don't think it has much impact.' Ian McKinnon, a former pollster with Decima Research, adds that most government officials are knowledgeable enough not to be swayed by biased research. Interest groups' presentation of polls to the media is more troubling, however, because journalists and the public generally lack the expertise to subject the data to the necessary scrutiny.

A major pollster's name gives legitimacy to its polls. McKinnon recalls that Decima would occasionally reach mutual agreements with clients not to proceed with planned research when 'we could not agree on something that met our test of professionalism and their view of what was an appropriate question.' An Environics pollster, speaking generally about clients who want to use intentionally loaded questionnaires, says 'I would not ask questions that are designed to elicit certain kinds of answers, because in the end you're not doing your client any good, and you're not doing yourself any good. It's just not worth it.'[15] Similarly, pollster Angus Reid says he has turned down prospective clients who wanted his firm to ask deliberately skewed questions and present the results in a way that benefits from the association with Reid's name.[16] The name of a well-known polling firm would attract attention to the results and enhance their credibility with the public and government officials.

Despite the claims of pollsters, according to *Globe and Mail* columnist Hugh Winsor, even well-known firms such as Environics and the Angus Reid Group have allowed interest organizations to place questions on their omnibus surveys with wording 'tilted towards the lobbyists' desired outcome.' One of Winsor's examples is research by Environics for the Canadian Drug Manufacturers Association, which represented makers of generic drugs.[17] A question mentioned that the Liberals opposed extending patent protection for brand-name drugs while they were in opposition and then asked, 'Do you think the Liberal government should shorten the period of patent protection, as they had earlier argued?' which Winsor considers a leading question. This kind of practice generates data which may be misleading.[18]

It should be noted that officials at Environics and the Angus Reid Group were not given the chance to respond to this criticism in Winsor's column; asked in interviews for this study, they firmly defend their companies' practice.[19] They suggest that the questions like those cited by Winsor are usually part of a series of several questions on the same topic. They acknowledge that interest groups sometimes want to selectively publicize the most favourable results, although Reid's contracts no longer allow partial release of the data. Reid pollster Mike Colledge says part of the blame lies with journalists: 'Why report them if you don't think they're good questions?'[20]

Despite the criticisms of this research, the interest groups evidently believe it is worthwhile for influencing perceptions of public opinion. One pollster, however, believes that there are growing doubts about the credibility of these polls.[21]

Media Polls

Newspapers and other media outlets sometimes sponsor opinion research to use as a basis for news stories. As well, news coverage can attract attention to polls that originate elsewhere, which may be either leaked or officially released.

For those knowledgeable about opinion research, media polls are typically viewed as less thorough and less carefully analysed than research commissioned for government or the syndicated periodical surveys.[22] Chris Baker of Environics warns that some media polls have a slant because 'a media organization doesn't want the results; they want a story.' They are often taken when public interest in an issue is high, which can affect results. Many are also conducted on the cheap with a limited number of questions and small samples. In fact, most media polls are cursory, because research firms usually do not make money on them and do them for the publicity.[23] Reporting on media polls is often superficial and, as Michael Adams points out, their presentation may be slanted to align with newspapers' editorial positions.[24]

Despite all their problems, media polls sometimes figure prominently in the policy process. They almost certainly have some impact on the public's perceptions of policy issues and perhaps even on citizens' participation in the policy process. More significantly, as Hugh Winsor observes, media polls reach politicians directly through newspapers or broadcasts; in contrast, results of government-commissioned polls may slowly filter through a series of public servants and aides before reaching the minister, sometimes in a modified fashion or after an issue has faded. Baker comments that some media polls attract more attention from government officials than specially commissioned polls of higher quality. Part of the impact of media polls occurs when officials deliberately pay attention to them, although few receive intense scrutiny. The job of public servants responsible for monitoring opinion research includes gleaning what they can from media polls, although syndicated and specially commissioned polls are of greater value.

At a more general level, media polls contribute to the political agenda. As Winsor explains, they help to 'set the overall environment in which politicians act.' They can raise the profile of issues and are referred to by officials during the process of developing policy. COMPAS pollster Stephen Kiar says a poll his firm conducted for Southam News on the fiscal dividend in late 1997 prompted at least ten telephone calls from government officials seeking more details. 'That [poll] will influence people's speeches,' he claimed. 'It will influence ministers' press releases. I don't doubt that that poll will have as much influence in the Finance ministry as their own polls, and the other ones on this subject ... The only reason it might have a little bit less is we're not there to actually deliver the point home in the same way as something they paid for.' Pollsters who receive calls from government officials about media polls report more contacts from civil servants than ministers' offices; in some cases the former make the inquiry on behalf of the latter, or in anticipation of interest from ministers' aides.[25]

Syndicated Polling

Syndicated studies are periodical reports sold to small subscription lists of public and private sector clients. The best-known of these publications used to be *Decima Quarterly*, which appeared from 1980 to 1995. The major national reports currently published include Environics' *Focus Canada*, Pollara's *Perspectives Canada* (each quarterly), and the *Ipsos Trend Report Canada* (six issues annually). Each of these firms also produces periodical reports on some of the larger provinces. While these studies report on a wide range of issues, there are also many specialized publications such as COMPAS's *The Business Agenda*, Ekos's *Rethinking Government*, and the *Berger Population Health Monitor*. Between fiscal years 1999–2000 and 2002–3, the federal government spent $3 to $4 million each year on subscriptions to syndicated research studies.[26]

Some of what applies to media polls is also true of syndicated polls. Civil servants refer to syndicated research more than media surveys, examining it because they wish to conserve resources and avoid purchasing unnecessary new research. For use by policy-makers, the main limitation of the syndicated reports is that, compared with specially commissioned research, they are too general. As consultant John Laschinger explains, 'Custom research is important, and stuff that's in the public domain doesn't quite fit the specific needs of any one company or one individual. That's why custom research is better than omnibus research ... [It is like using] a shotgun instead of a rifle.' Another pollster comments that syndicated polling is superficial: 'The big risk for syndicated polls is that they are to polling what the centrefold of *Playboy* is to sex.'

Still, syndicated reports are generally more methodologically sound than media polls. They usually feature more questions and may employ larger samples. Moreover, they are less driven by the desire to make news, and are more useful for gauging how public opinion changes over time. Syndicated studies are used most by communications branches; they are considered particularly useful for general 'environmental scanning,' which aids policy-makers' awareness of public concerns and priorities at a lower cost than specially commissioned polls.[27]

Party-Sponsored Opinion Research

Most of the opinion research conducted for political parties is used to fight election campaigns and therefore has little relevance for the policy process.[28] Environics pollster Donna Dasko explains why most party-sponsored research is not useful in governing: 'It's used as input into election strategy, for developing policy ideas, initiatives, and developing communications. And targeting voters, that's what it's used for ... A lot of the party polling would deal with certain ridings only ... Or it will be focused on supporters and potential supporters of the party, and sometimes won't even be [the] general population.' However, there are various ways in which opinion research conducted and paid for by parties enters the policy process from time to time.

First, opinion research may influence the positions taken by opposition parties, which occasionally affect the policy process. For instance, governments may address the issues highlighted by opposition parties, and these may be partly determined by polls. On occasion these are polls the parties initiate themselves, although more often they are syndicated or government polls.

Second, opinion research helps parties prepare election platforms.[29] A winning party's platform then becomes the basis for a government's perceived electoral mandate and subsequent policy, an agenda-setting effect. The following two cases illustrate different ways opinion research can help shape a platform. The first is the federal Liberals' campaign in 1993. Polls and focus groups by Insight showed the party that the public was sceptical of politicians and their promises; this finding helped inform the decision to release a platform, which was done through the document known as the Red Book.[30] 'The research for the Liberals behind [the] 1993 [campaign] showed that the number one priority was jobs,' explains Don Guy, whose firm, then called Insight, polled for the party. 'So, much of the content of that campaign, the platform and the government's messaging since have been related to job creation. And that's because that's what the public wants [the government] to do.' Polls on the policy issue, then, helped determine the planks of the Liberal platform. The second case is the Ontario Conservatives' campaign of 1995. Guy says the research helped the Conservatives understand the strategic value of their party sharply distinguishing itself from Bob Rae's unpopular NDP government. This, rather than evidence about public support for the substance of the Common Sense Revolution (which was not strong), helped with the development of the platform.

Third, some research stresses party activists and supporters, and it may be reported to the PMO along with research on the wider public. This research is a potential source of policy ideas, which are initially polled with party activists and then with the wider public.[31] Information about party supporters can be of greater interest to political officials than data on the population as a whole. 'You don't much care if a minority of Canadians support you if all your party guys are with you,' says a former senior governmental official.

Fourth, party polls can help to inform the government's MPs. This is not necessarily a neutral exercise. The research can be cited by cabinet ministers to try to bolster support for their policies in caucus. As minister of justice in the Mulroney government, Kim Campbell referred to opinion polling to help win the Tory caucus's support for her proposal to amend the Human Rights Act to prohibit employers from discriminating against gays and lesbians. She cited polling showing that 'Seventy-two per cent of Canadians agreed; there were regional variations but majority support across the country. Sixty-seven per cent of PCs who had voted in the last election – our winning coalition – were in favour, with 29 per cent against ... The issue was simply not a vote driver, one way or the other.'[32] Between 1993 and 2003, Michael Marzolini, the chair of Pollara, reported to the Liberal caucus about twice each year.

Fifth, party-sponsored polling can have a direct agenda-setting effect. Sometimes newly elected governments commission polls to explain, for example, the voters' decision in the election and their perceptions of the party's commitments. This kind of research is typically presented not to bureaucrats but to cabinet ministers, who use it to help determine priorities.[33] Alternatively, the research can be conducted when a government is anticipating an election and desires guidance about which issues to address before calling it.

Finally, party polling can influence the advice pollsters give to their clients. Decima chair David Crapper explains that 'Decima Research got [contracts to poll on] free trade and the GST and [the] Meech Lake and Charlottetown [Accords], because of an existing relationship between a pollster and his client ... And in the guy's head is all of that partisan stuff, and in his head is all the policy stuff, and in his head it all comes together.' He says Allan Gregg worked this way as the main pollster for the Mulroney government and believes Goldfarb also did for Trudeau's government.

Governments sometimes prefer to use party-sponsored polls because they can be commissioned faster than government-funded polls. More often, party-sponsored polls are used because either officials want to keep the results secret, or because a study's questions and objectives are too partisan to justify the use of public funds for the research. The latter reasons depend on reports of taxpayer-funded research being publicly available as a result of Access to Information legislation, while party-sponsored research can be kept confidential.

As the above discussion indicates, public opinion research from a variety of sources figures in the policy process. For most research that is not commissioned by government, its officials have little opportunity to directly influence the subject and content of the research. From the point of view of Gallup and Rae, who thought mostly of polls published in newspapers, it is desirable that government officials are also exposed to opinion research with questions influenced by external sources rather than merely questions they choose to investigate.

With media polls, and to a lesser degree the other alternatives to government-commissioned polls, the research helps to shape the environment in which policy-making takes place. Overall, their impact appears to be greatest in agenda-setting. Because these polls are general and oriented to political rather than technical concerns, they have more potential to affect the overall direction of policy than its details. They are even less useful for implementation or evaluation of policy. For these purposes, greater depth is needed, so officials normally prefer specially commissioned polls. The impact of externally sponsored polls should not be exaggerated: most of the opinion research that matters in the policy process is initiated by government.

How Are Government Polls Contracted?

The process by which the federal government awards contracts for opinion research is somewhat decentralized, increasingly complicated, and prone to change. Most taxpayer-funded opinion research undertaken for the federal government is commissioned by individual departments; for example, in the 1994–7 period, just 1.6 per cent was initiated by the Privy Council Office.[34] A recent exception is 'Listening to Canadians,' a series of surveys for Communication Canada with samples exceeding 4,700 respondents, an unusually large number. Subjects investigated included Canadians' awareness of government advertising and their attitudes on national priorities, economic performance, health care, and the quality of government services. The federal government's opinion research is currently administered by a unit within the Department of Public Works and Government Services, the Public Opinion Research Directorate (PORD).[35] Until the early 1990s, its predecessors focused on the content of the research, but the emphasis has shifted to the contracting process. The final questionnaires, therefore, are not necessarily received by the directorate. Its responsibilities include advising departments when they are commissioning opinion research, monitoring the contracting process, and helping to avoid duplication of efforts by different departments.[36]

Until 1994, polling contracts were awarded either without competition on a sole-source basis, or through a competitive procedure with firms bidding for individual contracts.[37] Asked what happened before 1994 when opinion research was needed quickly, a Public Works employee familiar with the contracting process replies, 'You'd phone Decima.' Sole-sourcing was perceived by many as unfair, however, and holding competitive bids for individual contracts presented several problems. First, it was time-consuming and expensive for polling firms to prepare proposals for individual projects – Baker estimates a preparation cost of $6,000 to $10,000 per bid – and considered a wasteful use of resources as several firms might compete for the same contract. Second, similarly, reviewing individual proposals for each contract proved a drain on the time of public servants. Third, because of the time taken by polling companies and the public service, the contracting process was slow, and on many contemporary issues (for example, military intervention abroad) users of polls need data quickly as the political landscape can change rapidly. Finally, with each contract being awarded individually, the chances of productive ongoing relationships between departments and polling firms were reduced.

For these reasons, and a desire for a cleaner system, the 'standing offer' process was introduced in 1995, which applied for most contracts valued at more than \$30,000.[38] This amount was later reduced to \$25,000. (Smaller contracts, which are largely for questions on omnibus surveys or qualitative research, can be sole-sourced.) The standing offer procedure enables departments to contact an approved polling firm directly for research, or to approach a company which PORD advises would be suitable for a particular project, rather than taking competitive bids for a specific study.[39] While the rules and procedures have often changed, polling firms present proposals to PORD to win positions on the standing offer lists and these proposals are evaluated by civil servants. Most government departments use the same set of lists. At present there are separate lists established for qualitative research, quantitative research, and mixed projects valued at up to \$200,000, as well as recently established lists for higher-valued contracts.[40] Many firms have qualified for more than one list. A few departments, such as Finance and Transport, operate their own standing offer list; PORD participates in choosing the firms for these lists and receives copies of the contracts.

Pollsters generally agree that the standing offer procedures have improved the contracting process. Although a recent auditor general's report harshly criticized the management of advertising contracts, the government's handling of opinion research was generally considered satisfactory.[41] Contracts are also spread considerably more evenly among polling firms than in the past. Moreover, according to a civil servant, this 'improves their stake in the department's mandate and program. They're not just data collectors [any more]; they become advisers.' This comment highlights the potential for pollsters to not merely gather and present data, but also to mediate it; it brings to mind Goldfarb's essay in which he speaks of the role of *pollsters* rather than *polling*.[42]

While patronage is not a major basis for the contracting of opinion research as it arguably was in the past, and as it was for some recent government advertising contracts, concerns about the sole-sourcing of certain contracts persist.[43] Gaudet's analysis for the Reform Party found

220 of 500 opinion research contracts were sole-sourced in the fiscal years 1995–6 and 1996–7. He also identifies several contracts with values such as $29,960, an amount which falls just under the former $30,000 barrier for sole-sourcing.[44] As well, the Department of Finance's past awarding of opinion research contracts to Earnscliffe Research and Communications, which contains such close associates of former Finance Minister Paul Martin as David Herle, is considered 'patronage' by some, or, more gently, a case where the minister was reputed to 'direct' research towards his favoured polling firm.[45] Concerns about politicization of contracting, then, have not been completely eliminated.

Which Departments Use the Most Opinion Research?

Government departments' spending on opinion research varies considerably, and there appears to be a somewhat random pattern.[46] In part, spending changes over time depending on what issues are highest on the public agenda. A change of minister or senior public servants can also alter the pattern of expenditures on opinion research, as some officials are simply more interested in opinion research than others. A civil servant explains that some ministers 'don't want to take a step without finding out what the reaction would be. Others are less concerned about that and don't place as much emphasis on it. So ministers' offices often set the tone for the kind of research that's undertaken and how much input research has into the policy-making process.'

However, a department's policy area is more important than its senior personnel in determining its use of opinion research. According to the Reform Party's calculations for the three fiscal years from 1994 to 1997, Health, Industry, and Human Resources Development Canada (HRDC) were by far the heaviest spenders on opinion research, each at around the $5 million-mark. These three departments accounted for more than half of the government's expenditures on opinion research during these years. Finance was well behind in fourth place, at about $1.8 million, and three other departments exceeded $1 million: Canadian Heritage, Revenue Canada, and Natural Resources. At the other end of the list, spending less than $0.5 million each over the three-year period, are the departments of Veterans Affairs, Transport, Justice, and the Solicitor General, along with the Treasury Board and PCO.[47]

Although Health is often mentioned as a department where opinion research is used heavily, Industry is not. The figures are also surprising in light of the impressions of several interviewees who commented that Paul Martin's Finance Department made considerable use of opinion research. Still, it could be pointed out that Finance was the fourth-heaviest spender on opinion research. Additionally, the close working relationship between Martin and his pollsters at Earnscliffe was well known in Ottawa (the firm's contract for services to Finance was cancelled following Martin's departure from the cabinet in 2002), while the research for the higher-spending departments assumes a lower profile and provokes less controversy.

Pollsters provide several explanations why some departments commission polls more than others and why these tend to be in social service areas. For instance, says Stephen Kiar, departments such as the former HRDC have many programs that directly affect people; as a result they initiate opinion research more than most other departments. Another pollster comments that issues such as health care require the most opinion research because they are the most complex. And Senator Michael Kirby, who has experience as a pollster and government official, explains that the high-profile and 'political' departments such as Health and HRDC are the largest users of opinion research. 'National Revenue doesn't need to do polls, Public Works doesn't need to do polls ... They're not going to get covered in newspapers, they're not going to be covered in public opinion, they're not going to swing votes.'

Government Clients and Their Use of Opinion Research

Which political actors initiate requests for opinion research? With whom do polling firms interact when they deal with government? And how do pollsters report to clients?

A distinction is frequently drawn between the 'political' or partisan level of government – primarily the PMO and cabinet ministers and their political advisers – and career public servants. While this is important, it is also useful to distinguish between two types of civil servants, those whose primary function is communications or public affairs, and those who work in strategic policy positions. In most departments the activities of communications and strategic policy units are not well integrated throughout the various stages of the policy process, and the communications sections are typically brought into the process only after the key policy decisions have been made. As one observer bluntly puts it, 'The communications people are by and large treated like a latrine cleanup squad. They only come in after [the policy-makers] act.'

Which Government Officials Initiate Opinion Research?

Even for those at the centre of the process, it can be difficult to identify the officials who initiate a request for opinion research: a *need* for research may be articulated in a meeting of several political and bureaucratic officials early in the process of planning policy, but the actual polling may be conducted several months later.[48] Moreover, a request for polling might come from a minister's office but travel through the bureaucracy, while larger research projects initiated by civil servants require a minister's approval. Nevertheless, it is possible to address the question of which government actors request opinion research. The minister's office, the communications/public affairs staff and the strategic-policy staff each have roles.

Contrary to the emphasis critics of polling place on its political element, a minority of requests for publicly-funded research originate at the political level. Baker estimates this proportion at 20 per cent and some suggest it is rarer.[49] For those requests that do come from this level, however, the research tends to be politically sensitive and oriented towards larger-scale political concerns, most obviously national unity. Political staff might be motivated to poll, explains a public servant, because 'they're hoping that if they're going to move in a certain direction, they'll have public support for doing it. And the polling hopefully makes a case ... For a minister's office, from a political standpoint, polling is at least one mechanism we have for consulting the public, so it lends a certain legitimacy.' Although staff in ministers' offices initiate more opinion research than the ministers, occasionally ministers personally request polling on, for instance, budgets or short-term crises such as labour disputes.

Public servants initiate much more public opinion research than the political side of government. Baker estimates that with about 20 per cent of research requests coming from ministers' offices, the other 80 per cent comes evenly from communications and strategic policy branches. Others suggest that a majority of all opinion research for government originates with communications staff.[50] In part, differences in pollsters' perceptions result from variations in the companies' work. Ian McKinnon, for instance, says that in the 1980s Decima's pollsters regularly dealt with senior public servants on strategic and policy concerns. He adds that firms such as Canadian Facts which conduct less strategic research have proportionately more contact with communications staff. Public servants are especially likely to initiate the research that deals with less contentious matters like implementation and communications.[51] In addition, Angus Reid comments that some research initiated by public servants probably never comes to the attention of ministers. He offers the examples of studies of holders of hunting licences and visitors to national parks.

Overall, then, public servants play a much larger role than ministers' offices in initiating opinion research, and among public servants, communications staff appear to originate research somewhat more than officials in strategic policy positions. The roles of the different officials in requesting research are by no means entirely discrete. Rather, there is a degree of intertwining and joint responsibility in the process of initiating polling contracts. Still, the predominant role of civil servants in commissioning opinion research has implications for the types of research conducted and the ways that it is used. Most importantly, civil servants are oriented towards applying technical skills and they lack the incentives of elected officials to be responsive to public opinion;[52] therefore they are less likely to commission the kinds of research that would potentially enhance responsiveness.

Which Government Officials Do Pollsters Meet?

Who meets with pollsters depends partly on the nature of the research and who commissioned it. Still, contrary to some journalistic images of pollsters feeding data directly to politicians, pollsters say most of their firms' contacts with government are with public servants rather than ministers and their staffs. Among the public servants, pollsters report more interaction with the communications staffers than with strategic policy officials.[53]

McKinnon describes representing Decima at meetings with government clients:

> When you are reporting, for example, on strategic research you had done, it would be routine for people from the communications shop to be there, if there was any relevance for communications. It was rare that [they] would be your direct client or the person that mattered most in the room, regardless of who had signed the contract ... [In] the majority of work that Decima did with government agencies, particularly at the federal level, the most important person would be the senior bureaucrat in the room. In fact, I would guess it was in a minority of cases that there would even be a staff member from the minister's office in the room.

Broadly consistent with this, Michael Kirby says the officials most likely to attend meetings with pollsters are the department's deputy minister, the senior policy-makers, and the minister's political staff; ministers themselves attend only occasionally. Other sources, perhaps because of their experiences with different kinds of opinion research and different kinds of meetings, downplay the appearances of ministers and their aides even more than McKinnon and Kirby. However, ministers and their staff are typically invited to presentations of the final report and sometimes request copies if they do not attend.

While this discussion emphasizes the role of civil servants as the main users of opinion research, this impression should not be over-stated. Even though the partisan side of government initiates relatively little research, elected officials and their political aides may still make considerable use of it in their contributions to the policy process. This point is evident from an observation by Reid: 'I've had meetings with people ranging from Mulroney to Chrétien and have always been struck at how [familiar] they are with all of the latest polls, and how much they know chapter and verse on ... the public mood on a variety of issues.'[54] Moreover, ministers' staff periodically approach civil servants for poll data to use in preparing speeches, and briefing notes and memoranda to cabinet often mention opinion research, which helps elected officials become informed about it. Still, as with the initiation of research, it is clear that communications staff and strategic policy staff are the usual figures who meet with pollsters. Personnel in ministers' offices are involved less; when they do meet pollsters it tends to be later in the reporting process. As well, politicians' familiarity with polls does not necessarily mean that the polls make a difference to their decisions.

How Are Findings Reported to Clients?

Clients in government rarely receive only raw data unmediated by pollsters, although some firms provide more analysis than others. Goldfarb writes that 'it is the interpretation of results – not the collection of data – that sets a good pollster apart from an ordinary one.'[55] One pollster says his firm always interprets the data for clients, and adds, 'Explanation, understanding – that's what they're paying for; that's the fun part of our job.' Interpretation takes many forms, he says. It could include, for example, assessing support for the government's position on the fiscal dividend to be 'soft,' and identifying factors – such as new information indicating a larger surplus than anticipated – which might shift public opinion in the future.[56] Generally, the pollsters' analysis of public opinion also draws on their knowledge of public affairs. In this way, pollsters can influence how their polls are received as they reach beyond the data they have gathered and mediate it when they present their results and recommendations. Clients in government do not rely entirely on their pollsters' interpretations, however, because some government departments, notably Health and the former HRDC, have specialized staff who conduct analysis of the data.

On most contracts, pollsters report to their clients both in writing and orally, although the relative emphasis on these varies from pollster to pollster. A few even say they rely more on oral presentations than written reporting. Oral reporting is often used when there are time constraints. Also, pollsters sometimes feel freer to give advice orally. Indeed, on occasion, recommendations are softened between draft and final written reports – or in rare instances left out entirely – when clients do not wish to have a written record; the pollster and client keep in mind that most final reports are in the public domain or may be requested under Access to Information legislation.

Pollsters' interactions with government clients sometimes extend beyond their written and oral reports on a given piece of research. A series of formal meetings might be held, or clients may contact pollsters months or even years after a research project is completed, and sometimes they ask pollsters for general advice that may not even relate to a particular study. Pollsters may even participate informally in public sector working groups dealing with a policy. This is another way that pollsters potentially influence the policy process.

Conclusion

Some key points about the practice and framework of government opinion research are as follows: federal government opinion research contracts are now divided between a wide range of companies; besides the opinion research commissioned for government, polls from other sources play a part in the policy process; PORD oversees the process by which departments obtain opinion research, and this process became fairer under the Chrétien government; departments spend on opinion research in different amounts, with those dealing with social services among the heaviest purchasers; and generally, staff in ministers' offices initiate fewer requests for opinion research than civil servants, and they interact with pollsters less; and among career public servants, those who specialize in communications use research somewhat more than strategic-policy staff. The role of public servants has implications for the kind of opinion research initiated as well as the way it is used. In particular, public servants, especially those in communications branches, are less likely than elected officials to use opinion research for directly responsive purposes relating to policy content.

4 An Overview of the Uses of Opinion Research in the Policy Process

How can polling play a role in the various stages of the policy process: agenda-setting, the development and study of policy alternatives, the choice of policy options, implementation and evaluation?

Before briefly examining these phases and then turning to answer this question, four general observations are worth making.[1] First, not all senior government officials use opinion research, and indeed a few question its value. Notably, some civil servants, particularly experts in specialized fields such as transportation and the environment, are reluctant to use polls. These officials have an outlook which one pollster suggests they would privately express like this: 'We're the experts ... People who are occupied with their daily lives don't really understand this stuff. Why should we get them involved? It would just muddy the picture.'

Second, several pollsters use the metaphor that polling provides a 'map' or 'road map' of the political environment. They apply the concept in ways that emphasize different uses of opinion research. The Angus Reid Group's Darrell Bricker employs the term to characterize the picture that opinion research creates; Environics' Jane Armstrong refers to using research to help understand the 'priorities, the choices and the trade-offs' of citizens, an orientation towards policy; and the Strategic Counsel's Michael Sullivan applies the map image to describe how polling helps with the communications of policy. Ian McKinnon explains that opinion research often serves 'much like a map. It doesn't tell you where to go, or tell you [that] you shouldn't go some place, or you must go some other place – but rather it gives you a fairly accurate picture of how hard or easy it is to get to various goals. And it lets you make a more sophisticated choice about both where you're going, and above all how to get there.' While it does not signal a major role for polling in determining policy goals, the map metaphor captures uses of polls across different phases of the policy process, as a map of the public landscape can help guide the timing or details of policies, and, more commonly, implementation and communications.

A third point is that governments commission polling partly because it is a quick and economical way of consulting citizens.[2] Canadians have higher expectations about government consultation today than thirty years ago, says Armstrong. Indeed, the government has recently hinted that it is taking seriously the capacity of opinion research to aid consultation. The Treasury Board and PCO have expressed interest in obtaining more input from the general public into policy development through consultations, town hall meetings, 'public juries,' the Internet, and focus groups and polling.[3] Andrew Sullivan explains that

> there's interest within government [in] ... citizen engagement – the idea stemming from looking at all of these polling results, that Canadians are growing more disaffected with government ... and there's a need to rem- edy that in some ways, one of which is to offer them some sense of inclusion as to how broad directions are set. A modified use of public opinion research is actually the best way of engaging Canadians. Picking up on sort of a Fishkin deliberative model, and taking a lot of the strengths of that, but [addressing] some of the weaknesses as well, [and proposing] a sort of iterative polling model, seems to test very well with people: they understand it, it meets most of the tests that they would hold an engage- ment exercise up to, it's deliberative, it's representative.[4]

To the extent that this reflects a genuine shift in government practices, this kind of consultation could influence the government's agenda, or help find solutions to policy problems, or offer some guidance for communicating about policy. However, it is probably less useful at other phases in the policy process.

Stages of the Policy Process

In order to identify the effects of polling and focus groups on the policy process, it is important to distinguish various stages. This will highlight different roles opinion research may play during the various phases of policy-making.[5]

In the first stage, agenda-setting is the process by which some issues emerge on the agenda of government while others are delayed or excluded. Governments partially express their agendas through party election platforms, throne speeches, and addresses by leaders. However, the government does not enjoy full control of its agenda. For example, news reports and public opinion can attract attention to various issues, affect which ones are addressed, and when they secure a place on the political agenda.[6]

The development and study of policy alternatives, the second stage, has two distinct components. First, on occasion, opinion research guides the broad strategic thrust of a government's policies. There are no clearly documented examples for Canada. However, in the United States, in 1995–6, political consultant Dick Morris employed polling to advise Bill Clinton to move towards the centre of the political spectrum and to take stands on so-called 'values issues' such as television violence, teenage smoking, and fathers' child support payments.[7] Second, opinion research can help develop specific options from which policymakers choose. The process that puts certain choices on the table and excludes others contributes to reaching policy outcomes.

The selection of policy is the most important category for examining the impact of opinion research on policy content, but it is also the most overestimated use of polling. First, polls may guide decisions about the direction and content of public policy. In its crudest form, this suggests that policy-makers refer to polls on public preferences and that the results determine their decisions. More realistically, polling can be one of several factors on a backdrop to certain policy decisions. Second, opinion research can affect decisions about the *details* of policy. A given policy decision may not be driven by polls but a particular element of it may be influenced by them.

Once a policy is in place, opinion polling can assist officials in making decisions about how to proceed with implementation, the fourth stage. Opinion research can help determine the most effective way of delivering a program.

In the final stage, while much evaluation measures policy outcomes rather than public attitudes, there is a place for polling and focus groups to measure citizens' satisfaction with, and awareness of, a policy or program. In evaluation, this research resembles commercial market research, which gauges attitudes of actual or potential consumers and clients.

Pollsters' and Practitioners' Views about the Effects of Opinion Research

An exploratory part of the research for this study included twenty-seven of the interview sources (twelve current and former civil servants, four former political aides, three former cabinet ministers, and eight current and former pollsters). These interviewees were presented with a list of eleven ways that opinion research potentially influences the policy process and asked which they considered most significant. Up to four responses were accepted. While most interviewees agreed that all applied at times, and a few suggested other classifications, some patterns emerged. Four of the twenty-seven said they were not familiar enough with how governments use polling to answer the question; the responses of the other twenty-three can be summarized as indicated in table 4.1.

These responses suggest that opinion research contributes substantially to agenda-setting. Most importantly, the results highlight the prominence of opinion research in communications. Six interviewees volunteered that it was the most significant use; one each made that claim for agenda-setting and helping to justify a policy externally. Several other sources not presented with this list also indicated that they viewed communications as the foremost function of opinion research in government; moreover, requests for examples of opinion research affecting the content of policy produced many responses relating to communications.

Agenda-setting

Dick Morris has explained how he used polling to develop the advice he gave to Bill Clinton which led the president to alter the general direction of his policies in 1995–6. This kind of strategic change in the character of policy is one type of agenda-setting; more commonly, the term refers to the process that brings individual issues to the attention of government officials and determines which are addressed. The term can also be used to apply to an individual department setting its priorities. Opinion research can help pursue two overlapping goals: learning which issues are high priorities with the public, and identifying issues which if stressed could increase the government's popularity.

McKinnon says pollsters sometimes deliver the message to politicians that their policies are less popular than they believed: this oc-

TABLE 4.1
Uses of opinion research in the policy process

Phase of process	Specific use of opinion research	Mentions
Agenda-setting	1. Agenda-setting*	10
	2. Affecting timing	4
Development and study of policy alternatives	3. Affecting the general direction of policy	7
	4. Helping to formulate policy options	5
Selection of policy	5. Affecting decisions about specific policies	0
	6. Affecting decisions about *details* of specific policies	4
	7. Helping to justify a policy *within government*	6
Communications of policy	8. Helping to justify a policy *externally*	5
	9. Helping to communicate policy	20
Implementation	10. Helping to implement policy/programs	3
Evaluation	11. Helping to evaluate policy/programs	6

*Agenda-setting was defined in writing as 'identifying policy issues and problems, and deciding which issues government addresses.'

curred with the Mulroney government on federal-provincial relations and privatization. However, this influence should not be overstated. McKinnon explains that 'I have never met a government that would go out and ask "What are the top ten concerns facing you?" [and] then try to mirror them back in the throne speech.' Senior government officials also contact pollsters for ad hoc discussions 'on what we see in a big-picture sense.'[8]

When sources are asked why policy-makers in government use opinion research, answers are often at a general level that suggests an agenda-setting function. This applies to the role of opinion research in monitoring the public environment; this also includes analysis of media coverage and monitoring the activities of interest groups.[9] Don Guy says polls help 'bridge the gap' between government and citizens by helping policy-makers address the priorities of the public. Consistent with this, Hugh Segal thinks of opinion research as one of several 'planning tools' used by policy-makers (of roughly equal importance to econometric analysis, 'traditional policy analysis,' and analysis of media coverage).

Angus Reid argues that polling influences agenda-setting at both strategic and tactical levels. The strategic level is the agenda of the government as a whole. Strategic opinion research is conducted to examine

> the broad landscape and help people in government use things like gap analysis to ask [the public], well, how important are the following policy areas? And you can actually go through a list of policy areas ranging from the environment, to unemployment and jobs, to reform of the health care system, etc. You can go through those areas of the importance of those, and you can go through those areas and get an idea of performance – how well people see the government doing. And you can end up with sort of a gap, and using that gap analysis you can at a very strategic level help to set agendas.

The overall agenda of the government can also be expressed through its throne speeches, and polling can help determine which issues are addressed this way. Agenda-setting for the government as a whole can occur in a less deliberate way, when survey research brings a specific issue to the attention of cabinet ministers or other officials. One pollster says the classic example of polling affecting the profile of an issue occurred with environmental policy in the late 1980s. Polling showed increased public concern and 'Environment became a senior cabinet post in the latter part of the '80s; the priority placed on the environment has shifted.' Ministers sometimes use polls in cabinet debates to try to justify moving their policy areas higher on the government's agenda.[10] Another example is external polls by Ekos which drew attention to proposals to address concerns about government accountability by producing 'report cards.' This has attracted attention in several departments and, for instance, was mentioned in a speech by Allan Rock while he was the minister of health.[11]

As well as strategic agenda-setting, Reid says tactical agenda-setting takes place within departments. Whether this is agenda-setting in the conventional sense – the term usually refers to setting government-wide priorities – might be debated. On this type, Reid explains, the Canadian Information Office deals with national unity, 'but within that file, what is the priority? Is the priority youth, is it women, is it Quebeckers, is it francophones outside of Quebec?' Similarly, departments can also use research to help set priorities in allocating their finite resources. A public servant describes a case where a department had

> established its own priority list. And polling showed ... a lack of synchronization here: 'I can see how you turn the priority list of policy people around.' And say, 'If I were you, I'd move item six up to item number one. If you want to get ministers' attention, and you want to get their support to go forward to get funding for your initiatives, change your priority list a little bit.'

Gary Breen, who has worked for both Decima and the PCO, adds that 'individual departments at times will use surveys in a very strategic way, [to] try to make a case for policy proposals and for resources ... It's a department saying, "We've got to prove to central agencies and ministers that there's public support for these ideas. So let's prove it." I'm not sure that George Gallup saw that coming.'

Sometimes the priority-setting is not deliberate and results from external polls. For example, opinion research revealing public concern about the problem of youth unemployment apparently helped pressure the minister's office and public servants in HRDC to address that issue, raising its position on the agenda. In this instance, the cause was Angus Reid polling appearing in newspapers rather than custom research. Polls affected timing in this case, spurring the government to address this earlier than it would have otherwise.

Polling, then, can contribute to agenda-setting in several ways, partly because the research comes from both internal and external sources. Polls can figure in agenda-setting following an election when there is a conscious and deliberate exercise covering all departments. They also can influence the agenda in a less deliberate way when external polls signal public concern about an issue. At a more tactical level, the agenda of a department can be influenced by either external or specially commissioned polls. In the less planned forms of agenda-setting, pollsters rarely advise clients, but the research can still help to shape priorities.

The Development of Policy Alternatives

While McKinnon says Decima regularly advised clients about the development of policy options, most other pollsters agree that this happens but they view it as less common.[12] What they describe could more accurately be called testing and comparing different policy choices as a contribution to the formulation of policy alternatives. For example, Guy says pollsters are asked to measure citizens attitudes towards different policy options, some of which are pursued while others are not. Another pollster, Andrew Sullivan, says that on policy areas in which his firm, Ekos Research, specializes, it 'would be in a position to say that, "Based on the views of Canadians, these are the types of levers that seem to work fairly well; these are the types that don't seem to. And looking at this specific group, we might suggest exploring this type of option."'

Michael Kirby agrees that polls can provide helpful input when governments are choosing among policy options. For example, a survey might ask respondents what they think are the pros and cons of different proposals to cut spending and which option they prefer. Similarly, a government seeking to raise additional revenue might try to learn which type of tax would be most acceptable to the public. Kirby warns, however, that officials 'won't follow that religiously, because in many cases there's spin-off effects of the tax increases that the public wouldn't understand.' Armstrong says polls are sometimes taken to assess the public's tolerance for tax increases, but she cautions that the findings are not very influential in the decisions. These comments underline the need to avoid overstating the impact of opinion research on the development of policy options; other factors, including assessments of the merits of the choices, play a part too.

Determining the Substance and Details of Policy

Central to Gallup and Rae's enthusiasm for the democratic promise of polling is the claim that it can significantly influence decisions about the content of policy. To what extent does this actually occur in Canada?

Pollsters readily acknowledge that opinion research can serve as an input into policy choices, although most indicate that this influence is limited. When this use of polls occurs, often it is without a pollster's direct advice. In fact, several pollsters state firmly that they would *not* give advice to policy-makers about whether to adopt a particular policy.[13] As McKinnon insists, 'It is certainly not a public opinion researcher's place to say, "Based on our results, you can't do this; you have to do this."'

However, some pollsters say advice about adopting specific policies is given from time to time.[14] Moreover, says McKinnon, pollsters advise their clients about the likely political consequences of a policy (which is distinct from advice about whether to adopt a policy). He adds that sometimes this is 'informed speculation.' Andrew Sullivan does not consider what Ekos gives clients about policy choices to be advice. Rather, he explains, 'We would say, "We've tested these policy options and there seems to be an issue there."' In his words, 'We would make recommendations on the broader public acceptability of an option.' Consistent with this, another pollster describes his role in interpreting public opinion to clients: 'You can usually give them a warning about doing something that's really dumb in terms of their own political situation. But if they want to ... proceed with doing it because they think it's the right thing to do, they'll do it.' He continues:

> I've said to clients before, 'I'm a mercenary, not a missionary' ... I remember saying to a couple of clients at one point, 'I'm willing to tie that bandana with a little red zero on the front of it, and put you in the cockpit of the zero airplane, bolt down the canopy, and send you towards the fleet if you want. But I'm just here to tell you that you're going to run into an aircraft carrier. If you decide to do that, that's up to you. I've done my job. I'm just telling you what the implications of doing it are.'[15]

While this vivid metaphor may not constitute advice, it would be perceived as an emphatic warning about the potential political hazards of a policy choice, and such a warning might well lead some clients to proceed more cautiously, or even change direction.

Asked for examples of issues where polling affected a policy decision, some pollsters suggest that the federal government's approach to tackling the deficit was partly driven by public opinion research. A former civil servant, who says polls rarely exert a major influence on policy content, recalls one case where he believes they were decisive. Polling showed that Canadians favoured retaining Canada's peacekeeping forces in Haiti in 1994–5: 'It largely resolved the debate that was taking place in cabinet ... We're talking here of knowing where public opinion is at, and in this case it confirmed there was no real significant opposition to us staying on in Haiti. That was a nice clear decision: do we or don't we extend [the peacekeeping efforts] another six months?'[16] Similarly, Hugh Segal suggests that polling affected

> the way in which the [Bill] Davis government decided in '80–81 that it had to move from a kind of 'if it ain't broke, don't fix it' approach to public policy, to a cohesive economic development plan for Ontario ... in terms of

its throne speech, its budget, and ultimately in terms of its electoral platform. Polling said that there was sufficient anxiety about whether the boom would last, and whether the recession would begin, and whether Ontario was competitive, for [the government] to address some fundamental questions of social and economic infrastructure. And I'm not sure that that would have happened in the normal course of events were it not for public opinion data.

This example indicates that a decision to abandon an ad hoc approach to economic policy in favour of a more systematic plan stemmed partly from concerns revealed through public opinion polls.

Michael Sullivan expresses a view shared by many pollsters and government officials when he reflects on his work for government clients: 'It's tough for me to find a situation where a poll has actually led to a particular policy. I mean, a policy might be refined, but it wouldn't necessarily lead to wholesale change.' Echoing the view attributed to Keith Davey in chapter 2, Chris Baker says that 'I can't really think of an instance where a poll was ... done and the government sort of changed its mind on the basis of the poll.' Bricker agrees, saying polling occasionally affects a detail or nuance of policy but, at least in his experience, 'This idea of policy by polls never happens.' These comments are consistent with the road map metaphor and the notion that, while opinion research does not help with a decision about where to go, it can assist a decision about how to get there.

This suggests that rather than opinion research serving as a major influence on the direction of a specific policy, often it is more likely to affect the policy instrument chosen or the details of policy. It can affect small-scale decisions about, for example, the amount of a transit fare increase. It also influenced the exact form that Employment Insurance assumed. Another example is that polling showing public concern about toxic industrial waste was crucial in the establishment of the Ontario Waste Management Corporation by the provincial government in the early 1980s. Without the polls revealing public concern, he says, the government would probably have taken a more modest step, such as enhancing the Environmental Assessment Act. In this case, the polls did not specifically show a desire for a high-profile body, but the creation of the corporation was a response to the data. The polling affected the timing and the policy instrument for addressing the issue concern but not the policy goal.[17]

Opinion research, then, is a factor in decisions about the content of policy, but plays a smaller part than is commonly assumed. Also, while it might be expected that opinion research is more likely to affect the general thrust of policy content more than details of policy, in fact there appears to be at least as much of the latter.

Implementation of Policy

In the process of putting policy goals into practice the necessary legislation is often quite general and leaves considerable discretion to civil servants.[18] Opinion research can affect the implementation of policy, including timing and communications. Timing can reflect political considerations such as avoiding unpopular policies shortly before an election; communications can be about determining what profile to give policies or certain components of policies, based in part on their popularity.

One example that illustrates the role of communications in implementation concerns Health Canada's regulations on health warnings on cigarette packages. Qualitative research has helped to anticipate consumers' reactions to different types of warnings, including pictures of cancerous lungs.[19] Another example comes from work by Decima Research which sought to encourage participation in a federal home insulation program during the 1980s. The research indicated that consumers could be categorized into discrete groups, and specific types of consumers should be induced to participate in different ways. For instance, some responded positively to the potential reductions in energy costs, others were motivated by nationalist reasons to save energy, and still others were 'home handymen ... who were reading things in Beaver Lumber or *Popular Mechanics* ... They went out and did it because, if you were proud of your house, [and it was] well maintained, then you *had* to have R-20 or whatever.' This research fed into a strategy of communicating different reasons for insulating a home to separate audiences, using different communications vehicles.[20]

There are also purer examples of opinion research exerting influence on implementation. For instance, it might help to decide whether storefront offices are required to reach the clients of a specific government program or to determine citizens' views of automated kiosks for providing government services. Kirby says that the kind of opinion research that affects implementation is administrative research, generally with focus groups: 'Typically what you would do, is you might launch a new program, and then do a set of focus groups with customers after they've been served, and get them to give you their reaction to it after it was over.' Opinion research can also be used to monitor implementation of policy.

Evaluation of Policy

Policy and program evaluation ranges from ad hoc judgments based on casual observation to systematic processes drawing on specially commissioned research. Generally, the main goals of policy evaluation are to assess the effectiveness of the policy and the efficiency of delivery of programs.[21] Policy evaluation addresses either performance or the awareness and support for a policy among its clients and the wider public. The latter is sometimes considered part of evaluation because citizens' perceptions are a factor in the success or failure of policies.[22]

   Most major polling firms conduct some research in policy evaluation, and pollsters with Ipsos-Reid and Ekos say their firms do a considerable amount. Ekos, in fact, originated as a specialist in evaluation. Opinion research to evaluate policy takes a variety of forms. It is most likely to be used when changes to a policy are being considered (*program* evaluation, however, is ongoing). Tracking surveys are conducted to assess changes in citizens' awareness, behaviour, and acceptance of a policy. Much of the evaluation research, generally done through focus groups, aims to study the attitudes of a specific program's clients or 'target group.' One pollster recalls explaining to a cabinet minister that much program evaluation research is 'basically polling, but it's asscovering stuff for civil servants. You know, you put out a program, you do this survey which says what a great idea it was.'[23] A former pollster explains that

   public opinion research ... tells you what the public think of [a policy], not what the specific clientele who [it is designed for think]. Effective public policy means how does it help the people who you were trying to help? Things like that. Effectiveness studies require that you do a detailed study of the specific individuals who have been affected by a policy. You could do a sample of that, part of an effectiveness study might include a public opinion sample of the customers, just as you do [with] customers of a car company or anybody else.[24]

Another source comments that it is rarely useful to ask the general public about technical questions, such as their opinion of the patrol frigate program.[25] Opinion research, then, is most likely to directly support evaluation in the areas of monitoring the performance of programs and clients' satisfaction with them.

Conclusion

Opinion research contributes to each phase of the policy process, although it is usually not the most important factor. The extent and nature of the use of opinion research varies from stage to stage; this is also true of the pollsters' roles interpreting data and providing advice. It appears that opinion research is a greater input in agenda-setting than in later stages of the policy process. Surprisingly, the impact of opinion research on details of policy, sometimes called 'fine-tuning' policy, may be somewhat larger than on the general direction of a policy decision. For agenda-setting and choosing policy options, the relevant research is usually conventional polling with large representative samples. On the other hand, in developing policy options, implementation and evaluation, greater emphasis on qualitative research is found. Also, in agenda-setting, and to a lesser degree in developing and choosing among policy options, syndicated and external polls play a significant part in conjunction with specially commissioned research, while the latter dominates in implementation and evaluation. This is partly because the effects of opinion research on agenda-setting and on formulating and deciding policy are in part unplanned and involve elected officials more. When opinion research figures in policy implementation and evaluation, however, it is largely because policy makers, mainly at the bureaucratic levels, deliberately seek it out and use it. Opinion research is used in many ways beyond the most obvious democratic function of influencing policy content as early pollsters anticipated. Some of these effects on the policy process – such as agenda-setting – are still reasonably consistent with their populist vision.

However, the role of communications complicates this picture. Throughout each of the phases of policy-making, communications is an aspect of the policy process influenced by opinion research. This is the focus of the following chapter.

5 Opinion Research and Government Communications

Governments communicate their policies to the public through speeches, media interviews, news releases, press conferences, brochures, advertising, and internet sites, often developing and executing extensive strategies to pursue their goals. Through these strategies they hope to gain support for their policies and to promote understanding, compliance, and legitimacy. Increasingly, opinion research helps government officials design and execute their communications strategies.

Although there are differences, the use of opinion research in government can be compared to private-sector market research. For instance, explains Michael Kirby:

> In anything to do with public communications, the polling is used in large measure as a market research study. The analogy is perfect. If you consider a new policy as a new product or service, then what would you do if you were doing a new product or service? You would want to understand what its likely receptivity is in the marketplace, and you also want to understand how you can best communicate about this potential product with customers. And sometimes, therefore, [depending on the policy] the customers are a small [subset] of the electorate, and sometimes, they're the whole electorate.

When pollsters advise government clients about communications, their work resembles that of public relations firms. Darrell Bricker says there are parallels, although he considers public relations more tactical, whereas a pollster's tasks are largely strategic. While a public relations firm actually prepares media releases, direct mail programs and sometimes advertising, the analysis by a polling firm influences the content of the material. In an effective communications strategy, the same message will be delivered through different vehicles, from advertising to media interviews. Therefore, the research can affect the entire range of ways that government communicates with the public.

First, although governments generally wish to avoid the appearance of governing by polls, opinion research is sometimes explicitly cited to justify a policy externally – to demonstrate support for a policy and defend a decision outside of government, usually after it has been taken.[1] These uses of polls have been particularly frequent on firearms control, as the Liberal government countered claims of public opposition, particularly in western Canada; although the loudest voices were indeed critical, most polls showed majority support for the government's position. This approach is illustrated by a government press release which stated that 'a large majority of Canadians agree that the registration of all guns is a reasonable approach to preserving Canadian values. A recent poll revealed that 82% of Canadians support registration including 72% of rural residents.'[2] Civil servants also cite polls in meetings with interest groups and concerned individuals. Similarly, cabinet ministers and MPs occasionally refer to polls in public statements to affirm popular support of their policies and to counter contrary claims. In 1997, for example, Health Minister David Dingwall defended his tobacco-control proposals, which faced singularly vocal opposition in Quebec. He said, 'I have a poll that shows 74 percent of the people in the province of Quebec support this legislation, a poll which shows 80 percent of Canadians support it. I am not going to be blackmailed.'[3]

Second, opinion research provides a general backdrop of data which informs the preparation of news releases and speeches, and ministers' briefings for Question Period and media interviews. When writing speeches, ministers' staff occasionally approach public servants for polling data, not to refer to explicitly but as guidance for content and phrasing.

Third, qualitative research is employed to test drafts of forms used for taxation, student loans, retirement planning, applications for programs such Employment Insurance, and other purposes. These documents are used by the public to 'communicate' with government, and they also explain government practices. It is therefore in the government's interest that the public understands and follows these correctly. Similarly, internet sites and interactive telephone message systems are tested with qualitative research. The research can produce substantial changes in communications. In most cases, this research is technical and uncontroversial.

Fourth, opinion research is used to help develop advertising and brochures by testing draft materials.[4] A former public servant explains that government advertising is normally tested: 'If you're going to spend private or public money on taking a public issue to Canadians, especially if you're using public money, what you want to make sure is that the message is the right one ... [and] that they'll be able to relate to the message that you're putting forward.' The cost of the research is typically a fraction of the total advertising expenses. An example of qualitative research generating a clear signal to the client appears in a study by Sage Research. Focus groups preferred an 'arrows' design to a 'stairs' design on a brochure describing the Canada Pension Plan's disability benefits program because the latter image could offend people who use wheelchairs.[5] Because of the cost and profile of advertising and the relative ease of using qualitative research to assess it, this the most purposeful, systematic, and intensive use of opinion research in government. The research influences the overall message and decisions about where to place advertisements.

Fifth, at a general level, opinion research helps to formulate, refine, and test communications strategies that government uses to promote acceptance and awareness of its policies. Among other things, polling informs policy-makers about the levels of public support for policies and the public's receptiveness to various arguments about them. Although governments are often reluctant to concede that they are spending public funds to promote acceptance of policies,[6] it is noteworthy that more than twenty interviewees for this study used the word 'sell' in this context. The selling of policy is the foremost purpose of government communications.

The Uses of Opinion Research for Government Communications

The main roles of opinion research in government communications are as follows: determining target audiences, measuring knowledge and awareness of policies, guiding the language and tone used in communicating policy, gauging the public's responses to different arguments, and influencing the content of communications. Overlapping with the second category is a further use, later in the policy process: evaluation of communications.

Determining Target Audiences

Polling is used to help decide which sub-groups of the population are to be targeted in government communications. Most *analysis* of polling emphasizes sub-groups, not the public as a whole. However, Andrew Sullivan warns against exaggerating this use of polls. He points out that government budgets for communications are limited compared to many large companies which allocate millions of dollars to *research* for communications. Another pollster indicates that marketing in government focuses on sub-groups of the population less than in the private sector because a government has some responsibility to serve, and communicate with, all citizens. While many policies affect particular groups, he states that the nature of a policy, rather than polling, determines whom government communications addresses.[7] Research is not entirely absent from such decisions, however. For example, a survey which reported high rates of smoking among teenagers influenced Health Canada's decision to aim an anti-tobacco campaign at young audiences.[8]

In practice, government opinion research and communications frequently aim at sub-groups of the population. Several pollsters indicate that research informs decisions about which demographic groups to target in government communications. For example, researchers look beyond the population as a whole to examine how differences in opinion correlate with language, region, age, sex, income, and education levels. Or the priority may be those groups that are the least aware of a policy or, more frequently, those judged most open to persuasion; addressing those who already know about a policy, and those who already firmly support or oppose it, is often viewed as a waste of time and money. More frequently, the government deliberately tries to reach those citizens who are considered most attentive to political news and likeliest to influence the opinions of others. The subsequent communications emphasize the media outlets to which opinion leaders are most frequently exposed.

Hugh Segal, who considers determining which sub-groups to address to be the foremost way that opinion research informs communications of policy, says that, for instance, 'senior professional women' are a very different audience from 'rural work-at-home women.' He explains that

the media that you choose are different, the language that you might use is different, and if you know you have a problem with that group, you test your messages qualitatively with the group with whom you hope to communicate, so that you'd have some validation ... [to show that] the language you're going to use and the message you're going to send is actually going to be receivable.

As an example where opinion research influenced the target of government communications, Segal points to polling conducted when the federal government allocated $25 million over five years for breast cancer research, starting in 1992. The opinion research showed that this issue was especially salient for young professional women, and this finding affected the way the program was communicated and the outlets where advertising was placed.

Measuring Knowledge and Awareness of Policies

Research often indicates that citizens desire information about policies. For instance, a survey of residents of the Quebec City and Abitibi regions showed that a majority of citizens believed that governments, especially the federal government, did not adequately inform them.[9] 'You could have a full page [advertisement], with every square inch filled with information, and they'd still ask for more,' comments a senior civil servant with a background in opinion research. Even when the government responds, however, and supplies information, this does not necessarily increase the perceived or actual levels of public knowledge. John Laschinger recalls opinion research in 1988 on the Free Trade Agreement (FTA) with the United States:

One thing they could all agree on was 'we don't know enough; we'd like to know more' ... So we produced three million pamphlets describing the Free Trade Agreement in explicit detail. And then we did some research, and said, 'now do you have enough?' Seventy-five per cent said, 'we don't have enough. We want more information' ... We just kept flooding them with information, most of which I'm sure they never read.

Indeed, the pamphlets had little effect on the proportion of respondents saying they lacked information.

In this and many other cases, opinion research measures the public's knowledge and awareness of an issue. This can help to justify a communications campaign or to determine what information to include or emphasize in communications. Often data are gathered periodically as part of the overall monitoring of the political landscape.

It is relatively infrequent that government polling measures the public's levels of knowledge, which pollsters distinguish from awareness. One pollster says awareness is measured more than knowledge because it is easier to test the former.[10] Another pollster explains that citizens know little about most issues, so it is generally not beneficial to practitioners to study knowledge directly. 'Most people will confess that they know very little [about the deficit],' he says. 'That really doesn't matter. The more important issue is, how strident are your attitudes about the deficit?'[11] Nevertheless, sometimes governments measure knowledge. An example of testing for both awareness and knowledge is found in a study Decima Research conducted shortly after the 1993 budget. The findings demonstrate that Canadians were generally unfamiliar with the budget: 31 per cent of respondents said that they had heard nothing about it. Moreover, given a list of eight policy options and asked 'whether each had actually been an element of the federal budget,' only 7 per cent of respondents could manage either seven or eight correct answers; 28 per cent offered five or six, 40 per cent gave three or four, 21 per cent provided one or two, and 5 per cent produced none. At least half the respondents incorrectly indicated that the budget had reduced transfer payments to the provinces.[12]

Most surveys attempt to measure awareness of a policy or program or some details, although this is frequently a minor part of the poll and it is not necessarily as important for straight communications purposes as determining target audiences and deciding which arguments to emphasize. The relevant questions are normally asked after a policy takes effect.

Guiding the Tone and Language Used to Communicate Policy

Opinion research, mainly through focus groups, helps to determine words and phrases to use in communicating policy, and the tone used in advertising and brochures. Many pollsters indicate that opinion research figures more heavily in selecting target audiences and choosing which arguments to use, although a minority consider guiding choices about language to be a major use of research. In Chris Baker's view, it is unfortunate that opinion research is not used more for this purpose because it could improve the way that government communicates with citizens: 'Bureaucrats or political people think that we are speaking to people. In fact, we're speaking *at* them. A lot of words are interpreted as code words for other things.' This reflects a sentiment also found in periodic calls for plain language in government.

Opinion research on government communications typically shows that audiences prefer a neutral, informational, fact-oriented tone to a promotional one. However, this message is not always followed. 'If we were doing print advertising for the government according to what a focus group tells us, it would be like this,' says a public servant, holding a white sheet of paper with twelve lines of black, 12–point type face. He summarizes the view of focus group participants: '"This is government, it has to be information. I don't want it to look like advertising. Because they'll try to sell me your policies. And information means a lot of copy, no picture."' However, he warns: 'the problem is that when you put this in the newspapers where you're competing with [advertisements by] Coca-Cola and Chrysler, and the news, nobody's going to look at it.' Still, during the referendum campaign on the Charlottetown Accord, messages from opinion research about a neutral tone led to greater emphasis on informational materials by the federal government. Another instance where research influenced the tone of communications took place in Human Resources Development Canada. Focus groups helped to ensure that letters sent by the department maintained a 'respectful' tone towards their readers.

As well as influencing tone, opinion research guides choices of vocabulary. Angus Reid says the importance of carefully-chosen language is evident from the tale about

> two priests who both have a similar question that they want to ask the pope. One of them writes him a question, 'Is it permissible if I smoke when I pray?' And the pope writes back and says, 'Absolutely not. Smoking's this very disgusting habit.' The other priest, meanwhile, is wiser. [He] writes and says, 'Is it okay if I pray when I smoke?' And the answer is, of course, 'There's no time you shouldn't pray.'

While the choice of language rarely has such a dramatic effect, it is recognized as important for influencing audiences. An aide to a cabinet minister explains that 'you might test a phrase like "We are fully committed to maintaining health care" with the intention of communicating that it's a critical priority – only to discover that people actually hear that since you say "maintain" you're not interested in enhancing the system. So you'd end up adjusting the phrasing to ensure that your full intention is well communicated and clearly understood.'

An example of opinion research affecting language involves opinion research by Insight Canada for Environment Canada. Don Guy explains that Insight's research helped to give direction to the vocabulary used to communicate policy. Several different terms were used by scientists to discuss climate change. Insight noted that communications on environmental issues such as climate change could be difficult because the public is not familiar with these specialized terms. The pollster's report explained that 'very few Canadians are comfortable yet with the term climate change ... In communicating on the issue of climate change, efforts will have to be made to explain the meaning of the concept and the specific term, in effect, branding the term with meaning.'[13] Guy recalls that 'there was no real value or meaning that was branded on any of those terms with respect to the public. So what they needed to do was to pick one [term] and start to explain what it ... meant, and basically sort of dig in ... the ground for the campaign, the ground for communicating that issue. So they did.' This illustrates how opinion research helps to clarify messages to the public.

More often, the main use of public opinion is not to improve clarity but to make a message more persuasive. Opinion research affected the wording used by Michael Wilson while he served as minister of international trade and industry. In 1991 he announced plans for consultations to improve Canada's competitiveness in the international economy. Wilson's use of the term 'prosperity initiative' was influenced by opinion research. 'People were interpreting competitiveness as [being about] winners and losers,' Baker explains. 'And they weren't very confident that they were winners. Michael Wilson was saying "competitiveness," he was [perceived as] saying, "you're a loser," which is why they regeared it to a "prosperity initiative," rather than a "competitiveness initiative."' This shift was spurred by opinion research conducted following the initial announcement; the term was changed roughly six months after that statement.

Similarly, in 1996 research for a new Industry Canada program called Technology Partnerships Canada helped make the public relations more effective. An interviewee explains:

They tested very specific language to be used in explaining programs like this. And essentially, 'government grants,' 'government subsidies,' 'government support,' all tested very poorly. 'Government-repayable investments' ... tested very well.

If you track how that program was communicated ... [at first, journalists] said, 'Repayable investments, I don't think so; we're just going keep calling them grants – government grants.' Constantly going back to that first message of repayable investments, the media was corrected: each and every time, a letter would be sent saying, 'Actually, these are repayable investments. You're being inaccurate in your reporting.' Over time, you saw that it began to be referred to as a repayable investment. Who could be against a repayable investment?

This contacting of the media represents a further way that the government communicates its message, in this case backing up the choice of terms that the opinion research helped to determine. The wording implicitly claims that the program is fiscally responsible. The impression that the words were not chosen for their accuracy is reinforced when we learn that, six years after the program was introduced, the claim that the investments were repayable looked shaky. Industry Canada's own report revealed that less than 1.3 per cent of the investments had been repaid as of March 2001.[14]

The impact of opinion research on language is mostly a matter of choosing among various words and phrases to promote clarity or, more often, persuasiveness. The selection can significantly affect public perceptions of a policy, especially in the choice of the terms such as 'prosperity initiative' and 'repayable investment,' which are intended to convey favourable images of the specific program. However, the selection of arguments is more consequential, and more widespread.

Gauging the Public's Responses to Different Arguments

Choices among arguments have more potential to influence the public than choices among language. Among the most common uses of opinion research is testing arguments to be presented and emphasized in government communications to promote policies. This use of opinion research is especially significant for potentially contentious policies and for the policies with the greatest profile and impact. Both qualitative and quantitative research assume significant roles in testing arguments.

A pollster explains that the questions which inform the choices of arguments to stress are framed something like this: 'there are many reasons why people are in favour of such and such a policy. For each of the following, tell me if it's a very good reason, [or] not a very good reason, for why this is a good idea.'[15] Sometimes respondents are divided, with different arguments in support of a policy being presented to separate portions of a sample; the most well-received argument is then emphasized.[16] CATI (computer-assisted telephone interviewing) has enabled pollsters to experiment easily with various ways of testing arguments.[17]

Another pollster observes that the use of opinion research to select the arguments employed to present policy is more frequent than its use to guide language, but often is indirect and less overt. He explains that research to select language must be intended to serve this function from the start. While some research has testing of arguments as its primary goal, it may also be done implicitly in the course of research when other purposes are more central.[18] Research on reactions to arguments may, for instance, evaluate actions the government might take.

Most pollsters and government officials agree that opinion research makes an important contribution to the choice of arguments for communicating policy. Angus Reid explains that opinion research can help guide the types of arguments presented to the public to justify a policy:

> During the period from 1993 to 1997, the Chrétien government ... on a lot of different fronts, [was] looking at that. We worked with Lloyd Axworthy when he was employment minister; he was redoing the UI Act. The question was, 'Well, what are the arguments that are going to be more persuasive? Which arguments are more conducive? Do you argue more about issues of equity, or argue more about issues of efficiency?' There's a lot of different ways to talk about this, recognizing that you're probably only going to get one soundbite [on the television news]. Which one is going to be the most effective?

The reference to expecting only one soundbite underlines the point that the finite amount of anticipated media coverage affects the decisions about communications.

Opinion research helped inform the Ontario government's advertising campaign when it introduced seat belt legislation in 1975. At the time, public support was '50–50 at best.' Hugh Segal, a key adviser to Premier Bill Davis, recalls that

> polling research was used to indicate what would likely produce the highest levels of voluntary compliance. And the highest levels of voluntary compliance would not be produced by police spot checks ... What would produce the highest level of compliance would be a communications program which [showed the dangers] ... of not wearing their seat

belt ... And that produced a very significant communications program, that showed ... pumpkins inside a car, if they stopped at 15 miles an hour with or without a ... seat belt. And we saw compliance levels soar.

The communications campaign was assessed as more effective than alternatives, such as relying on high fines and scrutiny by police officers. The opinion research, then, helped to decide the relative emphasis on communications and other means of persuasion – a matter of implementation – as well as the content of the ads.

Finally, polling firms sometimes gauge reactions to arguments that may be made by opposition parties or interest groups which oppose the policy. One pollster explains that opinion research is sometimes used to

test the opposition's arguments to see which ones work, and what arguments work against those. It sounds very manipulative, but it really isn't. It's helping people to anticipate so that they can better communicate – anticipate what may come as a criticism of you, so that you're able to respond in the best possible way. [Knowledge of effective arguments against a policy can help] decision makers to respond in a particular way to those issues, and sometimes it's as simple as acknowledging the concern.

The Department of Finance has polled to measure reactions to arguments for and against the GST, bank mergers, and proposals to reform seniors' benefits.[19] This was done partly so that the department would be prepared, if necessary, to address critical arguments in the public debate. Overall, the testing of arguments is the most significant use of opinion research in government communications.

Influencing the Content of Communications

Focus groups can serve as 'disaster checks' to confirm communicators' instincts that an ad should prove effective – before the ads appear in print or on the air. Sometimes, however, negative findings are not heeded because resources or time are limited.

Opinion research has tested speeches of particular significance. Qualitative research, with participants moving a dial on a 'perception analyser' as their impressions change, has provided immediate feedback to Paul Martin's budget speeches; this helped to refine the messages the finance minister delivered in media interviews. For instance, Quebec francophones disliked references to national unity in the 1995

budget speech, so Martin avoided the subject when he spoke to reporters a few hours later.[20]

In a quite different example of qualitative research guiding communications, Longwoods Research Group conducted focus groups to
analyse three versions of a print advertisement encouraging businesses
to register early for the GST.[21] In English Canada, the headlines 'Now is
the time ...' and 'In business, timing is everything ...' were preferred to
'It's easy and beneficial to register ...' In French Canada, however, the
first alternative was viewed as the weakest. The second remained if a
single slogan across Canada was considered necessary. The researchers
offered several more precise suggestions, such as specifying a registration deadline, explaining more about what registration involved, and
emphasizing through either words or graphics that the ad was directed
to businesspeople. The ad included information about a telephone help
line; Longwoods said the government should reassure readers that
their calls would be answered and, offering advice that moved beyond
the text of the ad, warned that 'the system [must] be in place to deliver
on the promise.' On the tone of the ad, the researchers exhorted that 'the
language ... should be convincing, not "selling,"' to improve the credibility of the ad and minimize readers' 'resistance.' The implication,
then, is that the most effective way to sell is to avoid appearing to do so.

Evaluation of Communications Efforts

A former civil servant explains some of the questions that might be
studied in evaluating the effectiveness of government communications:

> If you ask a question that's open-ended, [such as] 'Do you have enough
> information?' the answer will always be no. [If you ask,] 'Do you want
> more information?' the answer will always be yes. So that's not a poll
> [question] that's very helpful. It just tells you what you already know. But
> if you ask them, 'Do they believe that the information is useful? Did they
> get it the way that was least time-consuming for them? Do they think it
> was effective? Did they like the message? Was it too much? Was it too
> little? Was it a good message, but the wrong vehicle?' – then you get
> people to give you their opinion. Polls in that ... very general sense help
> give you the changing norms.

Assessment of communications involves both qualitative and quantitative research. It most often measures citizens' awareness of the commu-

nications campaign for a policy, awareness of the message (unaided and also aided), levels of support for a policy, and the intensity of support or opposition. From the point of view of government officials, evaluation of communications efforts addresses questions such as whether their advertising is working to inform and persuade the public, and whether ministers are successfully communicating their message. Having a communications campaign 'doesn't make any sense unless you're going to track results,' says Michael Sullivan; communications efforts that are judged ineffective are usually altered.

A full evaluation includes an effort to gauge whether public opinion has shifted, although care must be taken before crediting change to a communications campaign. One case of polling being used to evaluate ads is when high awareness of aggressive federal anti-tobacco ads suggested their success.[22] Another illustration of polling being used to evaluate communications is that growing public support for the North American Free Trade Agreement (NAFTA) was interpreted as progress for the government's communications strategy in a private conference call by James Ramsey, an aide to Michael Wilson, minister of international trade and industry.[23] Similarly, toward the end of Mike Harris's first term as premier of Ontario in 1999, opinion research revealed growth in both awareness and approval of his government's management of health care. While it is difficult to demonstrate causality, a pollster explains why he is confident that the government's communications campaign sparked the change: 'There are literally no other variables at the time that occurred that you could point to as reasons why there would have been a significant increase in support of the overall management of the health care system.'[24] Evaluation can also assess general awareness of, and attitudes about, government advertising.[25]

It should be added that communications campaigns more often produce incremental changes in public opinion than dramatic ones. According to Michael Sullivan, 'A successful campaign may raise awareness 10 [percentage] points.' It is not easy for governments to change public opinion, then, and the impact of opinion research and communications campaigns should not be exaggerated.

Conclusion

Consistent with the evidence in chapter 3 that public servants in communications branches initiate and use opinion research more than their counterparts in strategic-policy positions, interviewees typically indicate that opinion research contributes to communications of policy more than other phases of the policy process. Qualitative research is prominent, especially in the most explicit uses of opinion research for communications such as testing and refining forms, information brochures, and advertising; it also helps determine which arguments to emphasize and contributes to evaluation. Qualitative research is frequently used in conjunction with quantitative research: the former helps to identify effective phrases and arguments and then the latter evaluates them systematically – before and after their appearance in government communications. Quantitative research prevails in some other areas, notably identifying target groups and measuring public awareness.

Opinion research aids the communications of policy in a variety of ways, and these occur during different stages of the policy process. Communications often takes place alongside implementation, and the two are sometimes intertwined. The role of opinion research in communications is greatest after a policy has been determined, when attention turns to the means and message to communicate to citizens.

6 Opinion Research and Constitutional Renewal, 1980–1

This is the first of three chapters examining the uses of opinion research by the federal government in connection with specific policies: the constitutional agreement of 1981, the Goods and Services Tax, and gun control. Where the term 'officials' is used, it includes politicians, political aides, and public servants who served in government during part or all of the period under consideration and had some involvement with the relevant policy issue. Many of them now hold positions outside government.

The Context for Patriating the Constitution

Before the 1980s, Canadian governments had tried many times to bring about constitutional changes.[1] A key goal was to patriate the constitution and thereby end the embarrassment of the British government having formal control over amendments. There were further matters to resolve: patriation required a settlement on an amending formula, and many thought a constitutional agreement should address other issues such as fiscal equalization of the provinces, the division of powers, institutional reform, and protection of human rights by including a Charter of Rights in the constitution.

Following the 1976 election victory of the sovereigntist Parti Québécois, the federal government established the Canadian Unity Information Office (CUIO) in 1977. As well as assuming responsibility for advertising, the office coordinated public opinion research on national unity and the constitution. CUIO continued to operate during Joe Clark's short-lived Conservative government of 1979–80. In Pierre Trudeau's final term, Jean Chrétien was the minister responsible for the research program, and he reported on it to cabinet; a key PCO official, Michael Kirby, regularly briefed the prime minister on the data.[2] This research would contribute to the federal government's strategy and tactics as it fought to patriate the constitution. (CUIO also coordinated opinion research for other departments. As a civil servant aptly observed, 'It seems to be a role of this office to take the flak so that others can remain anonymous.'[3] The Mulroney government would disband CUIO in 1985.)

CUIO systematically polled on sovereignty in Quebec, and carefully monitored surveys from other sources. As an example of the latter, government officials were anxious early in 1979 when a poll for the CBC indicated that 51 per cent of decided Quebeckers would vote for sovereignty-association. An internal government memo took eighteen pages to analyse the survey.[4] Since other polls of the period measured backing for sovereignty at less than 40 per cent, the federal government wanted to understand why this result was different. If the Quebec government believed support for sovereignty was this strong, it might well call a referendum soon. 'A major part of what we were doing was watching them, watching the situation, trying to figure out whether they were going to have a referendum, [and] if so what kind of question they might have,' explains an official who served in CUIO. The government's memo concluded that it was a rogue poll, an inaccurate reflection of Quebeckers' opinions.

More generally, CUIO used polling to brief federal politicians about Quebeckers' support for independence, the PQ, sovereignty-association, and a mandate to negotiate sovereignty-association.[5] Referring to polling of this sort, a government official explains that 'a lot of this [was] tracking – are things getting better or are they getting worse? – as opposed to using the polls to say "Ah, that's what we should do."' An adviser to the government notes that an implicit question that interested officials when they discussed polls was how the federal government could best fight the independence movement. Even this was strategic, and intended to help with positioning, rather than the substance of policy positions.

During the Quebec referendum campaign in 1980, the federal government employed opinion research in its campaign strategy. One specific influence was apparently on the major speech Trudeau gave in Montreal on 16 May, four days before the vote. Martin Goldfarb, the Liberals' pollster, suggests that opinion research helped the prime minister to 'galvanize his thoughts and galvanize public opinion to vote against ... sovereignty.' The speech included a promise to Quebeckers to

'renew the constitution,' although the exact meaning of this commitment has been vigorously debated since.[6]

The Quebec Referendum and the Decision to Proceed
with Constitutional Renewal

After the defeat of sovereignty-association in the referendum, Trudeau
started to try to fulfill his promise by proposing a constitutional package that would include patriation and, more controversially, a Charter
to formally protect rights.

Trudeau had advocated a Charter of Rights long before he entered
federal politics. As prime minister, he had attempted but failed to reach
an agreement with the provincial governments to patriate the constitution. Against the recommendations of aides, he spoke of his plans for
constitutional reform during his losing 1979 election campaign. But
when Trudeau led the Liberals to victory in the campaign of the winter
of 1980, he downplayed the subject – apparently because his advisers
were concerned about polling that indicated that English Canadians
did not consider constitutional change a priority.[7] Shortly after the
federalists prevailed in the Quebec referendum, however, he set about
pursuing constitutional reform, not just to achieve patriation but to
introduce an entrenched charter to protect language and civil rights.
Consequently, a series of meetings with the premiers would take place
over the next eighteen months.

Well before spring 1980 the government knew from polling that the
concept of a Charter of Rights drew positive responses in every region.[8]
While support for the idea exceeded 80 per cent in some polls, and a
majority also favoured patriation, this was background to the decision.
Trudeau's enthusiasm for this project was not influenced by polling.[9]
Rather, he had advocated his position on the constitution for years, to
promote national unity and to protect individual rights.[10] The latter
reason was emphasized in the government's communications.

However, for Trudeau to pursue a package that went beyond patriation
and included a Charter to protect rights, it was vital to secure the
backing of his cabinet and caucus. In a cabinet meeting, minister Hazen
Argue spoke for many when he said, 'If you're going to do it, let's go
first class' and pursue constitutional reform including strong protection
of rights.[11] The crucial caucus meeting took place in September 1980,
following a first ministers' conference that had intensified federal-provincial battlelines. Although the prime minister viewed the cabinet and

MPs as Liberal 'family' much more than as representatives of public opinion,[12] polling may have contributed to their confidence and support.[13] 'He was contemplating going fairly far in the summer [of 1980],' explains PMO official Tom Axworthy, 'but he was persuaded, perhaps even taken aback, by how enthusiastic the caucus was.' Trudeau had apparently made up his mind to act after seeing the support for his plans at a caucus meeting. If the Liberal MPs had opposed his proposal, Trudeau still would have proceeded with patriation but probably would have either dropped or scaled back his plans for a strong Charter.[14]

While polling did not figure in the decision, contrary data could have produced a different outcome in the summer or early fall of 1980. Axworthy insists that Trudeau would still have been firmly committed if public opinion polls, hypothetically, had shown 75 per cent of the public were negative about the Charter concept. To the specific question of whether the caucus, the support of which contributed to the decision to proceed, would have been similarly supportive, Axworthy replied that he did not know. Given the importance of caucus support, this suggests that negative public opinion could have affected the government's resolve. Moreover, when Kirby was asked what might have been different if the polling, hypothetically, had indicated public opposition to the Charter, he replied,

> Oh boy, that's tough. Let's suppose the poll numbers had been reversed ... [in] the extreme example, 25 per cent in favour, 75 per cent against. We probably would have just gone with patriation ... Would we have [brought in a Charter]? I guess the answer is no, but I've never even thought about the question ... The issue was never even contemplated because the numbers were so good.

Even with results of 50–50, he says it would have been a tough call. Moreover, if one particular right had been unpopular, it might have been excluded from the Charter to avoid jeopardizing the whole package. In support of this interpretation, it is worth noting that Trudeau had exhibited flexibility, and had not always insisted on a strong Charter of Rights during the constitutional negotiations of the 1970s.

Several implications flow from these comments. If no polling at all had existed, the government would have made the same decision. The polls, however, confirmed that 'going first class' suited the government's political interests; the findings thereby quietly reinforced the Charter's inclusion in the government's plans. Public opposition to the Charter would have been taken seriously by the government and its caucus because it would have demonstrated the political difficulties of proceeding without support from most of the premiers. But the polls showed that Canadians were favourable to the concept, so they did not spark doubts.

The CUIO regularly took polls on constitutional issues in 1980 and 1981, most of them after the government had decided to proceed with its package. Consistent with the discussion above, the polls revealed approval for patriation, and especially high levels of support for the principle of a Charter to protect rights. For instance, in a July 1980 study which one official says would have been 'very secret' at the time,[15] Goldfarb Consultants reported that 'an overwhelming majority of Canadians' favoured patriation, a bill of rights, 'minority language education rights,' the concept of equalization (termed 'a sharing of economic wealth'), and mobility rights. Greater than 80 per cent support was found for each of these concepts. Respondents heavily favoured the idea of protecting rights: 85 per cent agreed with the proposal that 'the constitution guarantee basic human rights such as freedom of speech, freedom of religion, and so on to all Canadian citizens, in such a way that no law, federal or provincial[,] could go against them.' Among the other findings, 71 per cent favoured a national referendum to decide the constitutional issue if there was no federal-provincial agreement.[16] The report broke down results by province to affirm that attitudes were similar in each.

The need for the government to commission opinion research was lessened by the polling from public sources.[17] CUIO monitored these polls, although variations in question wording made comparisons difficult. An internal summary records that between July 1980 and April 1981, support for patriation ran between 59 and 81 percent. Two Goldfarb polls are cited showing more than 80 per cent approval of a Charter.[18] A later report presents additional polls on the Charter and shows levels of support for the federal government acting without substantial agreement from the provinces: over this period polls ranged from 28 percent to 46 percent in favour.[19]

Government Communications in 1980

Having decided to proceed with an ambitious constitutional package, the government developed an unusually intensive communications strategy to promote awareness and support for the proposal. The CUIO machinery could be easily mobilized after its active participation in the Quebec referendum campaign. More importantly, the stakes were exceptionally high. Axworthy argues that the constitutional package was one of the most dramatic initiatives in Canadian history. He continues, 'Behind these extraordinary steps we were contemplating – which [were] going to London over the opposition of most of the premiers [and] breaking constitutional convention – you wanted to carry the public with you as much as possible, as we were betting all that we had that this was the right course ... So the communications efforts on this were extraordinary.' He confirms that public support was especially important because it would legitimize the plans to patriate the constitution against the wishes of eight provincial governments. Opinion research, he explains, contributed significantly to the development and refining of the government's communications efforts.

Other federal officials agree. Roger Tassé, the deputy minister of justice, says he does not recall polling contributing to any changes in the content of the proposals but adds that it helped to advance issues of interest to the public. He explains that opinion research was used 'to try and address some of the concerns, and to try and explain better what the proposals were – in other words trying to change public opinion.' Hershell Ezrin, who headed CUIO, concurs, stating that the ideas for renewing the constitution 'were held for profound and powerful reasons by the leaders of our country, who really believed that it was important for our maturity as a country, our development of the rights of individuals, etc.' He adds that the government used opinion research to help communicate this message effectively and appropriately.

An early study gauged reactions to four television commercials that aimed, in the words of a CUIO spokesperson, to 'establish a climate of understanding and acceptance' of the government's constitutional proposals.[20] The focus group participants recruited by Goldfarb Consultants liked two of the ads, one suggesting that constitutional renewal would be analogous to 'the way a house is turned into a home' and the other 'comparing the trees and Canadians and the forest and Canada.' Naturally, in view of the positive responses, the researchers thought these ads should be aired.

Two other advertisements were panned in the focus groups and therefore by the researchers. One of these ads featured a kite and the researchers observed that 'many felt the approach overdramatized the issue with the simplicity of a kite.' They also discovered an unintended reaction to the visuals: 'Some felt there was a problem in the use of kites being held by strings. It did not suggest strength, stability or control. People wondered who was holding or controlling the strings.'[21] Surprisingly, then, the focus group participants were more sensitive to the metaphorical connotations of strings than the creators of the ad.

Finally, the fourth tested commercial featured flying geese. The ad opened with a scene of the birds above water accompanied by the tune of 'Oh Canada.' The voice-over narration says: 'Freedom is an important part of our heritage. As Canadians. The right of each and everyone of us to strive. To rise. To be free. Riding the wings of freedom, working together to make all of our hopes and dreams come true. For all Canadians.' When the image of the geese fades to black the words 'Brought to you by the Government of Canada' are spoken.[22] While people perceived the geese as a symbol of Canada, Goldfarb Consultants brought disheartening news about confusion expressed in the focus groups. The researchers reported a mixed response but their overall verdict was clear:

> Some [participants] felt they [the geese] represent unity because they have to fly together towards a particular destination. They also represented freedom in that they are free to go anywhere they please. Criticisms about the use of geese concentrated on their instability. Although they fly away together to a destination, that destination is outside Canada where it is a warmer climate. That is, under adverse conditions the geese leave the country.

In case any readers still held hope for the commercial, the researchers drove their point home: 'The symbol, then, is incongruous with the message.' And they observed later that 'people haven't the background knowledge or understanding ... to grasp the intent of this message.'[23] Indeed, words such as 'constitution' and 'Charter' are entirely absent from the ad. The commercial, probably the best-remembered government ad of the era, was subject to much criticism. For example, Bob Rae, then an NDP MP, complained that 'I'll never look at a Canadian goose again without thinking it's a Liberal in disguise.'[24] The publicly expressed criticisms, however, emphasized the ad's emotional approach and the use of public money – unlike those that emerged from the focus groups, which simply expressed confusion.

Unfortunately for the federal government, however, the qualitative research came too late. Because senior advisers and cabinet ministers who viewed the geese commercial were uniformly pleased when they saw it, the ad was aired – contrary to normal practice – without waiting for the focus groups. As Kirby recalls, 'The ministers who saw it, [and] the constitutional group who saw it just loved the ad, loved the emotional side of it. We were so proud of the ad; we thought it was awesome. So everyone said, "To hell with this, we'll put it on air."' The decision was ultimately made by Kirby, although other officials had shared his confidence in the ad. After completing its research, the Goldfarb staff would have needed about two days to finish the report. After receiving the unexpected news that the ad was not effective, Kirby considered the situation briefly before deciding to pull it from the airwaves, after it had been running for several days. 'It was pulled solely on the basis of that [report].' This case was the exception; other ads were tested in qualitative research before airing. 'It taught me an unbelievably valuable lesson,' comments Kirby. 'You never put an ad on that hasn't been researched, no matter how good you think it is.' The CUIO head says this failure was not quickly forgotten: 'I certainly lived with the fallout, or the droppings, of the geese thereafter.'[25] Despite this misstep, Kirby credited the government's advertising with generating public interest and demands for more information.[26]

The government officials understood the advertisement's purpose because they were very familiar with the issue; many of the less politically involved focus group participants were unable to grasp the intent. This illustrates the value of opinion research in helping officials understand the perspectives of citizens for whom politics and government are a minor part of their lives; with the geese ad, the focus groups were presumed to be accurate and they prevailed.

The Kirby Memorandum and the People's Package

Michael Kirby's memorandum to cabinet, dated 30 August 1980 and leaked shortly after, reveals some of the government's thinking about its constitutional initiative. Prepared in the context of escalating conflict between the federal and provincial governments, much of the paper is geared to enhancing the public's perceptions of the federal government's position – partly to prepare Canadians for possible unilateral action by the federal government. As indicated earlier, public opinion was unusually important, in large part because of the growing prospects of the federal government acting without the support of most of the provincial governments and thereby causing a full-scale intergovernmental battle. Among other things, Kirby's memorandum explains that the prospect of a constitutional agreement had been enhanced by the federal strategy in the negotiations. This strategy incorporated three prongs: treatment of powers over resources and the economy; statements to demonstrate that the federal government intended to proceed unilaterally if a federal-provincial agreement could not be reached; and the tactic of separating of the people's package and the powers package.[27]

Opinion research contributed to this third prong, which was both strategic and communications-oriented. The constitutional issues that were in play were split into two packages, as defined by the federal government. The people's package consisted of the federal government's agenda: a patriated constitution with an amending formula that included provisions for referendums, as well as the foremost goal of a Charter of Rights that would include language rights and a commitment to fiscal equalization between provinces. The powers package comprised the demands that some of the premiers were making for expanding provincial authority in areas such as resource ownership.[28]

Kirby states that polling played a more critical role in this than anything else he has been involved with in government. 'If you absolutely want to understand where polling was awesomely powerful, it was in the decision to separate the issues on the table into the so-called "people's package" and the "powers package,"' he explains. The polling was used effectively to refine and enhance the federal position. Examining individually the constitutional items raised by the various governments, polling enabled federal officials to separate those with strong public support from those without it. Rights elements, even minority language rights, consistently received about 80 per cent approval. (Most Canadians also supported patriation, but few felt intensely about this.) Depending on the issue, however, citizens' attitudes towards the premiers' positions ranged from lukewarm to negative.[29]

Conveniently, the results fit neatly with the federal agenda: the Charter rights were popular but the premiers' proposals concerning the division of powers were less so. Having learned from polling how the issues could favourably be divided into two sets for public communications, the question remained what names to give the two clusters of proposals, and Kirby recalls how opinion research contributed here as well: 'We knew from other communications research we'd done that talking about doing things for people was very positive, and talking about grubby politicians fighting over power was very negative. The words were emotive words, as in any good advertising. They were words that were designed to play to people's base view of what politicians do.' Kirby makes the point even more emphatic: 'We'd painted ourselves as altruistic, trying to do things for people, and then these power-grubbing politicians just wanted things for themselves, for the provinces. It was a terrific dichotomy.' With the issues framed this way, federal leaders were well positioned to respond to the premiers' statements. For example, when Brian Peckford tried to bargain that he would accept a Charter only if the federal government agreed to increase provincial jurisdiction over fisheries, federal representatives could reply, 'Isn't it interesting that the premier of Newfoundland wants power for himself, and will not give you people out there in Newfoundland the rights you want unless he gets more power for himself?'[30] More generally, the federal strategy was to try to keep the people's package intact during first ministers' conferences and bargain with the provinces within the powers package.

Among the components of the people's package, polling drove the decision to emphasize the Charter rather than patriation. It was important that polls showed strong support for the Charter and also that the salience and intensity of that support were greater than for patriation. As a result of this finding, an official explains, the Charter was placed 'front and centre' in advertising, speeches, media interviews, and briefings of MPs. Another official confirms that if opinion research had shown that Canadians were more enthusiastic about patriation and were either less favourable or less intense towards the Charter, the former would have received a higher profile in the government's communications.[31] Polling in 1980 and 1981 that showed continued majorities favouring Charter rights suggests that the strategy was effective.

Progress and Setbacks, Fall 1980 to Spring 1981

Following a first ministers' conference in September 1980 that resolved nothing, the battlelines between the federal and provincial governments grew deeper. After Trudeau received encouragement from his cabinet and caucus, he was prepared to proceed unilaterally.[32] Six of the provinces formed an alliance (which would expand to eight members in April 1981) in opposition to the federal government, which received backing from only Ontario and New Brunswick. With federal-provincial negotiations stalled, the federal government laid the groundwork for acting unilaterally, and in October 1980 it established a joint parliamentary committee to help legitimize the action.

The committee's hearings were initially intended to finish in early

December and report back quickly. However, the number of people who wished to speak prolonged them until January. While newspaper advertisements generated heavy feedback from people expressing interest in participating in the hearings, this response should not be confused with wider public opinion. Many who wanted to speak were not invited. Moreover, as one critic points out,

> It is difficult to avoid the conclusion that it [the list of speakers] was heavily weighted in favour of the more aggressive, vocal, and unrestrained, and also the best financed, of our burgeoning army of national pressure groups and special interests lobbies [sic]. There was an observable absence of balance – ethnic and cultural, religious, political and ideological, and above all linguistic and regional – in the list.[33]

This is an indisputable description of active public opinion.

The hearings were televised, building awareness and support for the federal proposals by enlarging the audience for speakers at the hearings. With a majority of presentations favouring the Charter, the hearings demonstrated its popularity and helped to end the provincial premiers' control of the issue.[34] The coverage on television helped move the debate from being a matter purely for the federal and provincial governments to one involving at least some members of the public, who tended to be sympathetic towards the federal position. Tassé says that the increased public awareness and support of Trudeau's positions showed up in opinion polls and other signals; the support was helpful later in strengthening Trudeau's hand in negotiations with the provincial governments. Without television coverage of the hearings, the final agreement might not have been reached at all.[35] Despite the unrepresentativeness of the hearings, their support for the Charter concept helped its advocates. On this account, active public opinion had an unmistakable role.

However, by the time the committee presented its report in February 1981, with a parliamentary resolution to follow, the federal government's position had grown more difficult. The alliance of six provinces had mounted court challenges to the federal position in Manitoba, Newfoundland, and Quebec. With Joe Clark's Conservatives obstructing business in the House of Commons during early 1981 to delay the federal initiative, governing became difficult. The federal government prevailed in Manitoba and Quebec, where the judges affirmed its right to proceed without the consent of the provinces, but lost in Newfoundland. In early April, Trudeau agreed to postpone the parliamentary resolution until the Supreme Court had ruled on an appeal of the provincial cases.

Government Communications in 1981

In the spring and summer of 1981, as the federal and provincial governments awaited the Supreme Court's decision, their relationship grew increasingly adversarial, and this heightened the prospect that Trudeau would decide to act unilaterally. In this context, communications with the public became even more important. CUIO continued to conduct opinion research to monitor support for the federal government's position, and to develop and refine its communications campaign. The campaign aimed to maintain and strengthen public support for Trudeau's plans.

Focus groups tested ads before they were aired; the government would not repeat the error made with the geese commercial. The qualitative research was not only used to decide whether ads should run or not; it had additional purposes. For instance, a Goldfarb study in February 1981 reported that the public welcomed a print ad explaining the federal government's position. The study found that an 'omnibus concept' which promoted the whole constitutional package was preferred to an approach with separate ads for each element.[36] A federal official comments that this advice amounted to 'sell the people's package – don't sell the individual items ... You were selling a concept, not the details.'[37] Two other officials agree that this type of advice was very important to the communications strategy. While the ad was well received, focus groups characterized the tone as impersonal and some explanations of rights as unclear. Reflecting the struggle that opponents of the federal government faced to effectively communicate their position to the public, Goldfarb's researcher reported that 'people agree with bringing home the constitution and guaranteeing the rights. They cannot see why this would be a problem for anyone or how anyone would argue against these rights.'[38]

Later, presumably because of the increasing federal-provincial tensions and publicity of the provinces' court cases, the ads were retested. A government official noted in a memo to a Goldfarb pollster that the retesting would be done in order to establish if it is still politically acceptable for the Government of Canada to run this type of ad. Basically, we want to know the following: Do people perceive the ad as *partisan*? ... Do people believe that this ad tells the *real story* and the *whole story* about what is in the constitutional motion? ... Do people think that the Government of Canada should *spend taxpayers' money* to run this kind of ad? (Is the government carrying out its responsibility to inform people or is it 'selling' the constitution?)

As well as investigating the legitimacy of the ad, the CUIO also sought the pollster's advice about its format and expressed interest in whether the signature of the prime minister at the bottom of the ad was appropriate.[39] Overall, the focus groups expressed positive reactions to the ad. Addressing advertising by the government, Goldfarb Consultants reported that many of the participants 'felt that irrespective of other ads, it was refreshing that the Government would make the effort to communicate broadly what it has done in this regard.' The researcher made several minor suggestions about design and content, and advised that the prime minister's signature drew mixed reactions.[40]

A benchmark poll in six cities was conducted in May. Asked separately about awareness of key rights covered by the proposed Charter, a majority said they believed they would be guaranteed. This finding had to be treated sceptically, however, as the public exhibited low levels of knowledge. Asked a more general question, only 40 per cent of respondents said the recently debated federal resolution 'provides for the protection of basic rights and freedoms which are not now guaranteed.' (Thirty-one per cent said it did not, while 29 per cent said they did not know. No doubt some of the affirmative answers were guesses.) Even more troubling, a majority also said incorrectly that property rights, a 'dummy entry' added to the questionnaire by thoughtful researchers, were protected by the proposed Charter.[41] As well, pluralities in Vancouver and Calgary wrongly indicated that there was no provision for an amending formula in the federal proposal, while outside Toronto, 'a majority think the motion does not protect rights or don't know if it does.'[42] This strongly indicates that the proportion of respondents with a genuine understanding of the contents of the proposed Charter was actually very small.

Commenting on this study, a public servant wrote that 'many Canadians are still not very informed about the constitutional motion and its contents. I think the results clearly justify our plans for an extensive information campaign once the motion is adopted by Parliament.'[43]

The justification would be to public servants, to politicians, and possibly the general public.[44] The memo concluded, 'Basically, we can't help but improve this situation [of low public awareness and misinformation] by running the print ad.' Kirby explains the significance: 'It tells you, one, if people know what we're doing they're supportive; two, there's a huge degree of ignorance.' He adds that the study contained enough information to persuade him of the need for an advertising campaign. This research leaves little doubt that the public's level of understanding and awareness was low; however, there is no sign that it shook the confidence of federal officials – who had absorbed the results of other studies – that their positions enjoyed strong public endorsement. Still, from their point of view, the polling showed general approval in a context of limited awareness and knowledge. If awareness could be increased, this was expected to help promote and maintain support.

Opinion research also helped the federal government to decide how its advertising campaign would vary from region to region. 'We had a concept which we were trying to sell,' states Kirby. 'And therefore we went at it the same way that you would go at any other product. Which is to say, let's understand the regional market and let's understand the sub-market. If there are particular demographic groups that are a problem, let's target an ad in the communications strategy at them.' One of the goals was to avoid emphasizing issues in regions where they were not important to citizens.

Using qualitative and quantitative research, then, CUIO identified different concerns in each region.[45] In Atlantic Canada, worries about the resource base and 'distrust of Upper Canada' were paramount, and a 'low-key logical discussion' was viewed as desirable. Fears of losing the French identity and culture were central to Quebeckers, 'based on historic feelings of being a second-class group.' CUIO planned an 'emotionally charged high "noise" level approach stating that the federal government has built the new Constitution to protect and develop the many rights Quebec is concerned about.' Quebeckers would see television ads featuring 'real people ... to explain the Charter of Rights with the commercials being skewed specifically to Quebec.' Ontarians presented the fewest problems but required more explanation of the proposals and 'the development of a sense that Canada is one country.' A logical, explanatory approach was indicated. Finally, western Canadians possessed a 'deep seated belief that the federal government and Ontario are gaining [sic] to use the west to assist the rest of Canada and that this is wrong.' The government planned to argue that the new constitution would protect and enhance the rights of westerners, but in a less emotional fashion than in Quebec.

Television, radio, and newspaper ads were to be used in different combinations in the four regions. While television ads would appear more frequently in Quebec, radio ads would be more prominent in the Atlantic and western provinces; newspaper supplements would also appear in the outlying regions. The CUIO document concluded with this jumbled metaphor: 'Rather than hitting the consumer on the head with high noise level, it is felt most important to convince through explanations and kid gloves.' In fact, the advertising strategy seemed to combine both the high noise level and kid gloves approaches. The proposals, prepared with the aid of opinion research, were important in honing the government's communications strategy to suit the different regions.

The Premiers' Poll

While the federal government was polling and advertising, the eight dissident provinces were also attempting to influence public opinion. In July they jointly commissioned a Gallup poll which would help them make the case that their positions were in line with the public's views. The questions reflected the provinces' agenda. For example, aiming at the federal government's threat to act unilaterally, respondents were asked, 'do you agree or disagree that meetings should be held between the Prime Minister and all of the Provincial Premiers in order to try to reach agreement on the issue of the Constitution?' Not surprisingly, 88 per cent agreed. Gallup also reported that 77 per cent said that constitutional amendments affecting provincial powers should have provincial consent. As well, respondents were asked, 'From your experience with this topic, do you think the Federal Government's action to patriate the BNA Act without the agreement of all provinces is working to divide or unite Canadians?' Not surprisingly, 60 per cent replied that the federal government's action was divisive, while just 26 per cent said it was unifying.[46]

While Quebec cabinet minister Claude Morin argued that the poll showed that 90 per cent of Canadians opposed the federal proposal, the survey's critics charged that it was designed to produce that kind of result. Several stated that some of the questions were leading. Maurice Pinard, a sociologist and polling consultant to the federal government, pointed out that the questionnaire contained a preamble that may have induced particular answers. Another sociologist, Pierre Bernard, observed that Gallup had not directly measured attitudes about the content of the federal proposal. He said, 'At least it is transparent. Gallup was hired by people who wanted to prove a point.'[47] The choice of questions and their design were each open to criticisms.

CUIO head Hershell Ezrin wrote an internal memo to discredit the premiers' poll. He argued that the preamble to the survey, and introductions to specific questions, would influence respondents. This applied to several questions, including the one about provincial consent to constitutional changes. Ezrin also contended that other questions did not supply adequate information. For example, he argued, a question about the Senate failed to explain that it has veto powers although they are largely theoretical. The memo challenged the finding of divisiveness by citing an earlier poll by Gallup that found a plurality of Canadians considered the patriation action unifying. As well, Ezrin wrote, Gallup failed to measure attitudes about the components of the federal proposals.[48]

Ezrin's note had two main purposes. First, it could be used to reassure federal officials who had learned about the poll through media reports. They could discount the poll, confident that federal positions still enjoyed strong support from the public.[49] Second, it could serve as background for federal officials in informal conversations with journalists, to try to influence the reporting of either the poll or the public opinion environment more generally.[50] While the federal government's questionnaires were not perfectly neutral either, this survey illustrates how opinion research sometimes is used to present a particular image of public opinion with the hope of gaining advantage in the public arena.

The Supreme Court's Decision

Late in September 1981 the Supreme Court ruled on the issues that had been fought inconclusively in the three provincial courts. By a vote of seven to two, the judges decided that the federal government could *legally* proceed without the agreement of the provincial governments. However, in a further ruling, the court voted six to three that *constitutional convention* held that 'substantial' provincial consent was required. (The meaning of substantial consent was not precisely defined.)

In the wake of the decision, according to a cabinet briefing note,

Trudeau was prepared to stay on course – which meant that he was prepared to act unilaterally. In this context, public opinion was stressed: 'The first, and far and away the most important goal is to increase understanding and political support in Canada for the content of the [parliamentary] resolution ... [W]e build on a strong support basis.' The briefing note then referred to an appendix, which summarized polling that showed strong support for patriation, the concept of a Charter, and fiscal equalization – but considerably less support for the federal government acting unilaterally. In short, Canadians supported the principles of the federal package but expressed serious reservations about the process. Having noted this poll-based finding, the briefing note drew the conclusion that future communications by the government should stress five items: 'the importance of constitutional renewal'; the content of the federal position (increasing awareness was explicitly viewed as a way of building public support); the failure to reach a federal-provincial agreement despite a series of efforts since 1927; the endorsement of the federal position from the Ontario and New Brunswick governments and the national NDP; and the Supreme Court's confirmation of the federal government's legal authority to proceed.[51] Kirby states that the polling was 'critical' in the development of this communications advice.

The Proposal for a Tie-breaking Referendum and the First Ministers' Agreement

Following the Supreme Court's ruling, Trudeau met with Bill Bennett, the spokesperson for the eight dissenting premiers. The British Columbia premier signalled the provincial governments' genuine interest in negotiating an agreement, which was important in the context of the Supreme Court's decision. Although the court's ruling was not immediately seen as a decisive victory for either side, a senior cabinet minister later expressed the view that the provinces won.[52] The ruling helped induce Trudeau to agree to a further meeting with the provincial governments, which took place in Ottawa in November 1981.

The decisive moment in that meeting occurred when Trudeau proposed that if the deadlock among the first ministers could not be broken, a referendum should be held. Although some details of the plan were never finalized, he was prepared to ask the British government to patriate the constitution. If agreement on an amending formula and a Charter could not be reached within two years, the issues would be put to Canadians to decide through a 'tie-breaking' referendum.[53]

Polling made a vital contribution to this manoeuvre: it guided the tactical decision that Trudeau would propose a referendum, and it affected the response of the premiers. Although Trudeau and other federal spokespeople had previously spoken publicly of the concept, the idea of proposing a tie-breaking referendum was prepared by the prime minister and his aides about three weeks earlier.[54]

The threat to break the log-jam this way was informed by polls that showed strong public support across the country for the federal positions, particularly for a Charter, and for the referendum concept itself. A senior official with a dissenting provincial government says that the federal government's strategy 'was dependent on knowing that they had the upper hand in public opinion terms.' He recalls that federal officials were quite bullish about their 'threat to go to a referendum as a whip in those negotiations.' He adds that the premiers generally agreed that the Charter was a popular concept. Axworthy confirms this impression: 'We were pretty confident that we could win on that issue. And we were confident, in part, because the polls showed us that if we did our job right, our message could be a very popular one ... [Opinion research] was a very large factor behind the gambit or manoeuvre that got us the [agreement on the] constitution, which was Trudeau's referendum threat.' Several federal officials had met earlier to try to anticipate how provincial governments might campaign against the 'people's package' in the event of a referendum. They believed the only reasonable argument was that of the prairie premiers, who thought the Charter represented an undesirable shift away from legislative supremacy and towards judicial supremacy. But the federal officials were also convinced that this argument would not persuade the public, which told pollsters that they trusted judges more than politicians.[55]

Crafted with the help of opinion research, the people's package was well suited to the federal cause in a possible referendum: 'The neat thing about separating powers from the people's package is all the things the feds might lose on were taken out of the package,' remembers Kirby. 'They were all over in the powers [package]. And ... there were polling results which clearly showed that. We were careful to test where [the public] were on each element of the powers package as well.' This comment highlights the major roles of polling in separating the people's package and the powers package, and in ensuring and demonstrating the force of the referendum threat.

When Trudeau explained the gist of his plan for a referendum to the first ministers' conference on 4 November, René Lévesque, the Quebec premier who had been a member of the 'gang of eight' premiers, quickly agreed to the proposal, breaking ranks with his colleagues in the other provinces and contradicting commitments he had made privately earlier in the day.[56] The members of the group had previously agreed not to alter their positions without prior consultation. Lévesque's defection was a gift to Trudeau but a shock to the other premiers in the alliance. The Quebec premier soon tried to backtrack, but the damage was done. With the group of eight's alliance shattered, the other premiers were more inclined to negotiate a deal without Lévesque. His decisive defeat in the 1980 referendum had weakened his position and probably made it easier to exclude him:[57] this effect represents an indirect impact of public opinion, although not opinion research.

Apart from Lévesque, the provincial premiers were reluctant to enter a referendum campaign that could undermine their governments' authority. Some, including Peter Lougheed and Allan Blakeney, feared that a referendum would be divisive.[58] More importantly, the prospect of a referendum, featuring the popular federal package contrasted with their own proposals, was unappealing and they faced probable defeat. Provincial governments had commissioned their own polling that signalled this.[59] As well, shortly before Trudeau made the proposal, Kirby had bolstered the federal position by showing senior provincial officials his own government's polling, broken down by province, which indicated that the federal government would have the upper hand if a referendum took place.[60] This demonstrated that the federal position was popular and suggested that the premiers faced greater political risks by remaining off-side than by compromising. The provincial officials replied sceptically, although Kirby believes they were bluffing. Indeed, a senior provincial official acknowledged later that the polling helped to make the provinces 'more pliable' and willing to accept a Charter of Rights.

While other factors, including the Supreme Court's ruling, certainly contributed, the referendum threat proved decisive to the outcome of the first ministers' meeting. The premiers' expectations that the federal position would prevail in a vote encouraged them to reach a compromise agreement with the federal government. Kirby explains that although many premiers doubted that the federal government would actually hold a referendum, the threat was 'absolutely crucial' to achieving an agreement. Axworthy concurs, calling it the 'tactic that got the premiers on board.' As he explains, 'There's no doubt that in the minds of the premiers, the referendum threat was a real one because they thought we'd win it.'

Indeed, the day after Trudeau's gambit, an agreement was reached that formed the basis of the revised constitution. Trudeau and nine provincial premiers agreed; only Lévesque was not included. Alterations to recognize the rights of aboriginals and women were finalized in December, as governments responded to pressure from interest groups – an example of the force of active public opinion. The compromise gave the federal government its entrenched Charter of Rights and Freedoms. Trudeau had to accept some demands from the provinces, however. Among them were the notwithstanding clause that permitted legislatures to override specified Charter rights for a five-year period. The federal government also abandoned provisions for referendums that were in its preferred amending formula and accepted instead a formula that enabled provinces to opt out of certain changes and reflected a principle of provincial equality. (Quebec did not receive a veto, and most important items in the constitution could be amended with the approval of the federal Parliament and seven provincial legislatures representing at least half of the population.) In Edward McWhinney's judgment, the provincial premiers were left with little to show for their protracted opposition to the federal proposal.[61]

Polling, then, was important to the development, and critical to the effect, of Trudeau's weapon of proposing a tie-breaking referendum. While the manoeuvre's success was not guaranteed, it helped to crack the premiers' alliance, thereby creating the conditions in which an agreement was possible. By strengthening the federal government's position, the weapon had the effect of presenting the majority of the premiers with a choice between fighting a referendum with a weak hand or reaching an accommodation with Trudeau. This choice helps to explain why the final agreement gave the premiers relatively little: they preferred a few slices of a loaf to a high risk of none. In the absence of the polling that strengthened the federal government's position, it is probable that the final package would have taken a form more favourable to the premiers – or, perhaps, no first ministers' agreement at all would have been reached.

Conclusion

'On the constitution,' says Axworthy, 'public opinion research was crucial to us in framing our communication and implementation measures, but on the substantial issue of what to do, it had very little role.' As this suggests, opinion research had little direct impact on the content of the federal position or the final agreement: the commitment and the decision to proceed were not driven by polling, and at most were reinforced by it. Indeed, the bulk of the research was conducted after the federal government announced its proposal. The inclusion of the Charter in the federal plans, and the content of that Charter, were also not the products of polling but of the government's beliefs. However, public opposition, or greater variation in public attitudes about various rights, might have produced a different outcome. While opinion research did not drive the initiative, it contributed to communications and strategy, as the federal government tried to maintain and strengthen its position with the public. The federal government lacked the backing of most of the provinces, and the support for the federal positions might have weakened the premiers' resolve. As well, the clearly favourable public opinion provided the federal position with legitimacy and reinforced the government's commitment to maintaining it; moreover, the government would have needed public support in the event of a referendum.

The opinion research showing public approval of the federal position assumed particular importance at two points on the path to constitutional renewal. The first was the development of the people's package, and the corresponding emphasis on the Charter, which enabled the government to position itself effectively. The second was Trudeau's proposal for a tie-breaking referendum, where the polling encouraged the tactic and made it effective. To the extent that opinion research framed the federal proposal and, through the referendum tactics, contributed to the fact and shape of the federal-provincial compromise, it indirectly influenced the policy outcome. This happened in part because the polls were used to project the likely result of a referendum; if the idea of holding a referendum had not been on the minds of the first ministers and their aides, opinion research would have had a smaller role. In an indirect way, the contribution of polling to the policy outcome, particularly the inclusion of a relatively strong Charter of Rights, was considerable.

While this assessment of the influence of opinion research might appear at first sight to be consistent with George Gallup's hopes that polling would promote responsiveness, a number of points should be made to qualify this impression. These concern the process that led to the agreement as well as the character of public opinion on constitutional matters. Four observations about the process stand out. First, as noted above, the impact of opinion research would have been much smaller if a referendum had not been a genuine possibility; Gallup hoped polling would be powerful enough to substitute for a referendum, rather than acquiring influence because of the prospect of one. Second, polling did not determine the positions of the politicians, it was used to lead much more than to follow, and public opinion was not a powerful enough force to make the gang of eight alter its position substantially until the endgame in November 1981. The role of public opinion was in part to exert indirect pressure on the first ministers to reach an agreement. Third, the impact of active public opinion, in the form of interest group behaviour, was more pronounced than polling, most obviously during the parliamentary hearings and the efforts by aboriginal and women's groups to achieve recognition after the premiers reached an agreement. And fourth, besides protecting rights, the government had a motive of promoting Trudeau's vision of national unity that was not highlighted in its communications or properly understood by the public that expressed its support in polls.

The character of public opinion also has implications for understanding the contribution of opinion research to the final constitutional agreement. The majority of the public did not follow the debate closely and was poorly informed. In one study, just 12 per cent said they were very involved in the subject of constitutional reform, while 28 per cent said they were somewhat involved.[62] Other research confirmed that the public did not feel well informed. And polling showed significant confusion about the issue, including vagueness about the plans to protect rights as well as the specific rights that the federal proposals covered: the most dramatic illustration is the widespread misconception that the proposed Charter covered property rights. Given the complexity of the issue, it is clear that surveys reporting solid support for the Charter tapped people's instinctive responses to questions containing phrases with positive connotations, such as 'guarantee basic human rights,' rather than more deeply-reasoned positions. The opinion research, then, did not report meaningful public opinion.

Consistent with this point, the design of questions in the Goldfarb study excerpted in appendix 1 reflects the wording of the government's proposals. Although less biased than the premiers' poll, the phrasing is not entirely neutral. As well, it does not begin to suggest the legitimate argument that could have been advanced about the anti-democratic implications of a Charter for ending legislative supremacy, although this position probably would have proven difficult to explain to the general public. Nor does this type of polling suggest the practical policy consequences of a Charter. These would, of course, have been hard to predict exactly before the Charter took effect, and persuasively presenting an argument along these lines would have been an even greater challenge. Still, the general pattern of policy consequences of the Charter could have been anticipated. The civil libertarian case for a Charter values the role of courts in protecting the rights of minorities, and especially unpopular minorities, from the democratic impulses of elected officials responding to public pressure. Indeed, Charter advocates refer to the internment of Japanese Canadians during the Second World War and other disturbing abuses of minority rights that were almost certainly favoured by majorities.[63] Since the Charter came into effect, most cases have been decided in a fashion consistent with its advocates' hopes: to consider some of the most challenging issues, many civil libertarians approve of the Charter's success in defending the rights of those accused of crimes, users of child pornography, and advertisers of tobacco – hardly popular causes. While the literature assessing the tolerance of the general public tends to assume the 'correctness' of civil libertarian perspectives, in many instances there is room to view these issues as matters involving two or more legitimate positions. In any case, the debate over the desirability of the Charter only ventured near such topics among the most attentive citizens; in 1980–1 most Canadians would have had no idea that the Charter could have unpopular results in many specific instances.

Survey questions that measure general attitudes towards the Charter deliver different signals than questions which measure support for specific rights. This is best illustrated by research conducted since the introduction of the Charter. In 1987, a general question about the Charter indicated that it had the support of 72 per cent of anglophones and 62 per cent of francophones.[64] However, specific questions show significantly less commitment to the spirit of the Charter.[65] For instance, in 1990, Decima found 40 per cent support for English-only or French-only laws in the local community.[66] The 1987 survey asked respondents whether homosexuals should be allowed to teach in schools. Only a slight plurality approved nationally, with majorities disapproving in seven provinces.[67] The study also showed that only 35 per cent of the general public endorsed the rights of a 'most disliked group' to rally, while 80 per cent favoured limiting public demonstrations if local officials are apprehensive. And 52 per cent concurred that 'if the cabinet says there is a national emergency and a majority in Parliament agrees, it is alright to suspend the usual civil rights.'[68] Since the Charter may have helped sensitize Canadians about minority rights, similar questions asked in the pre-Charter era might have indicated even less sympathy for specific rights. In any case, results of this sort indicate much less commitment to the principles behind the Charter than might be assumed from a quick glance at polls showing support for the concept at an abstract level.[69]

The opinion research that helped to bring about a constitutional agreement which includes a Charter, then, apparently did so not just because of some unusual features of the process but also because many Canadians failed to understand its implications. It is difficult to imagine, but if there had been widespread public understanding that the Charter would give courts an expanded role in protecting unpopular rights, the polls might well have given completely different signals about public opinion on the Charter – for reasons which its elite supporters would find discomforting. The majoritarian instrument of opinion polling ironically helped to build a counter-majoritarian element in the constitution, but the process was out of step with Gallup and Rae's hopes, and the polls were not reflections of the informed public opinion that a successful application of the early pollster's vision would implicitly demand.

7 Opinion Research and the Goods and Services Tax

V.O. Key argues that public opinion constrains, rather than determines, the decisions governments make.[1] He views public opinion as

> a system of dikes which channel public action or which fix a range of discretion within which government may act or within which debate at official levels may proceed. This conception avoids the error of personifying 'public opinion' as an entity that exercises initiative and in some way functions as an operating organism to translate its purposes into governmental action.

Key rejects the presumption that public opinion exerts *direct* influence on decisions about policy. Instead, he draws attention to the role of public opinion in setting boundaries that constrain or limit government actions. These 'dikes' define areas where political debate, and proposals or decisions about public policy, can take place. Key explains that some policy proposals fail to receive serious consideration because 'they depart too far from the general understandings of what is proper': they fall beyond the dikes. For instance, proposals to nationalize the American automobile industry would not be considered seriously because elected officials anticipate that pursuing them would conflict too greatly with the public's attitudes. Other policy proposals, however, may lack public support but still be acceptable to enough citizens and fall within the dikes. It is a plausible way of conceptualizing the role of public opinion, one gentler and probably more realistic than the notion of polls as 'sampling referendums.' It suggests that governments enjoy considerable autonomy from public opinion to pursue their choice of polices, but that public opinion still restrains them from making policies that fall outside the dikes.[2]

The introduction of the Goods and Services Tax in 1987-90 by the Mulroney government provides an unusually clear instance of a government acting at odds with the results of polls and every other indicator of the public's preferences.[3] Thus the opinion dikes, although more clearly defined than on most issues, failed to constrain what the politicians decided. Yet government officials commissioned and referred to polls and focus groups during the development of the tax.

The public's opposition could be foreseen. If a tax few citizens know about (the previously existing Manufacturers' Sales Tax, or MST) is replaced by one that is highly visible, negative reactions are hardly a surprise. The opposition was evident through active expressions of opinion such as interest groups, protest rallies, and media coverage. More than six hundred thousand people signed petitions against the tax and more than two million postcards were mailed to express opposition.[4] Virtually every poll result pointed the same way, many suggesting that Canadians opposed the tax by a margin of at least three to one.[5] Yet, having made its decision, the Mulroney government remained committed to proceeding despite the political dangers. Whatever doubts existed about the government's intentions largely disappeared once it was re-elected in November 1988. The decision is at odds with many assumptions about democratic government, about the impact of public opinion in general and polling specifically.

Although the government made its decision, and stuck to it in spite of hostile public attitudes, this does not mean that officials ignored public opinion. On the contrary, they commissioned a series of polls and focus groups. This research, broadly speaking, played three roles. First, it highlighted the public's hostility to the tax. Second, it provided a backdrop to several decisions about the design of the tax, which were made partly in response to public opinion – though not necessarily as shown in polls. And third, it contributed to the strategy for communicating the tax, to heighten understanding as well as alter public attitudes.

The Context for the GST

The MST was introduced in 1924. Charged on many manufactured goods, it operated with a narrow base and applied at several levels prior to the final sale. The tax was condemned by economists and business leaders throughout its life. It was attacked for its invisibility, variable rates, and narrow base. Moreover, most experts agreed that the tax induced many businesses to behave inefficiently and placed Canadian exporters at a competitive disadvantage. Long before the Conser-

vatives came to power in 1984, governments had examined alternatives, but apart from adjusting its rates, they left the MST largely un-
changed. Primarily because the tax was invisible, however, most
Canadians were unaware of it.

By mid-1986 it was clear that the finance minister, Michael Wilson,
had the will to tackle the problem. Allan Maslove suggests three reasons for this. First, there were growing concerns about competitiveness
because of the impending Free Trade Agreement with the United States.
Second, more generally, because of globalization, manufacturers were
trying harder to find ways to avoid the MST; this in turn made that tax
an increasingly unreliable source of revenue at a time of growing concern about the national deficit and debt. And third, with its narrow tax
base and harmful effects on businesses' behaviour, the MST was at odds
with the government's plans for other tax changes.[6] Interview sources
stress the role of the FTA and related concerns about the impact of the
old tax on exports.[7] For many reasons, then, the government wished to
eliminate the MST and replace it with a more neutral, broad-based, and
reliable tax; little consideration was given to alternatives besides some
form of value-added tax.[8]

The government initially planned to introduce the sales tax at the
same time as it reformed corporate and personal income tax.[9] During
1987-8, the extensive national debate over the proposed Free Trade
Agreement meant that tax reform attracted relatively little notice from
the media and even less from the public. What did receive attention
were cuts to personal and corporate income taxes in 1988; predictably
these did not create political problems for the government.

In June 1987 the government released a white paper outlining plans
to replace the MST with a new sales tax.[10] Prepared with little or no use
of opinion research, the paper announced that personal and corporate
income tax would be reformed the following year. A second stage of tax
reform would replace the MST. The government preferred a new sales
tax which would be harmonized with the sales taxes already charged in
every province except Alberta; if necessary it was prepared instead to
introduce a federal sales tax on its own. The white paper announced
several principles that the sales tax would follow. First was a broad tax
base with few exclusions (taxing food remained an open question at
this time). Second, the tax would be visible to taxpayers. Third, adjust-
ments to the income tax system would accompany the new sales tax;
these would include various tax reductions as well as credits for low-
income citizens. Finally, the tax, or at least the overall changes to the tax

system, would be 'revenue neutral.'[11] These principles would shape and constrain the development of the GST.

The Finance Department's Polling Program

Syndicated and media polls demonstrated Canadians' hostility to the proposed sales tax. But for more detailed information, the government had significant resources for initiating its own opinion research. In the 1988-9 fiscal year the Department of Finance commissioned only two opinion polls, but there were six in 1989-90 and thirteen in 1990-1.[12] In addition, at least one poll was taken in 1987 and two in 1991-2, and qualitative studies on the tax continued at least until 1993.[13] The bulk of the research, then, followed the announcement of the tax in 1987. Most of it was contracted to Decima Research and the Angus Reid Group.

Decima's ongoing polling tracked the public's attitudes on the issue. Opposition to the GST weakened slightly during 1990. One Finance official recalls, 'Opponents kept saying "We have to stop this thing or the sky will fall." And people kept getting up every day and the sky hadn't fallen. So it didn't seem like castor oil, it just seemed like Buckley's.'[14] The research also showed government officials that few citizens were aware of the MST. As long as the old tax was poorly understood, the GST would be perceived as a new tax rather than a replacement of an old tax. Overlapping with this problem, polling demonstrated that Canadians were sceptical of the government's motives and perceived the tax as a 'revenue grab.'

The opinion research was used by political officials and public servants. A Decima pollster describes his company's meetings with Finance officials:

> There was a group of people who knew each other ... Everybody would know the survey had been commissioned. People would have seen the questionnaire, but probably not made a lot of comments on it. [They] might have suggested that an issue area was missing or the minister had asked a question [and asked if we] could we get a read on this. So you'd have an hour and a half of ... [approximately] twenty slides with eight people in the room. And it would be very interactive, with lots of discussion surrounding each slide.[15]

Some of the research was prepared as background for Michael Wilson when he spoke to cabinet or the government caucus.

Anticipating and Learning the Public's Reactions

Most of the government's polling on the GST took place after the key decisions were made or at least signalled. Nevertheless, officials in the Department of Finance and the political arm of government generally understood that the tax would be unpopular with Canadians; however, they underestimated the reaction.

Indeed, Don Blenkarn, who chaired the parliamentary Standing Committee on Finance, says the government did not foresee the political difficulties. In early 1988, he recalls, 'We did not anticipate any objection to it at all; it was sailing along pretty well.' He says early statements from Liberal and NDP politicians indicated they would be supporting it.[16] Another source concurs that the government failed to predict the public's reaction: 'Nobody thought that this was going to be a really big issue.'[17] Asked if the government foresaw the extent of the opposition at the time of the decision to proceed, a Decima pollster answers 'not very well.' He explains that little polling had been done in 1987; only later when the government's research program was in full swing did it comprehend the extent of the hostility to the tax. As it was polling, agrees a civil servant, the government 'began to see the extent of the reaction: clearly they realized they had a tiger by the tail.'[18]

Others say the public's resistance was expected, if not its scale. Many civil servants in Finance and cabinet ministers foresaw that it would not be popular.[19] Yet the government was not fully tuned to public opinion on the tax in the early stages, largely because its attentions were diverted to the FTA and the Meech Lake constitutional accord. The energy and resources remaining for the GST in 1987 and 1988 were exhausted trying to establish a joint sales tax with the provincial governments.

While few Canadians paid attention to the issue before 1989, it became obvious during that year that the public opposed the GST. In July, John Bulloch of the Canadian Federation of Independent Business (CFIB) stated that public opinion was solidly against the government. Conservative MPs knew it. The same month, at least five of them publicly expressed doubts about the GST and warned of a possible tax revolt. For instance, Patrick Nowlan, a Nova Scotia MP, argued that 'the GST ... is political dynamite, especially without provincial agreement and small business support.' He predicted that the exemptions on some food would prove difficult to defend: 'I just don't want to see Mike Wilson on TV trying to defend the tax on his peanut-butter and dill pickle sandwiches while he nibbles peanuts on the side!' He added that the government should admit that the tax would raise more money than the MST rather than claim its revenue-neutrality.[20]

The government's polls delivered the same message as active public opinion. 'I think we were all aware that it was not going over well,' a civil servant recalls. Wilson opened one meeting by asking his Decima pollster, Bruce Anderson, 'What kind of trouble am I in now?' The polling firm's findings reinforced impressions that the political stakes for the government were high. As a result, PCO and PMO officials assumed larger roles in managing the GST.

External polls periodically brought the government further grim news. For example, in September 1989, Gallup reported that 72 per cent of the public opposed a national sales tax, with a mere 12 per cent in favour.[21] Two months later, CFIB released a poll which found that 87 per cent of respondents opposed the sales tax. Aiming its message at Conservative politicians, the interest group also warned that 59 per cent of respondents said they would not vote for an MP who favoured the tax.[22]

Despite its unpopularity, the government remained determined to press ahead with the tax in what David Dodge, a key public servant, called 'military fashion.'[23] The Finance bureaucracy was convinced of the rightness of its cause, as was the minister; with the support of the prime minister, the acceptance of cabinet followed. One Finance official explains that 'I think because the economics were so sound, [and] the whole federal sales tax was so broken, the determination to proceed with the replacement tax continued.'

A political element reinforced the commitment to proceeding, as the Conservatives stood very low in the polls. For instance, Gallup recorded that support for the party between January and October 1990 ranged between a low of 15 per cent and a high of 22 per cent.[24] In Darrell Bricker's blunt assessment, there was a perception within the PMO, the cabinet, and the Conservative party 'that it can't get much worse: "We might as well do all this stuff now, get it behind us, and then we'll spend the next couple of years of the mandate trying to fix it."' As well, reversing course would have shown weakness and risked creating a new set of political difficulties.[25]

Cabinet ministers such as Joe Clark privately expressed concerns about the political damage the tax was causing the government, but stopped short of urging that the tax be dropped.[26] Within the government, the GST was perceived as a communications problem. One Finance official recalls that public servants and senior Conservative officials shared 'a feeling that "if we can only explain it better to Canadians, then we'll be able to weather the storm."' The government officials did not perceive the opinion dikes to be as strong as they appear with hindsight.

The Decision to Proceed with the Sales Tax

The White Paper of June 1987 announced that the tax would be broad-based, visible, and revenue neutral. Wilson and his deputy minister, Fred Gorbet, both say they paid little attention to polling. As Wilson acknowledges, 'We [did] polling to try and find ways of making the tax more palatable.' But it merely served as background: 'Polling was not decisive, because we had to go ahead and change from the Manufacturing Sales Tax to the GST.' Wilson adds that it is difficult to precisely describe the impact of polling because he cannot separate in his own mind what the polls indicated, what the caucus said, the role of interest groups, and his own personal impressions from talking to people: 'that whole aspect of the introduction of the tax blended totally.' However, he believes the signals about the GST from polls and the other sources were broadly consistent.

While the government was determined to proceed regardless of public opinion, it faced several issues in the course of developing the tax. These were features of the design of the tax that potentially affected the willingness of the public to accept it. Officials were prepared to be somewhat flexible on these questions if this would reduce the obstacles to selling the tax. By examining these decisions individually we can consider what role public opinion and specifically opinion research played in the details and design of the sales tax.

The Calculated Timing of Tax Reforms

The government initially intended to bring in the sales tax at the same time as it reformed corporate and personal income tax. As New Zealand discovered in 1986, a sales tax could be accepted by the public if it was introduced along with other, more popular tax measures. If the Canadian government had followed that approach, laments a civil servant, 'at least we would have had cover.' Ultimately, however, the government introduced its tax reforms in two waves. Stage one, personal and corporate income tax cuts, took effect shortly before the election of November 1988; stage two, the GST, was postponed until January 1991. There is some doubt as to whether the government could realistically have introduced the GST during the first term had the will been there. Some federal officials suggest that the government postponed the tax because it feared the electoral consequences of introducing the tax before the 1988 election. Indeed, when the White Paper proposed to leave the tax until the second term, the government had a Decima poll showing that 68 per cent of respondents opposed the tax. Journalist Christopher Waddell wrote that 'the poll likely contributed to Mr. Wilson's decision to delay sales tax reform until some unspecified future date.'[27] However, some officials state that legislative and administrative overload forced the postponement of the sales tax. Another official says a mix of reasons explain the delay: the department could have introduced the tax in the first term, but this was held off for several reasons including the hope that an agreement could be struck with the provinces.[28]

Even downplaying the role of polling and accepting the claim that it was administratively impractical to proceed with the sales tax in the first term, it remains evident that the government could have delayed the income tax reforms and brought both stages in together. This was a clear political decision. The government wanted the benefits of tax cuts before the 1988 election and the fallout from the sales tax later. However, there is no reason to believe polls figured significantly here; the political judgment about the impact of the two tax reforms could be made instinctively. Polling would have contributed, says one official, but he notes that 'we didn't need polls to tell us that.' Another source suggests that if the GST had been introduced before the 1988 election, there was a risk that it would become a major issue in the campaign. If this had happened, he says, the government probably would have abandoned plans to introduce the sales tax.[29] The short-term benefit the Conservatives gained from the tax cut was ultimately outweighed by the longer-term disadvantage of introducing the GST unaccompanied by more popular tax reforms. One Finance official says splitting the two phases of tax reform proved a decisive mistake: 'The GST battle was lost the day we [announced] tax reform in June [1987]. We only did corporate and personal [income tax]. And we didn't include sales tax. And the day we did that, there was never going to be a hope in hell that we'd have an easy ride or even any level of comfort in handling the sales tax reform.' Overall, then, the timing was a decision made partly on the basis of anticipated public opinion – and it confirms that the government had some sense of the storm to come – but polling played a minimal role.

Exempting Groceries from the Sales Tax

The White Paper announced that the Manufacturers' Sales Tax would be replaced by a tax with very few exemptions. Although there was no firm commitment, this implied that groceries would be taxed. Finance officials and other experts considered this the soundest course in economic terms.[30] Fundamentally, they worried that exempting groceries would make the tax more complex.[31]

When the media, opposition parties, and public turned their attention to the proposed sales tax in 1987, it was usually to the idea of taxing food, and this sparked visceral objections. William Johnson graphically expresses the reaction: 'Taxing food in Canada is an unspeakable no-no, like proposing to tax widows and orphans, to tax the blind and the lame, or tax the aged gumming [sic] their cat food and the homeless foraging in their cold dumpsters.'[32]

Reflecting this sort of sentiment, the government's poll of March 1987 reported that 71 per cent of respondents were very uncomfortable and another 22 per cent somewhat uncomfortable with taxing groceries. In view of the poll results, Michael Cassidy, the NDP's finance critic, predicted that the government would rethink its tax reform plans and abandon any thoughts of taxing groceries.[33]

Following some debate in the public arena on taxing food, and a meeting with provincial finance ministers, Wilson announced in December 1987 that groceries would be exempted. Few observers were surprised by the retreat.[34] Why did the government exempt most groceries in spite of the economic arguments? 'My sense is it was too controversial, politics trumping policy,' says one civil servant.[35] Another concurs: 'It certainly was a political decision, not an economic decision. The argument for including groceries on economic grounds was extremely solid. The notion of taxing groceries was hard to sell politically.' Bruce Phillips, a key communications adviser in the PMO, warned the prime minister, 'Tax bread – you're dead.'[36] Others confirm the decision was political.[37]

However, polling mattered little in the decision. A Decima pollster says, 'I'm sure it contributed to the debate. I don't know that absent that public opinion [research] I would say the government was going to tax groceries.' Another source says polling might have contributed but he believes a combination of officials' instincts and informal contacts was more important.[38] Wilson says it wasn't necessary to refer to polling to learn of concerns about taxing groceries:

We just had the outcry, first of all, through [the] caucus; second, through things that we heard from various interest groups, and so on. It was very clear that that was a non-starter. I don't recall poring over public opinion polls to find out whether food was something that shouldn't be taxed. I didn't need [to] ... [Other officials may have referred to] polling to ... find out whether it was 93 per cent opposed or 89 per cent opposed.

While the decision was clearly political, then, it was not one where opinion research played a large part. While it had a slightly greater role than in the timing of the tax, other inputs, including active public opinion, were more critical.

Reducing the Rate of the Sales Tax

The White Paper tentatively signalled an 8 per cent tax. This assumed a broad-based tax, and certainly one that would include groceries. In 1989 the government announced that the rate would be 9 per cent. Department officials preferred this rate but accepted that lowering it might make the tax more palatable to the public. In the design of the tax, the rate was intertwined with the base and planned credits that would affect net revenues. Active public opposition to the tax grew throughout 1989 and this was reflected in public hearings held by the parliamentary Finance Committee in the fall. In November the committee recommended that the rate be reduced to 7 per cent, and in December Wilson announced this change. To offset the loss in revenue resulting from the shift from 9 to 7 per cent, it was accompanied by a package of trade-offs, including abandoning a planned income tax cut, as well as reducing forthcoming rebates to home buyers, grants to small businesses, and tax credits.

Calculations of projected revenue contributed to the decision to lower the rate, as did economic reasons, including the weakening economy of fall 1989 and the fear of fuelling inflation. There were also some concerns that a 9 per cent rate was simply too high.[39] But the economic merits of the possible rates took a back seat to political factors, specifically the hopes of weakening public hostility to the tax. In part the rate change was a response to what one official calls the 'poisonous atmosphere' of opposition, led by people like John Bulloch of the Canadian Federation of Independent Business. Clearly part of the explanation for the adjustment was the recommendation of the parliamentary committee – which heard primarily from interest organizations rather than the wider public. Blenkarn and other MPs also urged the rate be reduced in private contacts with Finance officials.[40] Business groups pushing for a 7 per cent rate had some impact, and the government hoped for political benefits from the endorsements of the GST that might follow. Many of the presentations to the committee urged that the rate be lowered, perhaps showing implicit acceptance of the tax.[41] A further reason for cutting the rate was the pressure from Conservative MPs as they reacted to the concerns of citizens.[42] In this sense, because the government hoped to reduce Canadians' hostility with an eye on its political standing and because greater acceptance of the tax would make its implementation and operation smoother, active public opinion had a central role.

What about passive public opinion? Roberts and Rose say that the rate was changed in response to polling data.[43] A Canadian Press news story similarly claimed that the change resulted from polls showing the unpopularity of the tax.[44] Still, the question deserves closer examination.

Decima's polling reveals that well into fall 1989, the rate of the tax was not only an open question but also a political one: the firm's survey on the GST in November included ten questions investigating reactions to altering the rate. Shown the survey, a Decima pollster says, 'You're not going to ask a question like that unless it's an issue.' Similarly, a civil servant explains, 'You wouldn't do that unless it was to see what would be an acceptable option, or to test out opinion on what the best option would be. No one likes a new tax. So the question is, what is the acceptable level? ... Policy just can never be divorced from that fact of life, and shouldn't be.'

In November 1989 Decima reported to senior officials in the Department of Finance that

> Public concerns are highest on two points: the impact of the GST on the cost of living and a worry about the government wasting the money raised. As a consequence, when offered options on the GST, people tend to be looking for a lower rate combined with a proven effort to reduce wasteful and inefficient government spending ...
>
> If a move is made to a lower rate, most of the required offsetting sources of revenue do not show any great appeal.

The public's impressions of excessive government waste appeared regularly in Decima's research,[45] and added to officials' problems: many

people believed the government should eliminate waste before introducing a 'new' tax. The study investigated attitudes to a 9 per cent tax
compared to a 7 per cent tax with various trade-offs: 'reduced transfers
for health and education,' 'less protection ... to the poor,' 'having all
housing taxed rather than just new housing,' taxing used cars, 'an
increase in income taxes for individuals earning $55,000 or more,' and
'an increase in the tax on large corporations which they say will hurt the
economy.' Predictably, Decima found that the last two options 'appear
to have more appeal than any others.' Of the other alternatives, only a 7
per cent rate with the tax applied to used cars also secured majority
support versus a 9 per cent rate. Only one finding offered encouragement for reducing the rate: the survey indicated that given a choice
between a 9 per cent tax and a 7 per cent tax 'with some combination
of the measures I just mentioned,' the lower rate prevailed by 69 to
27 per cent.[46]

A Decima pollster explains that despite this last finding, but in light
of the overall public opinion landscape, the firm advised Wilson that

> the reactions from the public were a little bit like, 'So you're going to hit
> me seven times over the head instead of nine. I'm supposed to feel great
> about that?' [The research] said that people would be ... more acquiescent
> to a 7 than a 9 [per cent tax]. But the differences as we interpreted them
> were at the margin, and nobody should assume that the difference be-
> tween nine and seven was the difference between political success and
> political failure ... Somebody else might have looked at our numbers and
> interpreted them differently, but our interpretation was ... 'Better hung for
> a sheep than a lamb. You may as well take the money.'

On this account, the data allowed different interpretations and offered
no clear guidance about changing the rate to seven or leaving it at nine.
Consequently, Decima advised Wilson that the government had little to
gain politically by making the change.

However, in part, the government was reacting to negative attitudes
towards the tax in general, as shown by both active public opinion and
polling. Some officials understood the polling to suggest the public
would be more receptive to a 7 per cent rate than a 9 per cent rate. Yet
different government officials drew different conclusions from the
polling.

One says lowering the rate 'was based upon research that suggested
that ... getting the rate down below nine might help.' Decima's results,

he says, 'would all go into the hopper ... We were looking for, would people loathe it less [as] a 7 per cent tax?' Another agrees polling was one of several inputs into the decision.[47] A third recalls that polling contributed to the decision, along with interest groups, the parliamentary committee, and the government caucus.[48]

Some officials placed somewhat less emphasis on the polls. One said that 'seven was obviously better than nine. Was it politically driven? Yeah, but you didn't need any polling to figure that one out.' Asked why the questions were posed by Decima, his reply was, 'Because you just did that. You wanted to be able to provide him [the minister] with all the information that you possibly can ... So you'd check out the possibilities.' He added that 'this would have been contributory evidence, but I don't think it would have driven it.'[49] Wilson himself explains:

> We did not sit there and study the polls and say 'that's how we're going to design this tax.' We looked at the policy considerations, the legal considerations, what we all sensed in the public domain, what the polling was saying. And we took all of that into account when you made the decisions as to which way we would go. I was never one to start with the polls. I started with that broad policy objective, and then came to a decision. And that was the conclusion of the decision [to change the rate from 9 to 7 per cent].

These explanations differ slightly but overall they indicate that opinion research was not a major factor behind the rate change.

Had the results pointed firmly in one direction, however, opinion research could have proven decisive. A Decima pollster explains that 'if it looked like 90 per cent of the public would come on side if the number was seven rather than nine, chances are there would have been a pretty vigorous debate about that.' A Finance official agrees, stating that if there had been strong support for a 9 per cent sales tax, the rate would not have been lowered.

Did the government obtain any political benefits from reducing the rate? The *Calgary Herald* predicted that Canadians' attitudes would shift to the government's advantage: 'The retreat to seven will probably swing enough corporate and public opinion to give the GST at least some semblance of popular acquiescence ... [O]n balance, the Tories have much improved prospects of riding out the storm at seven percent.'[50] However, a civil servant believes the actual effect on the public was minimal: 'That was a big change, and it was ... to try and craft the tax in a way that would make it more acceptable to the public. We probably won over five or six people. It helped a bit, but it didn't conquer the fundamental problem people have with the policy.' Analysis by the Angus Reid Group affirmed that the announcement of a 7 per cent rate 'has resulted in only a modest decline in public opposition to the proposed federal sales tax.' Its December 1989 poll showed 68 per cent opposed compared to 27 per cent in favour, a moderate shift from 76 to 18 per cent in August.[51] As Decima had anticipated, lowering the rate did not substantially alter the public's attitudes.

Partly because the opinion research did not provide an emphatic signal on changing the rate the way it did on overall opposition to the tax, it was only a minor factor in the decision. Economic factors played a larger role and political factors an even greater one. Active public opinion – relayed through interest groups, and especially through the parliamentary committee and the Conservative caucus – played a substantially greater role than polling.

Making the Sales Tax Visible

The White Paper committed the government to making the sales tax visible. This was partly because some viewed a transparent tax as more honest than a hidden one.[52] Additionally, the government would be able to argue that a visible tax would be more difficult to raise in the future,[53] and business groups that supported the tax preferred that it be visible. However, the matter was not entirely closed until 1990 as several government officials and external advisers explored the possibility of tax-included pricing as a way to make the GST more acceptable to the public. This was investigated in specially commissioned research and syndicated polling.

In June 1989, soon after negotiations to establish a joint tax with the provincial governments collapsed, Wilson announced that the decision whether to include the tax in the price of goods would be left to individual businesses. He said the promise of visibility would be maintained by requiring signs at cash registers to indicate whether the tax was included in prices.[54] Not only could the government claim to be keeping its promise, but it would also be in step with the wishes of business groups.

Several practical factors pointed to allowing individual merchants to decide whether to include the tax. One was logistical: businesses could choose the more convenient path for them. Another was the fact that nine provincial governments already had visible sales taxes. A hidden federal sales tax would probably be subject to the provincial sales taxes, and a 'tax on a tax' would invite criticisms. Finally, a constitutional argument, raised publicly by Wilson, was most important. The minister and other officials who were interviewed for this study referred to the Department of Finance's legal advice that the federal government lacked the authority to legislate in this area. If the federal government tried to rule either way, it could expect a court challenge from one or more provincial governments.[55] For these officials, the constitutional reason was central to the decision.[56]

Opinion research on the visibility of the tax was conducted for the government, which itself indicates that the matter was not settled. Interviewees' memories of public opinion vary. A few say Canadians preferred tax-included pricing to a visible tax.[57] Some suggest that opinion research showed support for a visible tax.[58] One of these says the government was open to either a visible or hidden tax and the research was critical in the decision. He adds that the research could not predict reactions once the tax took effect. Four others say that the opinion research did not give decisive signals. One of those who referred to the constitutional reason concurs, saying that if public opinion had strongly favoured tax-included pricing, the federal government would have considered risking a constitutional challenge.

The variation in sources' memories can be partly explained because they either interpreted the same research differently or were exposed to different research. An examination of three syndicated research studies illustrates how different polls can provide conflicting evidence.[59] Angus Reid's survey of January 1989 found the public supported tax-included pricing by a comfortable majority of 67 to 29 per cent. In September 1989, the *Decima Quarterly* recorded that the public preferred a visible tax: 64 per cent agreed the tax 'must be visible' while 35 per cent said 'it doesn't matter.' And in November 1990, Environics found the public divided almost evenly, with 49 per cent favouring tax-included pricing and 45 per cent opposed.

The timing might help to account for these results. But all three polls were conducted before the tax took effect, so the variation in the wording of the questions is probably the decisive explanation. Reid's question was: 'Suppose that the new federal sales tax were introduced. Would you prefer to have this tax as an additional charge calculated at the time that purchases are made, or would you prefer to have this tax already included in the advertised price of goods and services? (The total cost paid would be the same in both cases.)' The reference to an 'additional charge' may have created the impression of an extra cost which was not fully removed by adding the sentence in parentheses. For its part, Decima took a different approach:

> Some people say that if the new tax is going to be applied, it must be visible – that is, it must be shown separately on the price tags of all products that you purchase. Other people say that it doesn't matter if the tax is visible as long as there is a sign in the store telling you the tax is included in the price and your tax register receipt shows that it has been paid. Thinking of these two points of view, which one is closest to your own?

Decima's casual phrase 'doesn't matter' may have depressed opposition to a visible tax, which is defined somewhat strangely. Environics' question is the most straightforward of the three: 'If the GST does come into effect would you prefer to have the tax included in the ticket price of items or would you prefer the tax calculated and added at the cash register?' Whatever the reasons, the three polls – by respected polling firms which were presumably trying to write neutral questions – give contrasting impressions of the public's attitudes on this issue. Collectively, they would provide little direct guidance to policy-makers seeking to understand the public's preferences. Whatever exposure officials had to these particular polls, the variation in their results suggests why interviewees' recollections conflict: they remember different information.

Even if the data had provided a clear message, research before the tax took effect may have been a poor guide to attitudes after it was introduced. Some people almost certainly responded positively to the abstract notion of a visible tax, but after the GST was in place, they were reminded of it with almost every purchase and their anger was reinforced.

How can we best make sense of the conflicting evidence? Various sources had different impressions of the state of public opinion and its impact on the decision on visibility. While several individuals believed that the direction of public attitudes was clear, the government as a whole lacked a firm impression of public opinion. One of the Finance officials who cited the constitutional argument provides the best explanation when he suggests that the lawyers' advice prevailed in large part because the opinion research was not decisive. Wilson's early promise that the tax would be visible, and the views of business groups, reinforced the constitutional reason against tax-included pricing. Indeed, a different Finance official who cited the constitutional factor says that in its absence the department would have mandated a visible tax.[60] The inconclusive character of the poll results, combined with other considerations and the legal advice, meant that the government acted on the question of visibility with little help from opinion research.

In retrospect, the government's choice probably fuelled Canadians' opposition to the tax after it took effect. Don Blenkarn blames the minister of finance:

I frankly think at ... the cabinet end of things, Wilson screwed it up ... Early in the game, he said he was going to make the tax *visible*, alright? ... It's all very well to not know you're paying tax as you were with the federal sales tax, but to throw it in your face [with] a god damn purchase of every candy bar, for god sakes, is the most impolitic thing you could conceivably do, alright. But in order to satisfy the Chamber of Commerce view ... the god damn tax became highly visible.

Although their conclusions are gentler, several other officials agree that with hindsight a visible tax proved a political mistake and contributed to the public's resistance to the GST.[61]

Providing Income Tax Credits

As the White Paper projected, the GST ultimately included tax credits for Canadians with incomes below $30,000. The stated objective was to make them better off than they would have been without the GST.

A government poll in March 1987, while showing 68 per cent opposition to the general concept, found a narrow majority favouring a sales tax that 'would include a mechanism to protect low income earners against price increases.'[62] Polling and other signals of public disapproval were among the factors shaping the tax credits. More specifically, focus groups had some impact on the form the credits took: in response, says one Finance official, the government tried 'to err on the side of being overly generous.' More important was the government's effort to respond to the criticisms from interest groups that the tax was regressive (i.e., that it was more onerous for low income groups).[63] The anti-poverty organizations had a greater impact on the decision than the opinion research.

Debating a Revenue-neutral Sales Tax

The White Paper had promised that the new sales tax would be revenue neutral. While it was rarely spelled out, this meant that in its first year of operation the tax would produce the same projected net revenue as the old Manufacturers' Sales Tax. As revenue from the MST was expected to decline over time if it was continued, the GST would soon be generating more revenue than the tax it was replacing, although this was not widely understood.

The announcement that the GST would be revenue neutral was made by Wilson against some of the advice he received. Mulroney himself was initially sceptical when adviser Stanley Hartt advanced the concept.[64] Critics, including many Conservative party activists, wondered why the government was spending political capital to bring in the GST if it would be unable to argue credibly that the new tax would reduce the deficit.

Government officials hoped that the announcement would prevent the public from viewing the sales tax as a revenue grab.[65] Wilson judged that 'it is hard enough to sell a broadly-based consumption tax, but to say "by the way, we're going to [take] $5 billion" [would be even harder].' The notion that the tax would be revenue neutral in its first year of operation became 'part of the bible,' recalls an official.[66] This important decision was made without the aid of opinion research. It had consequences for the design of the tax: obviously a revenue-generating tax would have assumed a different shape. For example, the revenue-neutral commitment contributed to the decision to lower the rate of the tax to 7 per cent.[67] Moreover, it constrained the communications of the tax. The effects of the promise were felt throughout the development of the GST.

The revenue-neutral claim created two unanticipated problems in communicating the tax. It was not credible to citizens: most were unaware of the MST and therefore perceived the GST as a new tax. As well, it undermined the argument which many in the government wished to advance about the tax's capacity to help fight the deficit – one of the few glimmers of hope for selling the tax to the public. Polling showed that the promise was weakening the government's position.[68] As one of the government's advisers explains, 'We asked if in the government's mind each of [a list of possibilities] was a major or a minor motive [for introducing the GST]. And the number one response here was to raise the money needed to reduce the deficit. In part, people said "We don't believe you when you say it's not for that." And then they said "If we did believe you, we think that was foolish." It was a double whammy.'[69] This made selling the tax an even greater uphill struggle.

During 1989, then, it became clear from opinion research that the revenue-neutral concept was not resonating. Correspondingly, the research showed that the public was relatively receptive to the argument that the tax could help address the country's fiscal problems. For instance, Decima reported that 'most Canadians do not see any arguments in favour of the GST as overly compelling but the best of those available appears to be a combination of deficit reduction and the consequent guarantee of programs and services.'[70] The government responded to this and similar findings. The research helped to lead the government to subtly de-emphasize the revenue-neutral notion in its public communications and instead stress how the tax addressed the deficit.[71] A cabinet minister explains: 'We were looking for ways to try to sell it. And we didn't expect that it would ever be a vote-getter. But we were looking for ways to make it acceptable. And obviously, people were concerned about the deficit, so we put it forward as a deficit-fighting measure.'[72] Government spokespeople said that the tax would be revenue-neutral less frequently than they had earlier.[73]

While the shift in the communications approach is unmistakable, it is not so clear that the tax was altered in a way to make it revenue-generating. Maslove claims it was.[74] However, two officials dispute this, maintaining that the tax held to the revenue-neutral principle for its first year.[75] One, an accountant, adds that the government responded in a more specific way to the opinion research showing the relative strength of the debt reduction argument, by creating a debt servicing and reduction account. He explains that the fund 'was this notional argument that the GST revenues were going to go into this pot, and that pot would be used to reduce the debt. Which was nothing other than a total fraud ... It had no basis in fact. It was to fool the Canadian people into thinking that something was going to happen when clearly it was impossible.'[76] This accounting trick appeared, of course, to contradict the revenue-neutral claim.

Canadians were confused when the government tried to make both types of claims about the GST, with the result that the communications problems were compounded.[77] 'You're sort of sucking and blowing at the same time,' says one civil servant.[78] 'I think we just got killed, because we were riding both of those horses,' agrees another. He adds that it was logically possible to argue that the tax would be revenue neutral in its first year and would combat the deficit thereafter, but this did not come across.[79]

Although some defend Wilson's initial decision, others tend to believe that the early promise that the tax would be revenue neutral was a political error;[80] one official even calls it 'the Achilles' heel of the whole strategy for selling the GST.'[81] The government's communications task might have been slightly less demanding if it had taken a more flexible approach or tried to connect the tax to deficit reduction from the beginning. One of Wilson's advisers says the 1987 announcement, made before relevant polling data were available, illustrates how many details of the GST were determined 'in a bit of a public opinion vacuum.' If opinion research had been conducted earlier on this question, it might have helped the government predict the poor reception the revenue-neutral claim would have. Once the minister had made the announcement, of course, there would be political costs to openly changing it. However, in 1989, when opinion research was available, it contributed to the decision to gently downplay the revenue-neutral notion and communicate the idea that the tax would tackle the deficit.

Influencing and Informing the Public

How did opinion research contribute to the government's communications of the GST? As indicated above, opinion research helped assess the effectiveness of various arguments for use in advertising, brochures, media releases, and public statements.

The government was slow to address communications of the tax systematically, partly because it was not eager to draw attention to the tax prior to the 1988 election. However, the GST Communications Task Force was not established until late in 1989. The government's communications efforts on the GST had two main goals: to alter public opinion about the tax and raise awareness and understanding. Gorbet explains why opinion research affected communications more than the design of the tax: 'We knew what the polls were going to say about taxing anything. So it was more a question of trying to glean things from these various sources of opinion [research] as how best to sell the GST.' If opposition to the tax could be muted, that would be a step forward; if some support could be gained that would be even better. As well, the communications efforts aimed to provide information. A civil servant explains that 'some of the ads ... were really designed to deal with what we viewed to be confusion in people's minds, for example, about the tax base.' One advertisement pictured groceries on a conveyer belt; it sought to increase the public's awareness of how the tax would operate. Opinion research investigated whether such ads had affected attitudes as well as matters such as conciseness and clarity. It is impossible to separate entirely the two purposes of the communications: providing information could promote understanding, which in turn could alter attitudes.

One element of the government's strategy was to subtly persuade citizens that the tax was inevitable, and polling that inquired about the public's impressions of this helped to gauge the effectiveness of this approach. Consistent with the analysis in chapter 5, opinion research was also used to help to develop and pre-test the government's messages, and to learn whether these messages, delivered through advertising and public statements, were successfully reaching the public.

Opinion research also showed that many Canadians were not aware of the MST. As late as August 1990, Decima reported that 53 per cent 'disagree[d] with the government's assertion that the GST is not a new tax and that it is simply replacing an old tax.'[82] This revealed the scale of the task the government faced in trying to educate the public. It showed that some arguments for the tax would not resonate because they hinged on familiarity with the MST. In particular, the public was a long way from understanding the government's case that it was replacing a flawed tax.

One of the clearest messages from the opinion research was that a neutral, informational tone to advertising was preferred to one that appeared to be 'selling' the tax.[83] As indicated in chapter 5, this type of finding is common. A journalist criticized the government's advertisements on the GST as 'low-key, earnest, barely noticeable, [and] frequently boring.'[84] The research had helped to lead the ads to adopt a fact-oriented tone. However, according to one official, the most important reason for the ads' tone was a ruling from the Speaker of the House of Commons that criticized the government for running promotional ads before Parliament had approved the bill.[85]

Qualitative research helped to refine specific forms, pamphlets, and advertisements. One case was the Longwoods example described in chapter 5. In another instance, the government commissioned Decima to conduct focus groups to determine the colours of the signs that would be posted in stores to announce whether the GST was included in prices.[86] Decima presented the results at a meeting attended by several senior officials, including Wilson. 'They were not difficult choices: Do you want Tory blue?' says a Finance official, laughing. 'No. I think we'll go for green [and white].' It is surprising that this was considered a wise use of the finance minister's time, and it can be questioned whether the research on this question of detail was needed at all. Indeed, comments another official, who does not recall the study, 'I wouldn't have spent five seconds worrying about that kind of stuff. If somebody would have told me, I would have said, "Let me out of here. I'm going [to work elsewhere]. You're not focused. You deserve to lose."'

Opinion research also gauged the effectiveness of advertising, investigating what proportion of respondents recalled advertisements and what sort of impact they had. Government officials occasionally encountered good news in the polling. For instance, they found comfort in the slim 51 per cent majority which agreed that 'The government has a responsibility to send out information like this [pamphlet] about the GST.'[87] Yet there was plenty of bad news. For instance, only 23 per cent said the pamphlet made them more willing to accept the GST, while 47 per cent said it made them less willing.

On the whole, the communications did little to increase acceptance of the tax. It was not realistic to expect major changes in public opinion. However, the opinion research apparently helped modestly with the other goal of promoting awareness and it contributed to the communications that was a necessary aspect of implementation.

Implementing the GST

Many of the responsibilities for implementing the GST were borne not by the Finance Department but by Revenue Canada. One official says that 'Finance treated them [Revenue Canada] like poor, stupid cousins. They didn't think they were going to do a good job on it.' Implementation included technical tasks such as establishing procedures and purchasing equipment for processing tax returns. However, a considerable part of implementation involved communications with businesses and the general public, and opinion research figured here.

An example is research to learn whether businesses were ready to deal with the new tax.[88] Smaller businesses were slowest to adjust. Business people would have to understand and prepare for the tax in order to collect it and forward it to the government: for instance, bookkeeping systems and cash registers needed adjusting. Surprisingly, since contacts with business associations found many of them unable to provide the necessary information, qualitative research was viewed as the only way for the government to learn about businesses' preparations. Gary Breen remembers Decima's focus groups that asked business people,

> 'Have you heard about the plans for the GST? Are you getting ready for the GST?' Answer: no. That's what always scared me. Months before the GST [took effect] ... I remember one in Halifax in particular where small business people were saying, yeah, they'd heard of it, but they had no idea how they were going to work, they were doing nothing to get ready for it.

The research was conducted to take the audience's temperature and to try to anticipate policy and operational problems: how well were businesses prepared, did they understand what was necessary to prepare, and were they doing it? If there were major problems with compliance, then the entire implementation of the GST could have become a giant fiasco. The findings of the research then contributed to the communications strategy directed at these problems.

Passing the GST in the Senate

After the House of Commons passed the GST in April 1990, the government faced the threat that the Liberal majority in the Senate would obstruct the tax or perhaps even defeat it. The government employed polls to learn what the public thought of the Senate's threat. In June 1990 Decima reported that, despite the general unpopularity of the Senate, there was considerable support for it obstructing the GST: '[The] results suggest that any attempt by the Senate to delay or reject the GST enabling legislation would meet with the approval of almost two-thirds of Canadians.'[89]

In August and September, preparing for a fight in the Senate, Mulroney filled the vacant seats with Conservatives. In September the Senate Banking Committee recommended scrapping the GST. The government declared a deadlock between the House and Senate, a necessity to employ an obscure provision in the constitution that allowed it to appoint eight additional senators. As the government prepared for this, some foresaw public disapproval and an official suggested that credible people be appointed to fill the eight special seats, cast their votes for the

GST, and then resign from the Senate. This was proposed with public opinion in mind, he explains: it was 'an example of trying to respect public opinion [but] not based on a poll ... It was based on how I thought the public would respond.'[90] However, in late September Mulroney appointed the eight senators to sit until they turned seventy-five: this gave the Conservatives fifty-four seats to the Liberals' fifty-two, with six others. These six would divide evenly on the tax, giving the government a slim majority.

To help with the government's strategy to see the GST through the Senate, opinion research was conducted, some of it so political that it had to be funded by the Conservative party rather than taxpayers. The research was used to help develop arguments to challenge the tactics of the Liberal senators and deter them from continuing to block the GST. In particular, the polling helped to guide public statements of government spokespeople, including speeches Wilson made in Parliament. A participant in this strategy says the Liberal senators' filibuster was shut down because

> we called their bluff. We basically told them ... 'You can continue doing this, and you'll be right in the trough, you'll be basically in the mud pile with us' ... Our research indicated that, the longer they were filibustering on this, yes, people said 'I'd like the Senate to do one last thing before they' kill it, and that is to kill this GST stuff' ... But the longer they [Liberal senators] were out there, [there was] a political problem for them. I'm assuming they knew that; the political problem that was showing up ... [was that] people started saying 'You know what? I don't think these guys are any different.'

The polling, then, helped the Conservative government sharpen its message, delivered largely in public but designed to influence the Liberal senators. It also gave government strategists confidence that their message would strike a chord.

Conclusion

The decision to proceed with the GST was clearly not a political one, and polling assumed virtually no role in it. The decision was made, then, before government officials were fully aware of the opinion dikes, and when those dikes were less prominent than they would become in 1989 and 1990. However, political calculations figured in several subsequent decisions about the details of the tax, and so were potentially affected by opinion research; as the opinion dikes became more evident they led the government to explore issues in the design of the tax. Anticipated public opinion played a major part in the timing of tax reform, but this was through logic and instinct much more than polls. Active public opinion, again much more than opinion research, led to the exclusion of groceries from the tax. While economic factors helped determine the 7 per cent rate, political factors were larger: opinion research played a role here, although still a smaller one than active public opinion. A mixture of political calculation and policy constraints – including the constitutional factor – entered into the question of visibility; however, an early announcement was made and later opinion research did not produce clear results, so it had little chance to affect the decision. Opinion research exerted slightly more influence on the low-income tax credits. The decision to present the tax as revenue neutral, a claim with implications for design and communications, was an attempt to anticipate the reaction of the public, but this effort might not have occurred if opinion research had been used at the time. However, opinion research affected communications. It contributed substantially to the shift towards emphasizing how the tax would attack the deficit. More generally, the opinion research helped develop and evaluate the government's communications efforts. Opinion research also assisted with implementation.

Overall, although political calculations were important as the government tried to increase acceptance of the tax through decisions about its design, opinion research was secondary to active public opinion and even at times to officials' logic and instincts about public opinion. Opinion research confirmed other messages rather than acting as a primary indicator. Certainly it had more influence on communications and on some of the policy details than the initial decision.

Why did the opinion research not exert more impact, and thereby help the opinion dikes work as Key anticipated? First, as with most other policies, most of the research came late in the policy process, after decisions on details were finalized or at least difficult to reverse. While officials knew that public opinion would be against them, early exposure to polling would have increased their awareness and perhaps induced them to develop a communications strategy earlier. As well, earlier research would have had more potential to assist a communications strategy. Second, at times political considerations were not critical: economic factors (such as the Free Trade Agreement, the trend towards globalization, and growing problems with the Manufacturers' Sales Tax) were important and constraints such as the constitutional advice prevailed at times. Third, when political factors did apply, active public opinion was more influential than opinion research. Fourth, the public servants in the Department of Finance and their minister were determined to proceed with the tax regardless of the public's reactions. As unelected officials, the public servants saw the opinion dikes as obstacles to implementation rather than threats to re-election; the minister's view was that the tax was needed.

The failure of the government to manage the issue effectively was especially serious because it had initially ignored the opinion dikes. The failure depressed the government's popularity and contributed substantially to the catastrophe the Conservatives suffered in the 1993 election when they were reduced to two seats in the House of Commons. Assuming that abandoning the GST was not an option, what might have been done differently to try to reduce the government's problems with public opinion?

There are several possibilities relating to both policy and communications. The government could, for instance, have tried harder to achieve an agreement with the provinces. It could also have required tax-included pricing, and avoided claiming the GST was revenue neutral. As well, the government could have followed the lead of New Zealand and brought in the income tax reform along with the GST. Another lesson not learned from the New Zealand experience concerned communications. Gorbet remembers 'TV ads, where you had people who did the cleaning in a big bank tower talking about the new sales tax, and how they really liked it because the guys upstairs were going to have to pay it every time they bought their caviar and their steak. We were aware of that stuff, but we never really played that. And I was never quite sure why we didn't.' Whether this approach would have persuaded a sceptical public is uncertain. Still, any of these suggestions might have reduced the strength of the opinion dikes.

Marcel Côté, who served in the PMO until mid-1990, argued later that year that the government proceeded too slowly and thereby allowed opposition to build.[91] More plausibly, a Finance official says the opposite: the government acted too quickly, not leaving time for Canadians' attitudes to evolve. As he points out, their concerns about the deficit developed quite slowly.

Consistent with this notion, as noted earlier, much of the opinion research occurred too late to be fully integrated into the communications strategy. Reflecting on the problems introducing the tax, Wilson says that in retrospect the government should have 'much more aggressively ... advertised the negatives, the inequities, and the huge inefficiencies of the existing sales tax – in other words, set up why we needed to change the sales tax. And just blast the airwaves for six months, until people were down on their knees pleading, saying "If this one doesn't work, please give us something better."' He adds that it is uncertain how effective this approach would have proved. Still, if the government could have delivered its message about the MST, it is plausible to think that it would have encountered fewer political difficulties.

A source who served in the PMO says the government was poorly served by its advisers on this issue between the 1988 election and 1990:

> I think the people who worked on the communications of this at the front end were extremely lazy. They basically mailed in their advice. Nobody knew that this was going to end up where it ended up, and the best advice that they could give is 'Well, let's wait for the economy to turn around. And maybe people will accept what we have to say.' It was pretty muddle-headed stuff, pretty lazy direction in terms of both research and the communications advice that the government got. I do not think Michael Wilson was particularly well served.

He suggests that it was not simply a problem of who was involved: the advisers were oriented towards personal 'survival.' Their caution helps to explain the early failure to develop a satisfactory communications strategy.

Different decisions on design and communications probably would have lowered Canadians' resistance to the tax, although certainly not eliminated it. If more opinion research had been initiated earlier in the process, it would have enhanced the government's understanding of the opinion dikes and guided design and communications decisions that would have made the tax somewhat more acceptable to citizens.

8 Opinion Research and Gun Control

In 1995 the Chrétien government kept an election promise to strengthen Canada's gun control laws by passing Bill C-68. Among its features were heavier penalties for firearms-related crimes, safe storage requirements, licensing of gun users, and expanded requirements for registration.[1] Since the passage of the bill, the government has been implementing and communicating the policy and its rationale of reducing violent crime.

Public Opinion on Gun Control

The gun control issue features an unusually sharp contrast between passive and active public opinion. Most opinion polls produced strong majorities in favour of stricter gun controls. For instance, an Angus Reid poll in October 1994 indicated that 70 per cent of the public supported stronger gun control laws. In the same month, Environics found 90 per cent of respondents favouring a law requiring registration of all firearms. A few weeks later, Gallup reported 83 per cent support in response to a similar question.[2] Syndicated polls in the 1990s generally showed that each region of the country favours gun control, although support is strongest in Quebec and weakest on the prairies.[3]

Two factors complicate this picture of strong support for gun control. First, opponents of the policy have energetically scrutinized and criticized it, arguing that it would prove costly and ineffective. As well, many resented the announced fees and claimed that registration of guns is a step towards confiscation. They have disputed the mainstream polls and cited competing ones. One argument is that if the public is asked to rank gun registration and several other policies that address crime, registration appears to be a relatively low priority. More commonly, critics of the polls make the case that the public lacks basic information; when surveys provide significant amounts of information for respondents, support for gun control is depressed.[4]

The second and more important complication is that active expressions of public opinion are not consistent with the polls: the former create impressions that may mislead decision-makers. The most visible sources of opinion on this issue are the opponents of stricter controls, notably the National Firearms Association and other groups representing gun owners. More than supporters of firearms control, they hold rallies, organize petitions, and contact the media, politicians, and civil servants. Environics pollster Derek Leebosh comments:

> If you just concentrated on the calls to phone-in shows and the mail that MPs are getting to their offices, you'd think that 90 per cent of Canadians were overwhelmingly against gun control. But every piece of research shows the majority of people are in favour of it. It happens that middle-aged white men that own guns are vastly more likely to be the kinds of people that write their MPs and call radio shows than the rest of the population. So if there was no polling, the government might think, 'My God, we can't do this because it's going to be wildly unpopular,' and might cancel the policy, even though in actual fact most people were in favour of it.

Gun control activist Heidi Rathjen also believes that passive public opinion favoured her cause while active public opinion was expressed more vigorously by opponents.[5] For example, she refers to cross-country consultations undertaken by Justice Minister Allan Rock in 1994, when opponents of the bill outnumbered supporters at public meetings: 'An impartial observer could have been excused for believing that the country was 95 per cent against restrictions on guns.'[6] This image of public opinion was reflected when the Coalition for Gun Control urged 'the silent majority' that favoured firearms control to express itself to counter the loud voices of opponents.[7] The polls counteract impressions of public opinion that group activity might suggest, thereby undermining the gun users' groups and bolstering the government's position.

Gun Control Policy, 1989–93

Bill C-80 was the Mulroney government's first attempt at firearms control. The bill originated when Doug Lewis was minister of justice, in the aftermath of the shooting deaths of fourteen female engineering students at the École Polytechnique in December 1989. Indeed, the minister was meeting with officials from provincial governments and the RCMP when they were interrupted by news of the tragedy. Public opinion following what became known as the Montreal massacre contributed to the development of gun control, but it was active public opinion heard through the media and correspondence to the government, rather than polling. Although Bill C-80 was referred by Kim Campbell, the new minister of justice, for further study by a parliamentary committee, it was revived in a similar form in 1991 as Bill C-17. Campbell's adviser, John Dixon, neatly characterized the government's approach as 'all guns out of the wrong hands, and the wrong guns out of all hands.'[8] The law mildly strengthened existing restrictions on guns, including new prohibitions on several different weapons.

In 1991 the Department of Justice commissioned the Angus Reid Group to conduct a survey. The firm contacted slightly more than ten thousand households, and conducted interviews with people in the 23 per cent of households which owned at least one gun. The government was already committed to Bill C-17, so the survey was not taken to guide the content of the policy, and indeed attitudes were not investigated. Rather, it provided factual information that confirmed some of the analysis underlying the bill. Implementation of the bill would be helped by the data, including estimates that 2.2 million Canadian households owned guns, and that they possessed 5.9 million guns.[9]

The government also monitored syndicated research and conducted some polls, at least one of which was funded by the Conservative party. Campbell is apparently recalling this research when she writes that 'the majority of Canadians favoured tighter restrictions on firearms' around 1990.[10] However, the polling did not play a major part in forming the policy. Instead, active public opinion was assessed through correspondence, efforts to mobilize supporters of gun control to contact MPs, the organized expressions of opinions by the families of victims of shootings, and the associated media coverage.[11]

The Development of Gun Control Policy, 1993–5

Following the election of the Chrétien government in 1993, the new justice minister's office and the public servants became familiar with the polling that showed support for the general principle of gun control and specifically for registration. They monitored media and syndicated polling. The minister's office, however, was aware that even if the government enjoyed majority support, it did not necessarily follow that the policy would win votes: it was possible that most people who felt so strongly that their votes might be determined by this issue were opposed. While the polling was favourable, this was not a primary factor leading to the policy. During 1994 Allan Rock and Chrétien gradually committed the government to significantly strengthening gun control. The scope of the policy became clearer in the fall and included licensing of gun users and registration of rifles and shotguns.[12]

The government initiated little opinion research to study gun control during the development of the policy in 1993–5. Instead, officials relied primarily on public and syndicated research. These polls, however, did not supply the detailed findings that officials usually seek when they commission their own research.

The opinion research helped to put gun control on the political agenda. Polls helped the government recognize that crime was a major issue for many Canadians. This refers not just to polls on gun control specifically, but also to more general data on concerns about crime. As an example, a poll in spring 1994 found that one in three respondents considered crime and violence the most important issue to their community; 85 per cent believed the level of violent crime in Canada had risen during the previous five years.[13] A senior Justice official states that even if polling had shown the public opposed to the policy, the government would still have proceeded with most components of it. However, he adds that with unfavourable polls the government might have abandoned plans to require registration of guns. He also points out that polling did not affect the timing of the policy, since other priority issues were 'less divisive and less politically difficult.' To the extent that public opinion was a factor, this was realized largely through other means than polls. Indeed, it was partly a consequence of shootings such as the Montreal massacre and a series of murders with guns in 1993 and 1994; the subsequent news stories contributed to a political climate in which governments could strengthen controls on guns, as the Conservative government had in 1991. As before, the interest in gun control was gauged through active expressions of public opinion rather than polling. Justice officials stress other factors than polls in explaining why the issue arrived on the agenda and was acted on by the government.[14]

First, the Liberals' 1993 election platform, the Red Book, had promised action: 'To strengthen gun control, a Liberal government will, among other measures, counter the illegal importation of banned and restricted firearms into Canada and prohibit anyone convicted of an indictable drug-related offence, a stalking offence, or any violent offence from owning or possessing a gun.'[15] The platform avoided the controversial matters of licensing all users and registering their weapons – the main red flags the pro-gun organizations saw in the subsequent Liberal policy. Still, this promise helped gun control to secure a high position on the government's agenda.

Second, Allan Rock was a new star in the cabinet and he had the political will to proceed. The justice minister was able to secure support for his plans from PMO officials, the cabinet, and the prime minister. Rock's commitment to strengthening firearms control helped to ensure that the government would stick to the policy.

Third, an unusually influential interest group, the Coalition for Gun Control, supported and encouraged the government and thereby offset part of the pressure created by the gun users' organizations. Formed initially with assistance from the public service in bringing gun control activists together, the coalition developed in 1990–1 in response to the shootings in Montreal. The group's leaders skilfully held together an alliance of diverse affiliated groups, earned a reputation for being well-informed, courted the media, lobbied politicians, and developed strong instincts about which issues to treat as non-negotiable and which ones to compromise on. For these reasons, the group exerted substantial influence on the government. The affiliation of police chiefs further enhanced the group's credibility.

These three factors had a mutually reinforcing relationship with opinion research; for instance, the polls strengthened Rock's ability to advocate the policy within government. However, the contribution of mass opinion to the policy output was small. While the polling had a minor impact on the policy content, it was used mainly for what a public servant describes as 'environmental assessments: to understand what are top-of-mind concerns, and what are emerging concerns.' As well, the polls assured the government that the visible opposition to gun control was not reflective of the wider public. This factor was especially relevant to the contentious registration requirements of the bill. Polling was, therefore, consciously cited within the government to reassure elected officials and their aides, and it boosted the morale of public servants; it was also cited publicly to justify and defend the policy. Because their message showed strong majority support and contrasted with active expressions of opinion, polls were used more for these purposes with gun control than with most other policies.

Polling and the Gun Control Debate

As well as these uses of opinion research, polling was initiated and cited by political actors seeking to influence the federal government and the course of the public debate. Supporters and opponents of gun control each used polling to try to demonstrate public support for their position.

The Coalition for Gun Control commissioned an Angus Reid poll in the fall of 1993 which was presented in the syndicated *Reid Report*. Seventy-six per cent of respondents strongly supported firearms registration and another 10 per cent supported it moderately.[16] Additional analysis for the coalition separated those living in households with guns, 53 per cent of whom strongly supported registration and 15 per cent moderately supported it.[17] The wording of the key question, however, was not entirely neutral. It provided information which may have induced respondents to take a position in favour of gun control – the number of firearms in Canada, and the fact that registration would create a record of them (rather than, for instance, informing respondents about the costs of the policy).[18]

The coalition commissioned the poll partly to help it make gun control an issue in the 1993 election and to attract media attention to its cause. 'The poll proved to be one of the best investments we ever made,' recalls Rathjen. 'It showed that people who supported more controls were a majority in every province, and in both rural and urban areas. We used the results as a news item, a tag ending for our releases and a quote for all occasions ("If the gun lobby truly represented most gun owners, they would support gun control").'[19] The last point illustrates how the poll was used to demonstrate the support for gun control from a 'silent majority.'

Opponents of gun control also used opinion research to try to influence the public debate. For instance, one study by sociologist Taylor Buckner showed that undergraduates at Concordia University were poorly informed. Although the issue had become especially salient after a high-profile shooting at that university, few students knew that people could be jailed for owning a handgun without a permit, while most overestimated the proportion of murders accounted for by handguns. Informed of existing legislation, many indicated they were satisfied with it and did not support further controls on guns.[20] Consistent with other evidence, the general public appeared to be poorly informed about the issue, but this is hardly unique to gun control. The extent to which providing respondents with more information can de-press support for gun control is a topic that may deserve more atten-tion; unfortunately it has not been pursued in a neutral fashion and in some cases the research has been funded by pro-gun organizations. A civil servant in the Department of Justice does not completely dismiss Buckner's analysis but contends that some of the sociologist's questions set an unreasonably high standard of knowledge.

In early 1995 two provincial governments that opposed the federal plans commissioned polls in their provinces and released them pub-licly. Canwest Opinion's survey for the Saskatchewan government asked if increased registration of firearms would reduce crime; 86 per cent of respondents said it would not. Bob Mitchell, the province's justice minister, cited the poll to justify his government's opposition to fire-arms control, claiming that 'almost 75 per cent of the people polled agree that there should be an evaluation of our current gun control laws before further changes are made.'[21] Besides the fact that predicting the consequences of initiatives like gun control is a challenge even for policy experts, the questions were leading because they provided selec-tive information and probably induced answers that suited the Saskatchewan government. For instance, one question emphasizes that the 'Auditor-General has said that our existing firearms control pro-gram has not been properly evaluated.'[22]

At about the same time, Environics conducted a poll for the Alberta government, with unexpected results: the poll indicated that a majority of the province's residents favoured the policy. Even the controversial registry component received 64 per cent support. Justice Minister Brian Evans had commissioned the study in part because he doubted the federal government's claims of strong support for the policy.[23] He ac-knowledged that 'I was surprised, quite frankly, that over 50 per cent of Albertans would say, "We're not opposed to a gun registry."'[24] In fact, they indicated their support, not merely that they were not opposed. The poll produced this result, even though the survey design was considered potentially leading by a federal official because it outlined current regulations and restrictions on gun owners. Rock responded enthusiastically to the findings: 'It's very good news. I'm grateful for it. I will be making references to the poll's results as the week goes on.' A reporter suggested that he would cite the poll in an upcoming Liberal caucus meeting, and could argue that if Albertans favoured his bill, then the rest of the country must as well.[25]

This is a rare instance of opinion research not producing the results its sponsor wanted and expected. A Justice Department official explains how the poll reinforced the federal government's claims of public support: 'We could have done that survey twenty times, and Alberta would say it was faulty, it's biased, the questions aren't right – this kind of support you can't buy, because Alberta went and did its own survey, and got the same results. What do they do? It's great.' Nevertheless, the Alberta government continued to actively oppose the federal policy.

The gun control issue is a case where polls were commissioned and used to try to shape the public debate, as the provincial premiers had on the constitution and the Canadian Federation of Independent Business had on the GST. Apart from the unforeseen result of the Alberta government's poll, the provincial governments produced their polls too late to have maximum impact: by early 1995, the federal government was committed to proceeding and the Bloc Québécois was supportive, so the bill would pass even if a significant number of Liberal MPs were persuaded to vote against it. Opponents of gun control may have hoped that the public pressure would lead the government to modify the features of the policy that troubled them most, but they would have been disappointed by the final bill. In any case, because active and passive opinion diverged so greatly, there were unusually strong incentives to employ polls to publicly criticize or defend the policy.

Policy Details: Modifying the Policy

With the pressure from gun users and provincial governments to modify the policy in mind, we will now examine some of the questions of detail that were considered in the months before the House of Commons approved Bill C-68. The parliamentary Justice Committee discussed various proposals to amend the bill and exerted some impact on the final version.[26] But one Liberal member of that committee notes that it dealt with technical and legal matters, unsuited to the influence of opinion research.[27] One of his colleagues, asked if any discussion of public opinion on gun control took place in the committee, replies 'No. None whatsoever.'[28]

In May 1995 the minister told the Justice Committee that he would agree to several changes, most notably reducing the penalty for failing to register guns (to make it a summary offence in most cases); allowing gun owners to give certain weapons to their adult children rather than completely banning them; and narrowing the search and seizure powers of the police.[29] The acceptance of the changes by the government represented an effort to respond to pressure from both within the Liberal caucus and outside the government, as well as a genuine attempt to improve the policy.

There is no evidence that public opinion research had any impact on these changes to the bill. In fact most, if not all, of the available polling was at a general level and did not investigate such precise questions or provide much specific information about the attitudes of gun users – the group which would be directly affected by the legislation. The government initiated little opinion research between 1993 and 1997 and generally relied on syndicated polling. This research revealed the direction of public opinion and provided the desired results for defending the policy.

One official remembers signals of concerns about the policy details from critics in Parliament, the media, gun users' organizations, and internet chat groups, but cannot recall opinion research contributing to the impressions of public opinion. (This is probably because most available research was syndicated and lacked the detail and concentration on gun users necessary to be useful in this way.) Anticipated public opinion was a concern at a broader level. Rather than drawing on polling data, the government sensed that the critics were generating pressure that could have changed public opinion and potentially endangered the bill. The assumption of Justice Department officials was that shifts in public opinion 'could affect political and policy commitment.' They were thinking, of course, about active expressions of opinion rather than polling.

Policy Details: The Question of Restricting Air Guns

One of the few polls the government commissioned on firearms during 1993–5 was a study by Environics to investigate public opinion on restricting air guns, most of which were not covered under Bill C-68. While less dangerous than most firearms, these weapons use BBs or pellets; some can shoot through thin cardboard while others are many times more powerful. One in seven respondents told Environics in March 1995 that their household owned at least one air gun. While it is unlikely that many respondents understood the nuances of the issue, the pollster reported widespread support for restricting air guns. For instance, 73 per cent favoured requiring users of air guns to pass a safety test, and 59 per cent supported subjecting air guns to the same controls as 'real firearms.' Only when asked about an outright ban were

Canadians opposed to restrictions, and then by the tiny margin of 50 to 48 per cent.[30]

A Department of Justice official familiar with the poll confirms that this is a relatively rare instance of opinion research being initiated to assist with policy refinement. The Canadian Opthamological Society had urged the government to restrict air guns because they cause eye injuries.[31] Government officials held ongoing discussions on air guns as they developed the bill, and public opinion was a consideration in the decision. Yet despite the support the survey showed for restricting air guns, the government decided not to include most of these weapons in the legislation.[32]

Three factors help to explain why public opinion did not prevail. First, officials viewed the question of restricting air guns as a technical matter unsuited to determination by public opinion. As well, a comparison of the political costs and benefits did not clearly point to expanding the legislation to include air guns.

Second, the government had already spent considerable political resources to pursue gun control, facing the opposition from within its caucus, provincial governments, and gun users. Legislative overload was a factor. As a result, explains an official, the government did not have political capital to spare. Anticipated public opinion was a consideration once again; since the government already faced vigorous opposition from target shooters, it did not want to risk creating 'a concern that people would [think] that we'd just gone a bit too far.'

Third, the Coalition for Gun Control did not take a position on whether air guns should be included in the legislation. As observed earlier, the group enjoyed influence partly because it selected its battles carefully, and it did not choose to place air guns among its priorities. The absence of pressure from the interest group was not a reason for the government to leave the issue alone; however, if the coalition had spent its own political capital to lobby for it, this would have been influential and quite possibly decisive in leading the government to include air guns in its bill.

The poll on air guns was conducted to provide input about public opinion during the process of deciding on a policy detail. However, the favourable poll results were trumped by the technical character of the issue, the government's shortage of political capital, and the absence of pressure from the Coalition for Gun Control. The importance of the coalition suggests how group activity can weigh more heavily than opinion polls. More generally, interest organizations exerted more influence than mass opinion on gun control policy; for instance, the coalition's representatives met with officials to review policy statements and regulations. Overall, public opinion research exerted little impact on the details of the gun control policy.

Polling to Contain Dissent from Government MPs

The strength of party discipline in the Canadian House of Commons has been well documented.[33] As the second and third readings of the gun control bill approached in the spring of 1995, many Liberal MPs from rural areas faced a dilemma.[34] Many were under pressure from constituents and gun users' groups to oppose their government's bill, yet they knew that they could face disciplinary actions if they did so. At one stage as many as thirty government MPs had expressed their dissatisfaction with the bill.[35] The case of gun control provides an opportunity to consider how public opinion, and polling in particular, was used by a government and caucus members as a contentious parliamentary vote approached.

In this situation, as the second and third readings approached, some Liberal MPs referred to constituency polls. For instance, Andy Mitchell, a rural Ontario MP, had initially opposed the gun control bill within the caucus. After a poll in his riding showed 58 per cent support for the bill, Mitchell dropped his opposition. Another early critic of the policy from the Ontario caucus, Bob Speller, was influenced by a poll conducted by a newspaper with the cooperation of his office staff. The survey of 190 constituents found 62 per cent support for the bill. 'I'll look seriously at the results of this poll in terms of making a decision on my vote,' said the MP, who ultimately voted with the government.[36]

Some MPs initiated their own surveys, often using householder mail, with its non-representative character rather than polls with near-random samples. For instance, Tom Wappel used householder mail to survey constituents in his Scarborough riding, explaining later that he was much more interested in the views of the two thousand constituents who returned the survey than those who did not respond. Before the survey was mailed, Wappel asked some opponents of gun control whether the questions 'were – I hate to use this word, in view of the topic – loaded ... [They] thought the questions were fair and reasonable.' To the key question, 'Do you believe that all firearms in Canada should be registered with the federal government?' 62 per cent said yes. Wappel suggests quite plausibly that gun users would have been more likely than non-users to reply and to urge others to do so. (Three other questions did not clearly signal support for restrictions on firearms; for instance, only 37 per cent believed that universal registration would reduce criminal misuse of guns.) Asked if the survey helped him, Wappel replied,

> Yes, it was very helpful to me. Because my own personal view of the legislation was that it was overkill. And I didn't think it was necessary, and I didn't think that it was going to be cost-effective ... But this is not an issue of conscience ... And when my constituents advised me, to the extent that they did, 62 per cent, that they felt that the law was fair and reasonable, I saw no reason to go against that, and vote contrary to their wishes.

If his survey had signalled opposition to the policy, he indicates he would have seriously considered voting against the government. As with Speller, the survey gave Wappel some cover for defending his position to his constituents.

But while MPs are sensitive to constituents' opinions because they hope to be re-elected, surveys are rarely the most important means of constituency feedback. It appears that most Liberal MPs did not poll their constituents on this issue, even with a householder survey. Indeed, while many legislators initiate riding surveys for use in election campaigns, they can rarely afford to commission professional polling between elections. Some MPs do not even use their householder mailing privileges for surveys; even if they do, they are not necessarily guided by the findings. Moreover, when a small sample of Ontario MPs was asked generally how they learned about the public's attitudes,[37] their responses understandably stressed their ridings rather than province-wide or country-wide opinion. Dennis Mills of Toronto was the lone exception, describing himself as a 'national MP' and acknowledging that many of his colleagues are primarily constituency representatives. Apart from Mills, MPs' answers emphasized informal ways of learning about their constituents' views. Only two included polling on their lists of several sources of information about the attitudes of the public.[38] All referred to contacts with their offices by means such as phone, letter, e-mail, and individual meetings. Several sought out constituents by regularly travelling around their ridings to hold meetings or visit restaurants and coffee shops; a few spoke of talking to citizens while grocery shopping or attending local events such as hockey games and concerts. Some MPs indicated that they develop an instinctive understanding of their riding by living there for many years. 'If you're in touch with your community you don't need pollsters,' concludes one.[39]

When Bill C-68 reached second reading early in April 1995, three Liberal backbenchers voted against their government and two others abstained. Aware of substantial discontent within the government caucus, the party had already sponsored a confidential poll by Insight Canada Research on the issue, which was presented later in April to MPs by the company's chair, Michael Marzolini.[40] The restriction to a single issue is unusual in his addresses to caucus members; while these take place about twice each year, he normally stresses party standings or otherwise a range of policies. Also atypically, a written report of this poll was circulated to MPs.

Restricted to Ontario, where the caucus resistance to the gun control bill was centred, the poll was presented to MPs between the second and third readings. The poll confirmed heavy support for the bill: 54 per cent of respondents supported the bill strongly while 28 per cent said they somewhat supported it. Dividing the province into five regions, the poll indicated majority support in each one, even in the northern region (35 per cent strongly in favour and another 34 per cent somewhat in favour).[41] A similar pattern occurred with a specific question on registration of firearms.[42]

The survey also ventured into some political questions. Insight reported that the Liberal party was preferred to its rivals by 66 per cent of Ontarians at the time. Majorities in all regions of the province said that their MP should vote in favour of the legislation. Apparently trying to address concerns of wavering legislators, Insight concluded that 'Gun control also appears to be a voting issue. If their member of Parliament voted in favour of the proposals, almost four in ten people (38%) would be more likely to vote for their MP next election, versus 9% who would be less likely and half (49%) who would not be influenced by this issue.' Referring to the respondents who said they would be less likely to vote for a pro-gun control legislator, Insight argued that they tended to be Reform supporters and that therefore 'it is unlikely that these voters would consider changing their support to the Liberals, even if the Liberal MP voted for legislation they find personally popular.'[43]

From the poll's timing, its sponsorship, the topics investigated, the restriction of the sample to Ontario, and perhaps the use of the word 'voters' in Insight's report, it is evident that the research was not conducted to guide the government's position. Rather, the decision was already made and the poll report aimed to reassure MPs that despite the vocal opposition many were encountering in their constituencies, a silent majority continued to favour the policy across the province. As an interviewee explains,

> The purpose of that [poll] was to get the Ontario caucus to calm down ... Particularly the northern and rural caucus was very upset. They were getting all kinds of flak on gun registration, not so much on gun control ... The survey was obviously designed to be able to tell them, 'Well, cool it. Don't get so upset because there's no problem, everything's under control.'[44]

Specifically, MPs could cite the poll to defend the policy to their constituents.[45] More importantly, the government hoped that the poll would help to win the support of the roughly thirty MPs who it feared might vote against the legislation on third reading: the three dissidents on second reading could have been the tip of the iceberg. One MP who supported the legislation says the poll was taken to 'bolster people's resolve' in caucus.[46] And one of those who opposed it on third reading believes that 'it was directed at the caucus almost entirely.'[47] Another MP agrees that it was intended to persuade MPs to support the government.[48] And a Justice official recalls that 'there was a lot of talk about [the need to] shore up Liberal support'; he says the poll was initiated in this context. As noted earlier, there was little danger that the bill would be defeated; rather the concern was more about maintaining party unity.

Did Insight's poll help to contain the opposition from the MPs who were reluctant to support the bill? At first sight the answer seems to be no, since the resistance was greater on the third reading than the second: ultimately nine Liberal MPs voted against the legislation on third reading, and two more indicated their opposition but were unable to attend the vote in the House.[49]

Still, the poll may have helped limit Liberal dissent. One MP suggests that the Insight poll probably reassured some of his colleagues that 'the very vocal people and sometimes quite threatening people' who opposed the policy were not reflective of the public as a whole.[50] Another says it was a factor in the voting decisions of up to about twenty-five MPs, but their own views and contacts from constituents also contributed.[51] A third agrees that it would have contributed to the decisions of some MPs to support the government: 'Absolutely. We have people who believe that polls are divine revelation.' However, he adds that 'they were ... more influenced by the ramifications of voting against the legislation and what it might mean for their future in the party.'[52]

Other comments by MPs indicate that the poll was taken too late to have maximum effect. Two opponents of the bill believe that the impact of the poll was limited because it was not presented to caucus until after most members had made up their minds.[53] Consistent with this a supporter suggests that once some of his colleagues had publicly stated their opposition, it was psychologically difficult to reverse their position.[54]

More generally, while several MPs praise Marzolini, most of those interviewed express reasons for not relying heavily on polling. Like most polls, the Insight study was not detailed enough to provide results for their individual constituencies.[55] It was also pointed out that polls provide snapshots but public opinion is subject to change.[56] And several MPs volunteered their concerns that question design can shape the results of polls.[57] There are also some suspicions that the purposes of the research may have coloured Insight's results. One MP says, 'Because [Marzolini is] the Liberal pollster, and of course, the feeling is that if he doesn't bring in the numbers that we want to hear, he's not going [to continue] to be the Liberal pollster. So to some extent that's a risk. But Marzolini has a good reputation, even with me, for trying to ask objective questions.'[58] A different MP expresses doubts about this particular poll: 'Basically, [Marzolini] did what he was asked to do. He's commissioned, and he's being paid. So obviously you pay him to do a certain job. And he did that.' He says the pollster may present findings selectively to caucus and downplay bad news for the government.[59] Finally, another MP, who says he would have not have voted against the policy if he believed it had the support of a majority of his constituents, expressed distrust of the findings because contacts with his constituency office were overwhelmingly hostile to the bill; in fact, he even speculates that the poll may not have been conducted at all.[60] Although this is extremely unlikely, an MP with this sort of suspicion obviously would not be receptive to the pollster's message. It is an example of how active public opinion can be a greater influence on perceptions than polls.

Michael Kirby concludes plausibly that the poll helped address but did not eliminate the government's problem of resistance in its caucus. He adds, 'Let me put it this way, if the numbers had come out differently, we would have had a much bigger problem.'[61] The implication of this comment is that polling showing public opposition to the policy – if it had been presented to caucus – would have fuelled greater opposition among MPs. From this perspective, by highlighting the support for gun control in Ontario, the Insight poll contributed modestly to containing the opposition within the government caucus.

The Angus Reid Poll of 1998

After the House of Commons passed the bill in June 1995, the government worked to see it through the Senate, which finally approved it in November. In the following years the federal government successfully defended the new Firearms Act against a court challenge from six provincial governments, which were backed by the territorial governments and some interest groups.[62] The government also had to implement and communicate the policy – tasks that were delayed and would be unusually difficult because of the resistance among gun users. Indeed, the regulations were not in place until March 1998 and costs were many times greater than initially forecast.

In May 1998 the Angus Reid Group conducted a more substantial survey than anything previously initiated by the Department of Justice on gun control, at least since the Liberals took office. Public servants initiated the poll; staff in the minister's office did not have input into the questionnaire design and nor did they attend the pollster's oral presentation of the findings. This poll was taken almost three years after the bill passed the House of Commons, an even more pronounced case than the GST of opinion research following a key policy decision.

Officials wanted to obtain province-by-province breakdowns, and to analyse the views of gun owners. The former were for use by the new justice minister, Anne McLellan, and to cite in federal officials' discussions with their provincial counterparts, while the latter reflects a concern with the group most affected by the policy. Consequently, a large sample of 3,309 was used: approximately one hundred gun owners and two hundred non-owners from each province, and from the territories combined.[63] The poll showed that public support remained high for gun control, and specifically for the registration of firearms. For instance, 82 per cent support for registration nationwide was reported, with majorities in every province and territory. Support among gun owners for the Firearms Act was 47 per cent, higher than would be expected from the vocal signals of the gun lobby; 45 per cent of them supported registration.[64] The study also measured levels of knowledge and awareness of the act and attempted to gauge the intentions of gun users to comply with it. It was understood that the support was not intense, as an interviewee explains: 'The one Achilles' heel to the gun legislation is [that] the majority aren't going to vote against you if you wipe it out.'

Rather than providing guidance on the substance of policy, the poll had several other purposes. It monitored attitudes on the issues; demonstrating and confirming that public support remained strong – a welcome finding to the civil servants and the political side of the government. The poll was conducted in part to inform the new minister about the public opinion environment within which her department would continue to implement the policy. Civil servants understood the subject to be of particular concern to her since she represented Alberta, where there were many vocal opponents of gun control. Justice officials also anticipated that she could cite the poll in cabinet meetings.

Implementing Gun Control

The policy has proven unusually challenging to implement. As one Justice official explains, it involves

> massive change, enormous costs, and it requires the most complicated technology and technological reform that you could ever find. It's being implemented in the face of major resistance, in some cases being implemented by people who don't even want to implement it, and it's being done in an incredible goldfish bowl, under a spotlight ... I think [the Reform Party critic's] full-time job is trying to find a way to attack this [policy] every couple of days.

As well, the federal government has had to deal with an intergovernmental dimension, as six provincial governments were opposed to the policy. This proved an obstacle to securing their cooperation with implementation and diverted federal resources to fighting the provinces' court challenge.

One contribution polls made to implementation occurred when federal officials marshalled surveys to show their provincial colleagues that the public supported the policy in their own provinces; in this way the province-by-province results in the Reid study were helpful. This occurred when federal officials were negotiating with their Ontario counterparts to try to secure the participation of the provincial police force in implementing the policy (rather than establish their own administrative system). The federal officials cited polling, not to argue that Ontario's cooperation would be a politically beneficial move, but to strengthen their argument that public opinion would not create problems in implementing the policy. Research in early 1998 provided the Department of Justice with data on attitudes of Ontario residents on gun control; 76 per cent of respondents supported the legislation and 78 per cent supported universal registration. The proportions in gun-owning households were 42 and 46 per cent.[65] By indicating that the provincial government's risk of assuming a federal problem was small, the research probably contributed modestly to securing Ontario's agreement to participate, without which implementation would have been more difficult.[66] This tactical deployment of opinion research in intergovernmental relations is somewhat analogous to the use of polls by the federal government to show support for its constitutional position in 1981.

Another important implementation problem where polling was used was to try to anticipate the timing and rates of compliance with the policy. The Justice Department wanted to know whether licensing and registration would encounter significant resistance by gun users disobeying the law. And it hoped to learn the extent to which users would apply for licensing and registration early so that the government could project incoming revenue, the demands on police forces, and the requirements for forms, computers, and staff resources.

Research by Environics in 1997 probed the question of compliance. Asked if they intended to apply for a licence, 50 per cent of owners said they would, but 30 per cent said they would not. (Nine per cent claimed they were already licensed, another 6 per cent refused to answer, and 5 per cent said they did not know.)[67] Particularly since polling might be expected to understate willingness to break the law, the finding that only half the gun users surveyed indicated they would comply with the policy was, at first glance, alarming. An official acknowledges that it was a source of concern but observes that other data were less troubling and that, in any case, predicting compliance is difficult. Moreover, based on evidence from focus groups, he contends that the result should be understood as an expression of hostility to the policy rather than an actual intent to disobey the law; he points out that seat belt legislation initially met strong resistance but widespread compliance was eventually achieved.

The May 1998 Reid poll also tried to project compliance, and produced different signals from Environics' survey. According to Reid's data, 74 per cent of gun owners intended to comply with licensing requirements, many of them well before the deadline. Three-quarters claimed they would register their guns at the same time as they applied for a licence. Most who said they would not apply for a firearms licence gave the reason that they already held a hunting licence or certificate, which does not seem to reflect a genuine unwillingness to comply. Most also predicted that their friends and other gun owners would comply with the policy.[68]

Against the advice of the Angus Reid firm, Justice officials had asked the pollster to include questions on compliance in its survey.[69] One difficulty in predicting compliance rates was that survey research cannot be completely trusted to provide accurate estimates of the number of firearms in Canada. One government official cites an estimate that the country has about three million gun owners who possess about seven million guns. However, users' groups claim that some owners will not tell pollsters about their firearms and suggest that there may be as many as twelve million gun owners with about twenty million guns.

More importantly, the survey attempted to project when gun users would file their licence and registration applications. When the Angus Reid Group presented the report, it warned that data from people anticipating their own behaviour were inherently suspect and that the findings should be treated very cautiously.[70] Indeed, as Reid pollster Mike Colledge points out, 'There's a reason the Post Office stays open until midnight on tax filing day. That's quite simply, people procrastinate, people do things at the last minute ... No matter how much communication you do, no matter how much budget you put into making people aware that it's out there, you're going to be backlogged at the back end.' Despite the pollster's warnings about the need for cautious interpretation, the data were taken too literally by some Justice officials. As one of them explains, after they heard the cautions, 'There was general nodding, but still what sticks in your mind are the numbers.' The officials plugged those numbers into their projections of the volume of applications that would come in; they used what was probably the best data available, yet the result subsequently proved misleading, with fewer early applications than the research indicated. Asked in December 1999 if the department would in retrospect have been better off without this survey data, an official conceded, 'Probably, yes.'

Another official says he is reluctant to blame the research. He admits, however, that the methodology for anticipating timing of compliance is 'not very good ... We can get people to talk about feminine hygiene

products ... [and] all kinds of things that are quite personal and potentially embarrassing. The people who market those products seem to do
a relatively good job getting answers out of their target populations.
The polling methodology, I think, is not on that [level] ...' The problems
studying the use of sensitive consumer products, however, may be less
acute than the obstacles to projecting future behaviour relating to an
emotional subject such as firearms.[71]

Faced with research such as the Environics and Reid studies, it is not
surprising that public servants in the Justice Department drew different
conclusions. 'At a minimum,' recalls a senior official, 'we collectively
agreed that we were not sure what it told us. It didn't tell us that we
should change our approach.' Even if officials agreed on what the likely
compliance rate was, problems of interpretation would remain: sup-
posing, for instance, the research indicated that, say, 85 per cent of gun
owners would comply readily, it was unclear whether this should be
viewed as a problem. How far could the department go in trying to
enforce the legislation against a small minority who were flouting the
law? Aggressive enforcement that sent a few protestors to jail could
create martyrs; alternatively, if disobedience was widespread it would
have been difficult to cope and the legitimacy of the law might have
been undermined.

The research had further implications: the more compliance was
expected to be a problem, the more the communications would have to
address it, at least implicitly. Moreover, if the government anticipated
serious resistance, stronger exhortations would be required; if widespread compliance was likely, then a gentler message would be appropriate.

On the whole, Justice officials took the view that refusal to comply
would not be a major problem. Gun users, however, did not register
early to the degree that a literal reading of the Angus Reid data would
have indicated. This reflects a mixture of procrastination, genuine difficulties with the process, and intentions not to comply at all. This case
illustrates an attempt to use opinion research in implementation, but
one where disagreements and overconfidence in interpreting the data
limited their value. Indeed, despite officials' hopes, the research was
not up to the task and they would probably have been better off trying
to produce a more conservative estimate without the aid of surveys.
One official makes the general observation that 'there's a difference
between what people say they do, what people believe they do, and
what they actually do.' The problems are compounded when research-

ers attempt to project future behaviour on an emotional topic, and ultimately the efforts were unsuccessful.

Communicating the Policy

If the Reid poll had shown that opposition had increased since the passage of the bill, the department probably would have developed a communications strategy to rebuild support. The finding of strong support was communicated publicly by Anne McLellan and others to defend the policy against actual and anticipated charges that it was contrary to the preferences of the public. For example, a Justice official explains that to rebut claims at public meetings that Canadians oppose the policy, he has cited Angus Reid and Gallup poll results to demonstrate the acceptance of the firearms legislation by the general public. Another official observes that the department must be prepared to reply to journalists' demands for evidence when government spokespeople claim the support of the public. A similar approach is evident in the department's media release cited early in chapter 5.

Besides the periodic use of opinion research for the external justification of policy, the opinion research on gun control fed into the communications campaign that was central to implementing the policy. Unlike the communications examined in the patriation case and the GST, this campaign – and the opinion research to help develop it – occurred after the policy had been passed by Parliament. According to a Justice official, the primary goals were to inform and promote compliance; a secondary purpose was to sell the policy. Indeed, this official says the advertising steered clear of advocacy. He knows, however, that the issue is sensitive; he says that when qualitative research was used to test the tone and messages of ads, the government tried to 'avoid words that cause a huge outcry in terms of [perceptions of] selling the policy.'

Reid's quantitative study measured the awareness of gun owners and non-owners about the distinction between registration and licensing. The findings reflect the relative profile each had secured in the public debate. The research found low levels of awareness: even among gun owners, while 67 per cent were aware of the requirement for registration, only 15 per cent were aware of licensing requirements; even when asked an aided question, only 38 per cent of gun owners said that the Firearms Act required both registration and licensing. They were even less familiar with final deadlines for the programs. Offered five possible dates, only 7 per cent of them could give the deadline for registration, while just 13 per cent correctly identified the deadline for licensing.[72] This was troubling, as implementation was scheduled to begin later that year.

Reid's results highlighted the need for advertising to inform Canadians – primarily gun owners – about the two distinct programs and their requirements. An official in Justice explains, 'The challenge for us was to find the right way to clearly, very rapidly, show the difference between ... the two different documents that firearms owners needed to acquire.' Despite its higher awareness, registration would still be mentioned because of its real and perceived importance; ads would lose credibility if they omitted it. Unlike most government advertising, public servants in the Department of Justice prepared many of the ads. An external advertising agency initially worked on the project, but its creative approach was rejected by Justice staff who thought it was poorly informed about the public environment, even though the department had provided it with public opinion research.[73] Initially, the department ran print and radio ads; television advertising followed as implementation progressed.

More advertising appeared in rural areas than in urban ones. This is partly because gun owners live disproportionately in rural areas, and in addition, urban gun owners are easier to reach through other means, such as posters at gun clubs. As well, opinion research guided the advertising buy, by showing that rural residents were both less aware of and more resistant to the registration and licensing policy. Early ads proved effective in generating telephone inquiries to the toll-free information hotline – too successful, in fact, because the call centre was not equipped to handle the number of calls, roughly ten thousand a day at one stage. The ads were revised to make them clearer and they continued with a frequency that aimed to achieve a volume of about five thousand inquiries per day, the capacity of the call centre. The tone and messages of these ads were tested with focus groups of gun owners in urban and rural locations, and targeted at these audiences; some of the findings on print ads would be recycled when the broadcast ads were prepared. In contrast to the approach of Bill C-68, the advertising for the Conservative government's Bill C-17 had been tested with focus groups of owners and non-owners and aimed at a wide audience.

As happened with the government's communications on the constitution, the GST, and other policies, focus group participants wanted the advertising to provide more information and adopt a straightforward, factual approach.[74] The signals from focus groups were often heeded.

For instance, at one point a conversation between a youth and an adult was the radio ad most well received by focus groups and this was the version chosen to air. As well, a proposed television commercial was altered in response to focus groups. The story board and soundtrack included a scene with a woman walking up a country lane to a mailbox with her dog, collecting her mail, and returning to her home. Her mail includes either some licence cards, or applications (two versions of the script were prepared). The ad attempted to communicate the message that individuals needed to separately apply to license themselves and also to register each of their guns. Safe storage was also addressed.[75] This reflects earlier opinion research that encouraged emphasis on these areas. Yet focus groups reacted unexpectedly to the ad; participants did not perceive a need to take action and thought that the government would mail them the appropriate application forms. Government officials had thought their commercial clearly encouraged gun users to telephone for assistance; however, as it usually does, the visual image overrode the words. In response to the research, the script was modified, and the mailbox scene was omitted from the final version. In this case, it might be said that opinion research revealed the downside of the saying that a picture is worth a thousand words.

At other times, the messages from focus groups were not decisive. For instance, gun owners thought the ads should indicate where they could obtain forms for licensing and registration.[76] The government followed the advice when implementation commenced, and early ads directed owners to locations such as post offices. This proved a mistake because future clients were confused about which form to request and postal staff were not trained to help. To limit confusion and waste of forms, the government did not take the researcher's advice in its next wave of ads, preferring to encourage gun owners to telephone. When they did, call centre staff could specify the name of the form required and offer to send it by mail. Similarly, focus group participants asked that the deadlines for registering and licensing be included in ads; as these dates were a few years away, the suggestion was rejected because it might deter readers from telephoning the call centre and encourage procrastination. It would have been difficult for the pollster to anticipate these reasons for not taking the advice, as they were technical points relating to the efficient operation of the program.

As implementation progressed, opinion research enabled Justice officials to gain a more sophisticated understanding of their target audiences. Early focus groups were comprised of gun owners who were not active members of firearms associations. Later, after its opinion research showed the low awareness of licensing requirements, the department developed an understanding that there were three types of gun owners: those who use them at most once each year; those who use them somewhat more often; and those who use them more than five times annually. The last is the smallest group; some focus groups have been comprised of the less frequent users because they are the least informed.

Qualitative research was also conducted in which gun owners were asked to fill out drafts of licensing and registration forms.[77] Because of the sensitivity of the gun control issue, and the concern that poorly designed forms would provide ammunition for the policy's critics, the stakes were higher than in most research of this sort. There was also an awareness that the forms would need to be readily understandable to gun owners. Forms were tested in focus groups, revised, and then retested. Some of the errors made as participants filled out drafts were considered inevitable in a new program, but others could be avoided through redesign. The focus groups improved the design of the forms but a troubling number of errors occurred even when participants completed the revised forms. In any case, the research helped to transform the application materials. This included clarifying the connection between licensing and registration, and providing factual information such as the fee schedules and the toll-free number for assistance. Mike Colledge of Angus Reid Group compares the initial set of materials to

tax forms: 8½ by 14, drab grey, big long things ... It had lots of boxes on it. And if you saw what [the Justice Department] did to them based on our work, and the work of a good communications branch, they're down to like 8½ by 6, little custom things with a ruler on the side so you can measure barrel width. Everything you need is in that form. And in their print ads, they put in actual pictures of rifles and shot guns ... And really got them down to a simplified statement of 'here's what you need to know.'

Respondents in the second phase of qualitative research considered the revised registration forms a dramatic improvement: participants gave the redesigned form an average rating of 8.5 on a ten-point scale, compared to 1.5 for the initial version.[78] The Justice Department acted on many of the Angus Reid Group's recommendations for revising the forms before the final report was formally presented. It is clear, then, that research long after the policy decision had been made was used for communications. Broadly speaking, the quantitative research helped develop the general strategy for the communications campaign, while qualitative research was used to refine the details and tactics.

Conclusion

This case highlights several aspects of opinion research in government. First, the clashing signals of passive and active public opinion were a central feature of the politics of gun control. Polling played an important role by informing officials that despite the vocal opposition, Canadians supported the concept of firearms control. This reassured the government, and was publicly cited from time to time by ministers and MPs. It was also used by civil servants to justify the policy inside government and externally, and to present to provincial officials. But polling was not the only factor containing the impact of the gun users' groups whose powerful American counterparts have thwarted several attempts to strengthen firearms control south of the border; in Canada the gun users' influence was blunted because a well-organized interest group, the Coalition for Gun Control, supported the government's actions.

As Benjamin Ginsberg argues, polls can undermine interest groups. Firearms control represents perhaps the clearest case of this in Canadian politics. Pollster Derek Leebosh and gun control advocate Heidi Rathjen, quoted early in this chapter, would disagree with Ginsberg that this is undesirable, and of course their view is consistent with Gallup and Rae's. Although this chapter has argued that the overall impact of polling on the Liberals' gun control policy was small, a strong claim can be made that opinion research exerts democratic effects if it weakens the influence of an intense and vocal minority.[79] This is true if opinion research promotes an understanding of the state of mass public opinion and especially if this awareness affects the decisions of policymakers.

Second, partly because polling undermined the impressions created by the gun users' activities and revealed a 'silent majority,' it was employed in the public debate. The Coalition for Gun Control produced its poll to underline public support for its position, and federal officials cited polling for the same reason. Placed in a defensive position, opponents of gun control such as the governments of Saskatchewan and Alberta took polls to try to generate a different picture of public opinion. Both sides assume that perceptions of public opinion are important, and are worth fighting to shape; how they are believed to matter and how they actually do matter remain intriguing questions to which the answers are highly uncertain. In part, political actors are exhibiting habits shaped by the efforts of parties to spin their messages to the media in election campaigns, trying to create expectations of success. Relevant in understanding the potential impact of public opinion is the suggestion that the government might not have pursued registration if polls had shown opposition; as well, polling may have influenced wavering MPs. This sort of use of polling persists long after the policy decision. The government's poll of May 1998 was taken partly to produce numbers to employ in the public arena, and MP Gary Breitkreuz continued to challenge the accuracy of mainstream polls. While the polls reflecting gun users' interests tend to be biased, the point they highlight about citizens' limited knowledge reminds us of the need to interpret the major pollsters' data carefully.

Third, the impact of opinion research on the substance of this policy and its details was limited. Many of the issues and nuances were legal and technical, rather than matters where public opinion was brought to bear. On what was apparently the only policy detail where the government systematically investigated attitudes of the general public, the treatment of air guns, the poll's findings were not followed.

Fourth, polling on gun control was more relevant in the Liberal caucus than on most issues because many MPs were subjected to heavy constituency pressures to oppose their government and considered voting against it. Some initiated their own constituency surveys, if only with householder mail; the government sought to contain dissent in the Ontario caucus with the province-wide Insight poll. We saw, however, that some MPs distrusted or disregarded polls, placing weight on the signals of active public opinion and expressing suspicion of the Insight survey. The polling helped to offset the impact of active public opinion, contributing modestly to some MPs' voting decisions and also helping some defend their support for gun control. On this issue, then, polls reinforced the pressures to maintain party discipline.

Chapter 2 noted the judgment of Roger Gibbins that polling weakens the importance of government MPs as a channel for informing the cabinet about public attitudes. Polling served as a tool to counter the views of about thirty Liberal MPs who objected to the gun control policy and in many cases claimed the support of their constituents – but it was not wholly effective, and it was used to try to contain their dissent. Also, we should not exaggerate the effect of polling in weakening this function of caucus. A pollster says that while opinion research provides the signals of public preferences that are taken most seriously in government, the government caucus also remains significant and sometimes prevails over the research.[80]

Fifth, gun control provides an illustration of how opinion research was used in the implementation of policy. The data on mass opinion helped in urging Ontario officials to participate in implementing the firearms registry. Surveys were also conducted to project the rates and timing of compliance, but anticipating future behaviour in this area proved a task unsuited to opinion research, as the pollster had predicted. While Justice officials had excellent reasons for wishing to anticipate compliance, they were optimistic to think that the research could significantly help them to do so.

Finally, opinion research made a larger contribution to communications than implementation. It helped determine the general strategy of the communications campaign launched in 1998. The research was also employed at a tactical level to refine the communications vehicles, particularly advertising. In this case, officials used the research quite intelligently. While the signals from the qualitative research were generally predictable, they were taken seriously, and applied where officials thought it appropriate. However, they were not followed blindly, and at times the goal of efficient administration overrode the focus groups. Consistent with the findings of chapter 5, the most important roles of opinion research were to justify the policy beyond government and to guide communications strategy and tactics.

At times, active or anticipated public opinion had an impact on the process of developing gun control policy, but this effect occurred without opinion research exerting influence, or in some cases without it existing at all. Overall, polling had a visible but not a large role in the policy. As we might suspect after noting that the most comprehensive poll was taken long after the policy decision, the most significant uses of opinion research on firearms control were not to determine the general direction or the details of policy. Rather, it was employed mostly after the government was already committed to strengthening gun control: it was marshalled to counter the gun users' groups and justify the policy within government and externally; it had a role in the deliberations of members of the government caucus; it was used with mixed results in implementation; and it exerted the clearest influence on the government's communications. The character of public opinion on gun control had an impact on the politics of the issue without a corresponding effect on the content of the policy.

9 Constraints on the Use of Opinion Research in Government

Even if policy-makers were consistently motivated to use opinion research to guide their decisions about the content of public policy, and even if the research was not frequently trumped by other inputs into the policy process, there are other limitations on the use of polls and the desirability of them assuming a significant role in policy-making. These involve methodological problems in conducting opinion research, the characteristics of public opinion, difficulties in interpreting opinion research, some special concerns involving focus groups, the effects of Access to Information legislation on government opinion research, and sampling practices which are contrary to the normative ideals of Gallup and Rae. Many users of polls have a general awareness of these factors, and they are well understood by the pollsters who interpret data and provide advice; consequently these factors affect the use of polls.

Philip Converse warns of three dangers for practitioners who are not knowledgeable about polling and public opinion: they tend to be too confident in the accuracy of polling; they may perceive public opinion as a mix of firm pro and con positions without being alert to the differences within each perspective; and they often overestimate the stability of the public's attitudes.[1] These problems relate to the methodological limitations of opinion research, the interpretation of polling data, and the nature of public opinion. Although opinion research is often useful to clients, Converse's observations are justified. While many of the examples presented here are American, they are relevant in Canada.

Methodological Problems in Opinion Research

Numerous technical issues arise in opinion research. In many cases problems occur despite the sincere attempts of researchers to measure public opinion accurately. Difficulties may occur when polling firms cut corners to save money or meet tight deadlines. A former pollster and government official adds that 'if polling firms are given already-written surveys [by clients], they won't object to too many things unless there is really clear bias. I actually think some firms may pay more attention if they know a poll is going to be used for public relations purposes.'[2] Other effects result from the deliberate efforts of pollsters or their clients to produce particular results. One pollster says that 'the designing of polls to generate certain responses rather than seek the truth is a pretty common thing.'[3] Similarly, another explains that some companies engage in this sort of conduct because of unspoken business pressures: 'There are polling firms essentially for hire, in the sense of "What case do you want to make? What finding would you like to see? What result would help your cause?" These things are never said. But these things are understood by businesspeople who are in the research business, who want satisfied customers.'[4] Yet another pollster explains,

> We have done questions for clients [including government clients] where we have framed the questions ... And I said to them, 'Look, you know what people are going to say – they're all going to say "yes."' And they said, 'That's fine' ... These were people who were driving a particular agenda. And the stuff wasn't false. You could legitimately say this was what most Canadians believed. Were they willing to pay for it? That's another issue – we never asked that question. So when I stand up and talk about that data, I'd say, 'Read the questions. When you read the questions you know what the answers are going to be' ... The questions – were they leading? Absolutely. But they did tell us something really important: that Canadians really do believe ... in the principles about which those questions were concerned.

The pollster adds that his client had 'a particular process to go through within the ministry' to pursue a specific goal; he says the client would have acknowledged the survey's biases if challenged on them in internal government meetings.[5]

Opinion research is sometimes used within government to support arguments for adopting particular policies. Lowell Murray draws on his experience as a cabinet minister in the Mulroney government to make this judgment:

> The biggest waste of all in public opinion research is by bureaucrats and their political allies, manufacturing some public opinion research in order

to buttress their case for a new program or an increased expenditure on an existing program, when they go through the cabinet committee system. In that case it is more often than not, in my experience, misused by people who don't understand the uses and relevance of public opinion research. But they come in, and they try to persuade the cabinet, or cabinet committee, that they've got a poll that shows that people are just ready to break the doors of the Parliament Buildings down if they don't get this program, or this increased expenditure.

He explains that the polling is frequently used, or misused, to justify a new policy or an increased expenditure internally within government. He stresses, however, that questionnaires and analysis are often 'too narrowly focused' to justify the conclusions drawn. The skewing of research is most often a problem with polling that is to be released publicly, but it can also affect polls which are presented to political actors behind closed doors.

To turn to specific issues, sampling techniques and margins of error place relatively minor limits on the reliability of polling data: pollsters have achieved greater mastery of sampling than of most other elements of survey research.[6] Some difficulties remain, however. For instance, panel studies (in which attempts are made to survey the same respondents at different times) may produce misleading results. This is because they may overrepresent those with a high interest in politics, because they are likelier than others to participate in later polls. Moreover, the achievement of mastering sampling may be undermined because of the increasing use of cellular phones and the advent of call screening. Margin of error is mentioned in most press reports, partly because pollsters' media releases acknowledge it. Unfortunately, awareness of this sort of information leads some users to overlook other more significant threats to the validity and reliability of opinion research. Among these are less well-understood threats to accuracy, such as the rising proportion of people who decline to participate in polls, and the tendency of some respondents to give 'don't know' or 'no opinion' answers for certain questions – factors affecting the representativeness of the results if, for example, these people's demographic characteristics or information levels differ from those who do participate fully in polls.[7] Interviewer errors and effects are a further source of problems. (For example, an interviewer's accent may influence answers to questions on immigration; similarly, female interviewers find respondents of both sexes more likely to say they support affirmative action.) These types of difficulties with polls are potentially compounded – with sampling distortions becoming likelier – if speed is a factor, as on fast-moving events. These can be the very times when public opinion is of greatest interest to officials, as with American entrance into the Gulf War and the nomination of Clarence Thomas to the Supreme Court. On both issues, polls provided less accurate signals than was widely thought.[8] Similarly, the survey that led Dick Morris to advise Bill Clinton to conceal his sexual relationship with Monica Lewinsky was apparently conducted in a single evening, shortly after public allegations surfaced in January 1998.[9] The growing pressures on pollsters to produce data quickly, and the threat this poses to the quality of research, are recognized by public servants responsible for monitoring government polling.[10]

As country-wide questionnaires must be prepared in English and French, translation sometimes creates problems. Some translators lack sufficient knowledge of the subject to translate accurately, while others are not fully aware of the nuances of their second language. A civil servant points out that 'what that means, sometimes, is the results are meaningless for certain questions.' For instance, this happened with a question asked for the Department of Justice on benefits in same-sex relationships, where sensitivity is needed to the meanings of words such as 'couple' and 'partner.' This part of the research had to be repeated on another survey, but the timing and context of the questions would have affected the results. Similarly, a poll on the constitution in 1981 mistakenly translated 'right to veto' into 'droit de parole.'[11] Moreover, some errors may not be identified in time for a correction to be made. In any case, translators must strike a balance between a literal translation and a fluent one. This is always an art, and it can be especially challenging with a questionnaire, particularly when dealing with tight deadlines and words with legal meanings.

It is also known that some respondents give opinions on issues they have little or no familiarity with, and even provide opinions on made-up issues. Some respondents do not want to appear uninformed and use cues in the question to help find an answer. In a disconcerting study, researchers discovered that one-third of a sample of Cincinnati area residents provided opinions on a non-existent Public Affairs Act.[12] We can safely assume that the people of Cincinnati are not unusually dishonest. Rather, as the research showed, this owes much to question design since it can be mostly contained by reducing 'pressure to answer' with 'filter' questions which inquire whether respondents have opinions. Some pollsters still do not follow this procedure, perhaps because it lowers the proportion of usable responses by up to 25 per cent and because these researchers have not digested the implications of 'pseudo-opinions.'[13] This is a problem which stems from the nature of public opinion, but it can be minimized with careful research design.

Question design is a major source of variance in results. Among the explanations, the reduction of complex issues to yes/no or agree/disagree or numerical forms is controversial, with no clearly superior approach. Whether to provide a neutral option – and how to present it – are also debated.[14] Even with the best intentions, questions may inadvertently lead respondents in one direction or another. Opinion researchers also face some risk that respondents will misunderstand their questions, particularly if they are long or deal with complex subjects. Even apparently straightforward questions may not have the same meaning to questionnaire writers and respondents. In one study, opposition to school busing might have been understood as resistance to anti-segregation policies; in reality, 'Overwhelmingly, white kids were bused, and ... most of the busing was not for any racial purposes.'[15] This type of case shows that polls do not always succeed in measuring what they appear to.

A more common difficulty is that question wording often substantially affects responses, as Angus Reid's story about the smoking priests in chapter 5 and examples from the case studies suggest. Many illustrations result from variations in surveys by respected polling firms. For instance, Gary Mauser refers to a study that found 'Canadians' support for abortion rights ranged from 28 to 79 per cent, depending on how the question was worded. Some of these questions appear deliberately slanted, but others were probably the result of subtleties that even the pollsters may not have fully understood.'[16]

Similarly, two American polls taken in May 1993 reported 36 and 65 per cent support for U.S. air strikes in Bosnia. The key difference is that the latter survey included the words 'along with its allies in Europe.'[17] A pollster provides a further example, when two surveys on nuclear submarines gave contrasting results:

One was 'Are you in favour of nuclear powered submarines to protect Canadian sovereignty?' Something like 70 per cent said 'of course I'm in favour of that.' And the other one was 'Are you in favour of nuclear submarines at a cost of $5 billion to the Canadian taxpayer?' ... [About] 70 per cent were opposed. They were fielded the same week, they both had national samples. Those who were for at DND were quite willing to point to their 70 per cent [support], and those [interest groups] who were opposed were quite willing to point to their 70 per cent opposition. The government added 'sovereignty' and 'nuclear powered.' And it was more correct: they were nuclear powered, they weren't nuclear armed. By leaving off 'nuclear powered' and adding in ... taxpayers' money, you've loaded it.

This illustrates how polls can be cited selectively as policy debates unfold. The effects of question wording lead some to conclude that public opinion on issues can not be understood without reference to multiple questions.[18]

One further complication in assessing question wording deserves noting. While published sources typically treat non-neutral questions as completely undesirable,[19] at times researchers deliberately probe attitudes by asking a pair of leading questions. Ian McKinnon explains how this can be useful:

rather than ask[ing] two neutral questions about a topic, ask one that is strongly towards viewpoint A and another that's strongly towards viewpoint B ... Because the two neutral ones ... often tend to be ambiguous and a little hard to understand. [Instead,] try to make them as stark as possible, and it tells you not only who is consistent and strong A, [and who is] consistent and strong B, but it also points out for you right away, who's in the moveable middle. Which are often in public policy, and in marketing, the people you actually want to deal with.[20]

McKinnon is certainly not alone in using this type of technique. While it is easy to imagine how a question could be taken out of context by a client or a journalist, his comment highlights how question wording effects can be used to refine an understanding of public opinion. It is noteworthy that McKinnon refers to people who are 'moveable'; this kind of analysis is more useful for communications than policy development since it probably measures the public's preferences less well than neutral questions and may signal majority opinion less clearly.

As well as question wording, question order periodically influences responses too. One study found that responses to a general question on abortion rights varied according to whether it was asked before or after a specific question about abortion 'if there is a strong chance of a serious defect in the baby.'[21] Similarly, a civil servant argues that questions about immigration levels must be asked prior to questions about employment: 'If they came after questions on ... employment, we had a 5 to 8, and at times 10 per cent difference ... in terms of [attitudes towards] present immigration levels.' These effects of questionnaire design are understandable with hindsight but not always recognized when surveys are prepared.

As well as occurring in social science experiments or unintentionally, the techniques can be used by pollsters to manipulate results and therefore perceptions. Loaded questions can produce substantial bias, warns McKinnon. 'For example, if you have a real axe to grind on a particular topic and you ask six or seven inflammatory questions on that topic and then asked an unbiased final summary question – "Well, then, generally speaking are you in favor of or opposed to X?" – you can create enormous biases. Twenty and 30 points.'[22] This shows how the combination of question wording and question order effects can produce misleading results, especially if data for the final question are reported in isolation.

Closely related to question order effects, the preamble or context of the question can affect responses. For instance, Herbert Asher suggests, 'A survey about the American military buildup posed in the context of Soviet military strength would probably elicit more supportive attitudes toward defense spending than would a similar survey framed in the context of the huge national debt.'[23] Similarly, a poll commissioned by the Michigan Tobacco and Candy Vendors Association was tainted because its opening questions asked respondents to agree or disagree with the statements that 'There is too much government in people's lives' and 'Government should not be in the business of regulating private, personal behavior.' These questions increased the likelihood that respondents would oppose laws restricting smoking in public places in response to subsequent questions.[24] More generally, political scientist John Wilson argues that omnibus questionnaires measure public opinion inadequately because the shifting of topics affects how people respond.[25] Referring to polling on Americans' support for SALT II in 1979–80, William Lanouette comments aptly that 'the numerical percentages themselves are not "public opinion," but reflections of the public's reaction to certain statements and questions.'[26]

While question wording is normally readily available, the entire questionnaire frequently is not released. Consequently, the effects of question order and context are often hidden. Moreover, even with the questionnaire in hand, it is easier to judge whether a question is worded fairly than whether the results are affected by question order or context. Michael Marzolini agrees that these effects are difficult to eliminate:

> If I switch two questions in a survey I can have a complete set of different responses. That becomes very difficult when you have a hundred questions to ask on a questionnaire. And you have to ask it the best you can ... If there is going to be bias in your responses, you have to be able to understand that bias, in the interpretation and the analysis. You can't completely remove 100 per cent of it out of a large questionnaire. You can remove it from the questions, but the inter-item bias will always haunt you at some point in the survey.

The aspects of polling methodology discussed above suggest some of the limits on using polls: they do not necessarily produce clear signals of public opinion, and even when they do those signals are not always trustworthy.

A pollster says that in accounting for difficulties interpreting polling, 'question wording is the chief culprit. There are also things like question order – that's very important as well. It's like religion. These are matters of debate, rather than ... an iron-clad methodology.'[27] The effects of question wording and order on survey results bring to mind the saying that 'a person with two watches never knows the correct time.' Weather forecasts sometimes present similar problems. Indeed, polling varies more than watches and weather forecasts, so a policy-maker with more than one poll may become confused and uncertain about what public opinion 'really' is. Even with just one poll, there are often many reasons to question the clarity of the signal and uncertainty about what in fact that signal is. At times the doubts are enough to reduce the utility of polling as a guide to decisions about policy.

The Character of Public Opinion

Even if polling was a flawless measuring instrument, present-day public opinion has its limitations as a guide to policy-makers. One reason why public opinion is difficult to measure is that people may conceal from interviewers attitudes which are controversial or socially undesirable. As COMPAS acknowledges, 'One of the biggest threats to valid research is the desire of respondents to portray their own motivations as saintly.'[28] This tendency is captured by Will Rogers's comment on prohibition of alcohol in Oklahoma: 'Oklahomans will vote dry so long as they can stagger to the polls.'[29] Consequently, for example, polls may underestimate support for racist views and tax cuts. As pollster Christian Bourque and others have observed, no 'long-distance polygraph' is available to help interviewers determine who is lying to them;[30] moreover, some respondents may hide their views by saying they have no opinion.

It is also well documented that large numbers of citizens are uninformed about politics.[31] For example, a poll during Chrétien's first term as prime minister found that, offered a choice of five definitions of 'deficit,' only one-quarter of respondents made the correct selection.[32] Patrick Fournier cites National Election Studies to show, for instance, that a majority of Canadians could not give close estimates of the national unemployment or inflation rates in 1993, or identify the minister of finance – the second most powerful politician in the country for the previous 3½ years – in 1997. As he explains, 'Canadians are largely uninformed, but not misinformed, about political facts. Most Canadians ... manage to get on with their lives without having much information about political matters.'[33] Government officials in Canada and the United States often recognize the lack of knowledge among the public.[34] For instance, in August 1992, an aide to International Trade Minister Michael Wilson reported to other government officials on a recent poll about NAFTA: 'We do find in the survey unbelievable ignorance out there.'[35] The shortfall in basic knowledge, while understandable, indicates a widespread lack of attentiveness to politics which casts doubt on the likelihood of respondents having meaningful opinions on many issues.

In any case, some issues are too complex for most citizens to deal with, at least with their present state of knowledge. The issue of drug patent legislation is an example. A comment by Hugh Segal highlights the importance of the generally low levels of public knowledge. He questions whether,

> if you poll outside the target group of a particular program, you're going to get any analysis that helps you understand that program ... Asking the vast majority of Canadians about whether they think the patrol frigate program's a good idea, is probably unhelpful. Asking Canadians, however ... to choose between patrol frigates ... and a series of new infra-structure programs to

build new bridges and highways across Canada might be a worthwhile question. It really depends on how the question is framed.

Even at a non-specialized level, similar arguments can be made about many other issues, from trade to trucking to telecommunications. On topics such as these, with most citizens poorly informed, polls are measuring 'non-attitudes'; therefore analysts must avoid treating the responses as genuine opinions. As policy grows increasingly complex, it becomes more difficult for citizens to achieve even a basic understanding of major political issues. Many questions found in polls, then, set unrealistic expectations of respondents.

Even on straightforward and salient issues, some responses have little meaning, and many people have opinions which are inconsistent, weakly held, and subject to change. This is a fundamental characteristic of public opinion, not simply a matter of factors such as question wording. Phillip Converse's classic study compares public opinion in three different election years. He reports that for many individuals, 'opinions' on some issues changed apparently at random, so that individual answers in 1956 and 1958 were equally weak predictors of answers in 1960. This results from a combination of genuine responses that are weakly held and change, and 'pseudo-responses' that do not reflect real opinions. Converse argues that, even if aggregate public opinion remains relatively stable, 'large portions of the electorate do not have meaningful beliefs, even on issues that have formed the basis for intense political controversy among elites for substantial periods of time';[36] overall, people possess more non-attitudes than attitudes. This analysis remains relevant for understanding contemporary public opinion in the United States and Canada.[37]

Converse's study also illustrates that public opinion can be volatile. As Peter McCormick commented in 1991, 'The major issues of the last five years ... have swung public opinion so often that the pollster's graphs look like blueprints for a roller-coaster.'[38] Referendums illustrate this point: while public opinion is relatively stable on a few issues, such as capital punishment and marijuana law, voters' intentions on most other issues are prone to change during campaigns.[39]

Policy-makers often use polls to try to anticipate future public opinion. Polls, however, are snapshots of public opinion at a particular time. Robert Fulford extends this metaphor to argue that 'there is no reason to think that the people in a snapshot will remain in the same position for even one second after the camera clicks.'[40] It is often difficult, therefore, for government officials to affect public opinion since attitudes are subject to the influence of many factors that cannot be controlled or even predicted.

Similar concerns about the reality that opinions are subject to change, particularly after the public acquires more information, are expressed by a former civil servant. An observer with experience in government says that 'Governing on the basis of the polls is governing through the rear-view mirror.'[41] In this spirit Robert Young warns that polls are of limited value in preparing for the future if Quebeckers vote to secede from Canada:

> public opinion data are not reliable guides to what people would do or what policies they would support during the course of a secession. The questions are hypothetical. The respondents are not in the context of a momentous event, as they would be following a Yes vote. Poll data also do not allow for the trade-offs that would have to be made in the actual context of a Yes: there might be considerable support in the abstract for northern Quebec Aboriginals to remain in Canada, but would this stand up if the value of people's houses and savings were declining sharply? And, out of context, neither do poll data allow for the changes in opinion that can be brought by persuasive leaders in uncertain times.[42]

Even when dealing with current public opinion on sovereignty, pollsters sometimes appear to understate the extent to which attitudes are subject to change. When an Ekos poll late in 1999 showed 62 per cent support for the federalist position on the 1995 Quebec referendum question, company president Frank Graves said, 'I don't remember numbers for federalism any better than that in 30 years. It's a pretty compelling case that the sovereignty movement in Quebec is dormant.'[43] However, Quebeckers' attitudes on this issue have changed over time, and they may again.[44] Most notably, during the relatively short periods of the 1980 and 1995 referendum campaigns over sovereignty, their attitudes shifted significantly. In 1995, in keeping with Converse's observation about users of polls overestimating the stability of public opinion, the consistently comfortable poll margins for the federalist side in the months leading up to the referendum seemed to induce, or at least reinforce, the overconfidence of federal officials. During this period, as Young notes, the federal cabinet took the view that 'there was no danger that Quebecers would vote to secede. The polls confirmed that the majority of the public wanted to remain in Canada.'[45] In fact, of course, the final margin of victory was just over one percentage point. If fluctuation of opinion is found on this issue, which has assumed a long-term place high on the political agenda, it is also to be expected on less salient issues.

All these factors affect the evaluation and utility of public opinion research. Even when public opinion is relatively well informed, citizens may still express ambivalent and apparently contradictory attitudes. For instance, as noted in chapter 6, Canadians endorse the Charter of Rights at a general level but give significantly less approval in response to questions about specific rights. Similarly, the public tends to oppose regulation in the abstract but favours it if concrete purposes such as environmental or consumer safety are identified. As well, polls simultaneously show support for tax cuts and for increased spending in many policy areas. Results like these may be understandable or even rational, but they do not deliver clear signals to poll users who desire guidance about citizens' preferences.

Problems Interpreting Polls

Even when polls minimize the pitfalls discussed above, interpretation of data is not necessarily straightforward. A few media and government polls have explicitly asked respondents to address trade-offs in policy-making in order to better understand public opinion.[46] However, most surveys do not ask respondents to make the kinds of trade-offs and choices that policy-makers confront. Questionnaires that fail to present balanced alternatives risk producing misleading results.

Many polls have considerable scope for interpretation. For instance, pollsters may choose to emphasize particular questions or create an 'index' combining responses to several questions. They must also decide whether to present analysis of sub-groups. Herbert Asher explains that 'two investigators can interpret identical poll results in sharply different ways depending on what perspectives and values they bring to their data analysis.' While some would attribute this to pollsters' personal biases, Asher explains this subjectivity in analysis of polls as a matter of different 'professional judgments about the importance and relevance of information.'[47] Government officials are at least as capable of drawing different conclusions from polls. At times ministers in the Chrétien government have interpreted public opinion in conflicting ways, either citing different polls or analysing the same poll differently.

Some questions do not allow straightforward analysis. Robert Weissberg refers to a 1972 survey on American withdrawal of troops from Vietnam. Using a seven-point scale running from 1, support for 'immediate and complete withdrawal,' to 7, support for 'increased military efforts,' the survey produced the following results: 21.2 per cent chose position 1; 9.8 per cent picked 2; 13.6 per cent selected 3; 24.9 per cent opted for 4; 12.1 per cent chose 5; 6.3 per cent picked 6; and 12.1 per cent selected 7. As Weissberg points out, various interpretations are possible by collapsing categories. Most obviously, 44.6 per cent favour a degree of withdrawal, 24.9 per cent favour a 'balanced policy,' and 30.5 per cent favour increased military action. But it could also be argued that '69.5 percent (categories 1–4) reject increasing the country's military commitment; or 55.3 percent (categories 4–7) reject withdrawal; or even that 50.6 percent [the three middle categories] favour a "moderate" position.'[48] The force of this example stems in part from the vagueness of a numerical scale: it is unclear, for instance, what the difference between positions 2 and 3 means to respondents. Further, if this example included respondents who do not give opinions, additional interpretations would be possible.

As indicated earlier, questionnaire design often affects results. Previous chapters established that the premiers' poll on the constitution gave different signals from the federal government's surveys, leading pollsters produced conflicting results on the visibility of the GST, and opponents of gun control legislation have generated their own data that challenge the major firms' polls.

Another example of different pieces of research giving contrasting signals occurred in 1980. The Ontario Ministry of Health had initiated surveys which indicated that few respondents were concerned about the possibility of doctors opting out of the government's medical insurance system. At about the same time, Goldfarb Consultants had taken focus groups for the premier's office and reported widespread fears of this prospect. The health minister, Dennis Timbrell, understandably expressed confusion. Jerry Conway, a ministry official, analysed the results. He noted that a small number of people participated in the Goldfarb project, and pointed out that they lived in Toronto rather than across the province. Conway also reported that the qualitative study contained 'assertions that have a ring of authority and [are] generally not warranted by the method used to generate the information.'[49] This case was relatively easy to resolve because of obvious differences between the projects.

Another instance in which competing polls produced divergent findings is from 1997.[50] With the federal deficit eliminated, a public debate followed about the relative importance of reducing the debt, cutting taxes, and restoring funding for social programs. In September, Earnscliffe submitted a poll to the Department of Finance, reporting that 'Canadians ... first want to secure a balanced budget, then reinvest in health, education, children and youth and having done that, they want a reduction in taxes. When it comes to taxes, personal cuts would take preference over business tax cuts.'[51] That fall, the Angus Reid Group produced a poll which signalled that Canadians' priorities were tax relief and debt reduction. Shortly afterwards, Ekos released a poll which appeared to suggest the opposite, that the public's priority was funding social programs. A COMPAS media poll tended to reinforce the Reid perspective. At the invitation of Ed Greenspon of the *Globe and Mail*, Darrell Bricker for Angus Reid, and Frank Graves for Ekos explained their positions in his newspaper.[52] The polling attracted sufficient attention that, in a very unusual development, the Coordinating Committee of Deputy Ministers invited the pollsters to make presentations to civil servants. David Herle spoke first for Earnscliffe, and Bricker and Graves appeared together at a later session. The apparent differences between Bricker and Graves became smaller. What remained was Graves's stress on Canadians' stated desire for social policy changes, while Bricker argued that Ekos overstated their support for action on this front by the federal government. The Earnscliffe poll, with a message part-way between Reid's and Ekos's, carried most weight with Martin; not surprisingly the finance minister had most faith in his own pollster.

In part, timing and sampling may explain the conflicting messages, but many of the differences hinge on methodological issues on which leading pollsters have disagreements, including how to design questions, and what kind of information is appropriate to give to respondents. These types of results illustrate a problem faced by practitioners when they are trying to draw conclusions from different opinion research studies. When the polls do not point the same way, officials may be confused and have trouble getting independent advice to help sort out the differences. They show that policy-makers exposed to more than one poll may at times find themselves confused about the state of public opinion. Those who have access to a single poll may receive a more decisive signal but not necessarily one that is trustworthy.

Special Concerns about Focus Groups

Focus groups are unrepresentative of the overall public. This is often intentional – when researchers deliberately target client groups, opinion leaders, or those whose opinions may change. Accordingly, generalization from focus group findings must be undertaken very cautiously. While they are occasionally used to measure public preferences on policy issues, it is questionable whether the results of this measurement tool are of much value to policy-makers seeking information that might help with decisions about policy content. The limited samples are merely the most visible part of the problem.

During a focus group session, participants learn through debate, hearing alternative perspectives and acquiring information. As a result, warns Gary Breen, their attitudes may diverge from the general public: 'People sit there for two hours listening to others talk, and listening to the moderator; they suddenly learn more and more, their attitudes change and they [become less] reflective of the general population. And that's always the [concern]: how do we handle this discussion so that they don't become experts? That's a tough one.' This point is the reverse of an argument James Fishkin makes for deliberative opinion polls: the changes in the participants' attitudes caused by information provided during this type of research are a virtue because the quality of deliberation is enhanced. Breen is concerned that the change in the respondents' views threatens the representative character of opinion research – to the extent that qualitative research deserves such a claim at all. Both objectives can be viewed as democratic but they are difficult to reconcile.

Some other aspects of focus groups provide further reasons why policy-makers should use them cautiously. One former public servant argues that they are artificial because the context of focus groups differs from real-life exposure to advertising and other communications vehicles. He also believes that some participants know too much about what researchers expect of them and act accordingly.

Another potential problem is that results of qualitative research are increasingly reported in quantitative ways. In part, this involves using technology for quantification within the focus group. But it also reflects pressures of clients for reports with graphs and charts and even percentages. As shown in discussion after a panel spoke on qualitative research held in Ottawa in 1999, opinion researchers themselves are uneasy about this because they know that generalizing from small samples is dangerous.[53] Even if a qualifying statement is provided, clients may be misled by the quantification. In addition, one opinion researcher in attendance criticized the practice of quantifying results of focus groups because some respondents give different responses in a group setting than they would in individual interviews. However, knowing the competition for government contracts, researchers feel pressure to 'tailor the product to suit the buyer.' The meeting featured some discussion of whether it was the responsibility of pollsters or clients to determine and maintain appropriate standards; at a minimum it is reasonable to expect researchers to explain to their clients the problems with quantifying results of focus groups. While it should not be assumed that all quantification in reports of qualitative research is unjustified, some firms go too far and risk misleading their clients.

Finally, interpretation of focus group results is more subjective than analysis of quantitative research. Moreover, a former opinion researcher warns that clients sometimes draw hasty conclusions from focus groups: 'They see what they want to see, and they hear the sentence they were waiting for. It's like it's over: "I've got the confirmation; that's what we should be doing."' The impressions from watching a focus group can be more powerful than the analysis of relatively objective data from quantitative research.

Several distinctive features of focus group research, then, limit their value to policy-makers: they are unrepresentative, and may become more so during the course of the research; they are somewhat artificial; they are sometimes presented in quantitative ways; and they are difficult to interpret.

The Unforeseen Constraints of Access to Information Legislation

So far this chapter has focused on the technical aspects of opinion research and the characteristics of public opinion that together limit the utility of the tool to policy-makers. The following paragraphs will examine a specific 'external' constraint on opinion research, that of Access to Information legislation.[54]

Introduced in 1983 with the goal of promoting government openness, the legislation ensures that most government documents are available to the public. This includes reports of polls, most of which can be obtained within a few months of their presentation to government.[55] As polling reports are essentially the aggregated opinions of citizens, there is a strong prima facie argument against keeping them secret. More generally, most commentary on Access to Information focuses on problems applying the letter or spirit of the law, such as the tendency of public officials to withhold rather than release information and the common delays when they agree to release it.[56] As Hugh Winsor explains, many civil servants work in a 'climate of fear' that induces cautious behaviour. The result is an unforeseen consequence of Access to Information legislation: it has altered the character of information about public opinion that is produced and its availability in writing to users.[57] While much opinion research for government unfolds as it would in the absence of the legislation, pollsters and their clients know that reports of opinion research will become accessible to opposition MPs and journalists. The practice of opinion research is affected in several ways because pollsters and government officials anticipate potential political problems.

First, as noted earlier, Access to Information can affect the content of written reports. Analysis of sensitive questions may simply be omitted from these reports, although the questions and results themselves would normally appear in appendixes. Moreover, the legislation can constrain what analysis and recommendations are included in written reports. A pollster bluntly explains why:

> You're writing for the public, because it's all accessible under Access to Information. And so some things that you would like to have known, you don't want to put it onto paper in a certain way. Just because of that. Private sector clients have the opportunity of always hiding their research, and looking at it, and saying 'we don't like that, we'll bury it' ... The federal government can't do that ... So you get very good at writing where you're straddling that line of providing the advice but using language where people can feel comfortable with it, and still conveying the clear meaning without going too far. At the same time, typically there's more room to take that same interpretation a little bit farther verbally.

Recommendations in final reports, he says, are sometimes expressed more softly than in drafts, or occasionally omitted from the final written report altogether, since only the last version is subject to the Access to Information Act. Another pollster explains that government clients 'may say "Write the report, tell us your advice"' because of the legislation. A third says that by the end of the 1980s, research firms were regularly 'asked on high-profile things to give pretty flat descriptive reports'; he adds that often details of sensitive research are only discussed orally in part because of 'concern ... at being seen to be controlled, or have overtly strategic advice, coming out of external parties.' The fear is not always appearing poll-driven; at times, journalists may allege government waste if it appears that officials ignored the recommendations of a polling firm, or may simply be critical when government acts at odds with public opinion. These types of constraints on written reports apply more to research reported to the political side of government than to research primarily for civil servants. The constraints can make officials more reliant on oral reporting. Not only does this violate the spirit of the Access to Information legislation, in some cases it may mean the pollster's findings and advice have less impact. The oral messages are not supported by a permanent record and they are not necessarily received at all by officials who review a written report but do not attend a pollster's presentation.

As well as causing some analysis and recommendations to only be delivered orally, Access to Information sometimes affects the character of research more fundamentally. This is not merely that partisan questions are avoided because they are a misuse of public funds. Rather, some questions are not asked because they are sensitive: officials want to avoid possible political embarrassment if reporters or opposition MPs learn that their polls are including certain questions, using particular question wording, or researching certain topics. An illustration of concern about the effects of public release of polling results is that the Mulroney government did not want to publicly release its opinion research on national unity.[58] As well, testing arguments is sometimes difficult on government polls.[59] A pollster explains that while he recognizes the legitimate reasons for Access to Information, 'the downside is that the public servants have to follow the medical dictum that you do your patient no harm. And so you don't commission a poll whose first impact above all is going to be to cause embarrassment in question period – where the poll reveals the public doesn't like something the government is either doing or thinking of doing ... The biggest problem for government research is Access to Information.'

Even if the last comment overstates matters, the effects are varied. For instance, pollsters may be reluctant to ask a pair of intentionally leading questions that point in opposite directions, in order to compare the responses, rather than asking neutral questions. The fear is that the media will report the results selectively and create a misleading impression about either public opinion or the government's plans. Certain questions are not asked at all because they may attract public attention.

Indeed, this concern is so strong that Jean Chrétien has personally reviewed draft questionnaires and eliminated certain questions.[60] A government might have good reasons for investigating reactions to an increase in the rate of the GST, even if no policy alterations are under consideration, to track opinion in case circumstances change in the future. However, says a pollster, if the Department of Finance asked the question, 'it would be [headed for] the front page of the paper the minute the Access to Information request went out.' At other times, officials are anxious about the results of their polls becoming public, especially if they show public opposition to government policies. A more general wish to avoid the appearance of governing by polls compounds the constraints.

As well as avoiding specific questions, governments may be deterred from polling on certain topics. The Chrétien government was reluctant to conduct surveys on the war in Kosovo, anticipating criticism if it polled on a highly sensitive subject. Similar concerns have limited the amount of opinion research initiated on national unity by the same government. In both cases, however, government officials monitored and analysed syndicated research. While this research produces a general overview of public opinion, it could not have served some of the government's specific needs or provided the depth of specially commissioned research.

The desire to maintain the secrecy of information contributes to some decisions to commission research using party funds. This enables the findings to be kept private, a particular concern during Chrétien's time as prime minister with controversial issues such as the treatment of hepatitis C victims and protestors against the APEC conference in Vancouver. Still, this is only a partial solution for government officials and sometimes they proceed with only incomplete written records of opinion research, or with the research itself muted to avoid embarrassment, or without their own research at all. Access to Information practices have unquestionably decreased the overall utility of opinion research in government by diminishing the availability and flow of information and advice, and this effect is largest on sensitive issues where its potential to assist officials would otherwise be greatest.

Developments in Selective Sampling

When Gallup and Rae argued that opinion polls could function as 'sampling referendums,' they were advocating the principle that the opinions of all members of the population counted equally. This enabled polls to contrast with, and offset, the views expressed by organized interests. Pollsters still can and do claim that this representativeness is a democratic feature of quantitative research,[61] and some government officials appreciate this. In practice, however, Gallup's own polling often did not meet this ideal, and more recently polls have departed from this model in other ways. This is more than just threats to the representativeness of samples coming from rising refusal rates and technological advances such as answering machines, call display features, and cellular phones. When Dick Morris took a poll to anticipate reactions if Clinton confessed to his relationship with Monica Lewinsky, he included only likely voters in his sample.[62] Beyond this, pollsters sometimes deliberately emphasize particular groups rather than using polls as anything like sampling referendums of the population as a whole. While this may serve clients well, it weakens the democratic aspect of polling.

Early market research surveys tended to oversample the heaviest consumers of goods; this practice served business well and was transported to political polling. Early polls tended to be judged on their ability to forecast elections, and understandably overrepresented groups with the highest turnout rates. While Gallup publicly referred to the ideal of a sampling referendum and highlighted the potential of polls to blunt the impact of organized interests, his early polls failed to represent equally all demographic groups. Specifically, they substantially underrepresented women, blacks, and low-income Americans. As Daniel Robinson observes, the 'egalitarian ideal was constructed on a commercial foundation that was purposely inegalitarian.'[63] Gallup's theory was not followed in his practice.

Some recent opinion research for governments has also emphasized or oversampled certain groups, to more accurately measure their attitudes. This was the case with research on gun control that zeroed in on gun owners. Another example is a survey on immigration that oversampled residents of large cities.[64] Similarly, as the Mulroney government tried to save the Meech Lake Accord from collapse in 1990, some of its polling oversampled Newfoundland and Manitoba, where the provincial governments were obstructing passage of the agreement. Some qualitative research emphasizes the most attentive members of the public rather than the population as a whole, as happened with research on compensation for hepatitis C victims. Other research focuses on policy elites. This can mean a sample of journalists and public sector policy-makers of issue areas including free trade, the deficit, the constitution, and privatization.[65] As a COMPAS brochure for prospective clients explains,

> Our multi-audience perspective makes us alert to the importance of special audiences. Standard practice is to stress the general public in public opinion and marketing research. Yet CEOs, journalists, experts, government officials, and other special audiences can be key opinion leaders ... [COMPAS] undertake[s] proportionately more special audience projects than other firms.[66]

While this approach presumably serves clients well and is probably justifiable in many cases to stress the attitudes of those most affected by a policy, it represents a large step away from Gallup's egalitarian principle by emphasizing the views of certain groups.

One of the most intriguing developments in this direction is quantitative research that samples the whole population but singles out members of the 'attentive public' for separate analysis. Pollsters recognize that this portion of the population – 15 to 30 per cent, depending on the precise definition adopted – is most aware of public affairs, has the most sophisticated understanding of politics, and is most likely to influence the opinions of others.[67] This approach of separately analysing members of the attentive public is followed in some research by firms such as Environics and Pollara, which use the term 'opinion leaders.' This type of research, employing surveys to measure active public opinion, is used in policy development but to date has exerted more influence on communications.

This approach of emphasizing the most attentive segment of the public has been developed furthest in Earnscliffe's work for Finance and other departments, which uses the term 'involved Canadians.' As Earnscliffe pollster David Herle explains,

> We almost never do focus groups with anybody other than involved Canadians for the government or the private sector. Because people outside that 30 per cent really don't care much ... And no matter what the government does in its communications efforts, it's unlikely to be received by them: they're not paying attention, they won't notice.

Herle says that while no consistent ideological patterns have emerged, differences regularly appear between involved Canadians and the general population.[68]

In 1997, partly because of a perception among some Finance officials that the government was 'wasting a lot of money sending the wrong stuff to the wrong people,'[69] Earnscliffe explored the concept of involved Canadians systematically. Earlier research by the firm had indicated that 30 per cent of the public were relatively attentive to politics. Compared to the remaining 70 per cent, this segment of the public was more likely to receive the messages communicated by the government and more likely to influence others (through discussion and contacting the media). Drawing on this research, Earnscliffe conducted a mail survey to learn more about these 'involved Canadians,' and 328 of its 900 questionnaires were returned. Comparing these responses with the firm's data for the general public, Earnscliffe described involved Canadians as 'the key target for public communications efforts like the federal budget.' The firm proceeded to suggest that Finance's communications with this group must be fast because its members form their opinions rapidly. Earnscliffe's analysis of involved Canadians' media consumption generated proposals such as these:

> ... In the allocation of resources, it is more important to concentrate on beat and general news reporters than columnists ...
> ... In the search for third-party endorsement, communications strategies should take account of the need to monitor and promote letter writing.
> ... Radio news should become much more integral to media strategies ... This implies strong, directed outreach to radio stations, whether the CBC or privately-owned, and an attempt to understand how radio sources its information. Radio networks are one obvious key because of their news distribution systems.

The significance of radio to involved Canadians came as a surprise to at least one senior Finance official. Earnscliffe also noted that 'Canadian Press broadcast summaries and clip distribution are key,' that clips and interviews should be provided, and that regional ministers can play a role in home markets. Morning and midday news cycles were identified as the most important. The memorandum later advised that 'given the propensity of activists to monitor live events and to seek updated information, communications strategies should be geared to multiple appearances, quick response and new information delivery within short news cycles.' As well, it returned to the point that third-party opinion is valued, recognizing the credibility of non-government sources: 'Quoting and encouraging that sort of opinion will probably be more useful than [directly] defending against Opposition or interest group criticism.'[70]

While Earnscliffe continues to survey the general population in much of its research, this refined technique enabled the firm to advise Finance officials about how to target their communications. While other Canadians would still be exposed to the department's messages, greater efforts would be made to communicate with the most attentive and influential portion of the population. For instance, the information helped to lead officials to put greater weight on radio and be alert to multiple news cycles, and similar findings helped them understand the importance of weekly community newspapers.[71] Herle explains that distinguishing between involved Canadians and the general public can aid communications in another way:

the most compelling [reason for a particular policy] for involved Canadians may be very different from what the most compelling [reason] is for the other 70 percent ... If you just looked at that 100 per cent, you might say, 'Gee, minister, the best argument you can put forward for your policy is this argument.' But it actually isn't, because to the people who are paying attention, the best argument for what you're doing is this [other argument].

In this hypothetical example, even though one argument resonates best with at least a plurality of the sample, the government would place greater emphasis on another argument which strikes a chord with involved Canadians.

As well as assisting communications, the views of involved Canadians can be analysed to help with policy. A Finance official says that in examining policy details, there is more reason to be concerned with the involved Canadians than the general public: 'When it comes to details of policy it's the involved [people] that will kill you' by causing political problems for a government. Changes to details of policy may make it easier to sell and communicate the policy to the public – specifically, the involved Canadians. Herle offers the example of changes made to provide for the reporting of names of certain offenders when they are released from prison; the analysis of the attentive public indicated high levels of concern within that group.

As in this case, once analysis of involved Canadians is undertaken, it is likely to have some effect. The presentation of separate results for the attentive public in poll reports almost certainly means that at times officials' understanding of public opinion places more weight on that group than the population as a whole. Since the involved Canadians are understood to be the most likely to receive government messages and most likely to influence others, this is probably quite rational from the point of view of pollsters and their clients. If it means, however, that the views of the more attentive members of the public are more influential in the design of communications or the refining of certain policies, this is somewhat troubling. While incorporating weakly-held opinions of the remaining 70 per cent of the public into policy-making is not necessarily desirable either, the separate analysis of involved Canadians partially undermines a key strength of polling, the democratic claim that it equally reflects the opinions of all citizens and contrasts with active expressions of public opinion.

Conclusion

Several factors unforeseen by Gallup and Rae have affected the use of opinion research in government. First, many technical features of opinion research such as question design make opinion polling a less precise and less useful tool than is commonly understood. Second, public opinion can be unknowledgeable and volatile; this compounds the difficulties of drawing conclusions from polls. Third, the characteristics of opinion research and public opinion, including the presentation of data by pollsters and the existence of competing polls, produce difficulties in interpreting research. Fourth, focus groups present several specific problems. Fifth, beyond this, Access to Information legislation constrains the presentation of polls and the kind of research that can be done for government; this means that at times opinion research is unable to serve officials to its full potential. Collectively, these points make it clear that the analysis of opinion research is more of an art than a science – and that it not does consistently provide the clear and useful signals that many observers implicitly assume. Finally, pollsters have sometimes deliberately departed from attempting to achieve near-random samples, and while this may serve clients well, it weakens the democratic element of opinion research.

None of these points should be taken as arguments that opinion research should not be used in government. Indeed, they only apply to some opinion research. They alert us, however, to limits on the value of opinion research in government. They constitute a partial foundation for arguments for why it would be unwise for practitioners to rely on opinion research as heavily as some observers presume they do, why opinion research sometimes simply does not provide trustworthy or useful signals to policy-makers, and why some polling falls short of the democratic ideals advanced by Gallup and Rae.

10 Conclusion

The widely held belief that opinion research regularly influences the substance of public policy is not entirely false. Nevertheless, this study has shown that it is in large part a misconception, even a myth. As one observer with both government and polling experience puts it, 'The people who think that governments make decisions on the basis of polls are people who are not close enough to really see it and know it.'[1] Or, in the words of another source with a background in both spheres, 'The bottom line is that governments use polls not to decide what to do but to decide how to sell it.'[2] The fact that polls are used, and occasionally cited publicly, does not indicate how they are used. It is also very likely that when governments act responsively towards the public, other forces besides polls are at work. As we have seen, the greatest impact of opinion research is on communications – mainly after a policy decision has been made.

Observers have usually assumed that polling affects the content of policy without adequately considering how it influences other stages of the policy process. As a consequence, for example, the role of polling in agenda-setting has been neglected. Chapter 4 suggested that this was the case with environmental policy, and a hint of this impact of polling is present in the gun control case. Similarly, opinion research can significantly contribute to implementation. This was evident with both the Goods and Services Tax and gun control.

As chapter 5 and the case studies have shown, the biggest omission has been the failure of many observers to recognize the range and extent of ways that polls and focus groups contribute to government communications. Further, the conventional wisdom about the influence of opinion research on the content of policy does not take into account the pitfalls of polls and focus groups and the character of public opinion.

Overall, polls make a limited contribution to what Joel Brooks calls democratic linkage between public opinion and public policy. Although cases that fit Gallup and Rae's concept of sampling referendums are rare, it can be argued that the early pollsters would have approved of some modern uses of opinion research. Thus, in late 1981 polls helped to reinforce the federal government's position on the constitution, they contributed modestly to some of the details of the GST, and they were cited to defend the Chrétien government's gun control policy. More often than polling, however, various forms of active public opinion, along with factors such as officials' instincts about citizens' preferences and their interpretations of election results, contribute to democratic linkage. Clearly there is much more to be learned about the mechanisms and degree of responsiveness to public opinion – including the contributions of polls and other indicators of citizens' preferences – but neither the impact of polling nor the extent of democratic linkage in Canada should be overestimated. To the extent that opinion research helps elites lead public opinion, as it did with the constitution and various cases discussed in chapter 5, this may promote what Brooks terms a counterfeit consensus on some issues. However, we should not forget the substantial amount of inconsistency between opinion and policy in Canada reported by Brooks and Pétry, nor the findings from cases such as the GST that government communications have only modest effects on public opinion. Together with the evidence that many policy decisions are affected by the activities of interest groups that do not reflect majority viewpoints, this demonstrates the relevance of the democratic frustration model in which governments' decisions are often at odds with public preferences.

A Final Look at the Case Studies

Each of the three case studies features what David Easton called stresses, or at least potential stresses, to the political system if public opinion was ignored. If the Trudeau government had tried to patriate the constitution unilaterally, particularly after the Supreme Court ruled that to do so would breach convention, its legitimacy could have suffered dramatically. The Mulroney government's pursuit of the GST cost it considerable public support and officials could not be sure that compliance with the tax would be widespread. Later, gun users' resistance to the firearms registry posed a problem for the Chrétien government. In each instance, government officials used public opinion research to understand the problem but not to determine the policy position. The polling and focus groups were handled skilfully in the patriation case, and the research indirectly affected the policy outcome as well as the communications. The research appeared too late to have much impact on the GST, although government officials did employ polling to examine proposals for modifying the tax and it modestly influenced how the policy was communicated. While the gun control policy was developed independently of opinion research, the polling and focus groups had a substantial impact on the nature and content of the communications efforts.

Each case, then, illustrates how government officials can use opinion research. Together they show a range of ways that the feedback from the public provided by opinion research contributes to governments' communications with citizens. In all three instances, the governments knew what they wanted to accomplish and polls did not determine their position; rather, as the road map metaphor indicates, they used opinion research to try to help them achieve their goals.

They experienced varying degrees of success, however. Officials in the Trudeau government could be pleased with the contribution of opinion research to constitutional policy, as it helped them manoeuvre to maintain public support and gain the upper hand over the dissenting provincial governments. The research contributed to the development of the 'people's package' and a communications campaign by the federal government which aimed to maintain and strengthen public support for Trudeau's position. And polling helped indirectly to swing the final outcome in the federal government's favour because of the skill of officials such as Michael Kirby, the special circumstances of the negotiations among the federal and provincial governments, and the way that evidence of public support for Trudeau's position enhanced the credibility of his threat to hold a national referendum to resolve the intergovernmental disagreement.

In contrast, opinion research offered limited help to the Mulroney government when it faced the challenge of introducing what Canadians perceived as a new tax. As chapter 7 indicated, there are solid reasons to doubt whether the research was used effectively and the government would have benefited if polling had been employed early to highlight the public's opposition and lack of knowledge; this could have sparked a communications campaign to educate Canadians about the old Manufacturers' Sales Tax. Still, the opinion dikes were perhaps too strong to be overcome even with effective use of opinion research: the government's task was particularly difficult because opposition to the GST was both intense and widespread.

The role of opinion research on gun control was smaller than in the patriation case but larger than in the sales tax case. In contrast to the surveys showing heavy opposition to the GST, polling assured officials that vocal opponents of firearms control did not speak for the public as a whole. There was, therefore, little need to try to alter public opinion and much of the opinion research could be directed to a less formidable task: examining attitudes of the minority of people who own guns and helping the government communicate with them about the procedures for registration and licensing.

The variation among the three cases, then, resulted primarily from different patterns of public opinion, the range of ways that government officials used opinion research (caused in part by the differences in public opinion), and the special circumstances that made the referendum proposal relevant and powerful in the constitutional case. Yet they share the important similarity that opinion research affected policy content less than communications.

Why Does Opinion Research Affect Communications More than Policy Content?

Five interrelated factors explain the relative importance of opinion research in government communications compared to the decision-making and other phases of the policy process.

First, it is essential to consider who uses the research. Public servants in communications branches of departments initiate and employ opinion research more frequently than their counterparts in strategic policy areas, or staff in ministers' offices. As a result, much research is used by civil servants whose primary tasks are to inform and persuade the public about policies, rather than their colleagues who develop and deliver those policies. Moreover, the civil servants have fewer incentives to be responsive to public opinion than elected officials and their staffs.

The research that is initiated and designed to help communicate policies that have already been determined often does not provide useful signals to policy-makers, even if they are seeking guidance for their decisions about the content of policy. At most, research of this sort might provide inferences if, for instance, it reveals that selling a particular policy will be an uphill struggle. As well, this communications research is frequently qualitative, and therefore offers little guidance about the popularity of policy proposals. Related to this, pollsters give their clients more, and more explicit, advice on communications than on policy content.

Second, connected to the first factor, the timing of opinion research affects how it is used. As we saw earlier, most opinion research is commissioned relatively late in the policy process, after a government is committed to a policy position. Most communications branches are not well integrated into their departments' policy-making activities and they play a small role in the policy process until after a decision has been made. After a decision, the communications staff of a department has the responsibility for marketing the policy and informing the public about it. They then initiate opinion research to help with communications, but even if that research suggests that the policy is unpopular and perhaps should be changed, it is frequently too late to alter the decision significantly. Therefore, opinion research most often helps communications branches develop the messages to inform and persuade the public. However, research conducted at the policy-development stage may contribute later to communications of the policy.

Third, contemporary governments place significant emphasis on communications. For instance, federal cabinet documents must contain a communications plan. This frequently requires opinion research to prepare and to describe the political environment. As well, the research is often cited explicitly in memoranda to cabinet. Consequently, more opinion research is conducted for communications purposes than in the past.[3]

A fourth reason lies in the nature of public opinion. By contemporary standards, pollsters in the 1930s and 1940s perceived mass public opinion in a very optimistic light. Today, as indicated in chapter 9, it is more widely understood that many citizens frequently lack meaningful opinions on issues, especially at the time a policy decision is made. A Decima pollster argues vigorously that this reality contains the impact of polling on policy content:

> If you ask people, like we did in '84, if they favour a free trade deal with the United States, you get [approximately] 85 per cent saying 'sure.' And they don't know. How could they? How in the world can some housewife in Scarborough know the policy ramifications of a free trade deal with the

United States? Yet we phoned her, and asked her at dinner time whether or not she favours it. And because we asked her, she says, 'Maybe I should have a view ... It sounds okay. "Free" is in there. Can't be too bad' ... Now, if you're a government, and you're making decisions based on that house-wife in Scarborough, being one [member] of [the] 85 per cent of the public who tells you they support free trade, when the issue isn't even on the radar screen ... you're stupid beyond belief ... You cannot ask somebody who knows nothing about the issue to tell you what you should do ... Public opinion [research] explicitly asking people whether it was a good idea or a bad idea had absolutely nothing to do [with the decision to proceed on the Free Trade Agreement].[4]

On this account, public opinion was not driving this policy and the public developed meaningful opinions on the Canada–U.S. Free Trade Agreement only after the government committed itself to it. Later in the policy process, when the government was trying to maintain support for the agreement, opinion research showed greater public awareness and assisted mainly with communications. With the Charter of Rights and the GST, and arguably with gun control, a strong case can also be made that the majority of Canadians did not understand the issues well enough to have genuinely informed opinions. If this is true of these high-profile policies, it applies to numerous less salient issues. Govern-ment officials are often especially sceptical that public opinion can provide useful guidance on technical policies and matters of detail.[5] As well, many understand that it is volatile.

A final explanation for the relative significance of opinion research to communications compared to policy content is based on the nature of the policy process. Decision-makers are more inclined to follow the recommendations from pollsters on communications matters than on the substance of policy. This is partly because the advice on the former is usually more emphatic. A pollster explains a more fundamental reason: 'There are many tools that can help support policy develop-ment, and opinion research is simply one.' He continues:

There are few tools that can better help a government communicate policy than public opinion research. There it will stand out as a pre-eminent tool. Because you're understanding what people think about the subject, what messages will move them, what are their concerns, what are the strengths of some of the policies? So you can really craft messages, it really does stand out as ... particularly useful there.[6]

The point is that many inputs affect decisions about policy content, including letters and telephone calls from the public, interest groups, the mass media, expert and bureaucratic opinion, the views of politicians and their parties, institutional factors, financial constraints, international pressures, and the experience of other countries. However, for communicating to the public about policy, these inputs are less relevant and most of them do not deliver any clear signal to officials about how to communicate: the strongest suit of opinion research is its ability to help with communications.

This has significant implications. A policy option shown as popular by polls might be rejected by decision-makers for a host of possible reasons. On the other hand, the opinion research usually signals the 'best' approach to communicating policy because good communications depends heavily on how audiences receive it. Reinforcing this point, politicians do not want to be mere ciphers: decision-makers usually hold stronger views on the substance of policy than communications strategies and tactics.

Several factors, then, explain why opinion research contributes more to the communications of policy than policy development. These relate to who tends to use the research, the timing of the studies, governments' concerns with communications, characteristics of public opinion, and the nature of the policy process.

Opinion Research in Election Campaigns and in Government

Impressions that opinion research influences policy content may be reinforced by reports of polling affecting the strategy and tactics of parties during election campaigns. However, not only do many observers overestimate the impact of polling on policy positions taken in campaigns, but there are several important differences between the behaviour of political actors in election campaigns and in government. Politicians often make campaign promises that polls suggest will be popular, but some of these are broken after elections. Linked to this, the relative influence of pollsters and consultants is generally stronger on candidates during election campaigns than it is for politicians-in-office. The latter, who must pass and implement policies as well as propose them, are affected more by other inputs, such as advice from civil servants and the views of other politicians. Moreover, the proximity of election day strengthens the influence of public opinion on elected officials. This is because politicians have greater incentives to be responsive and because a larger proportion of the public is attentive during election campaigns. Lastly, polling presumes approximate equality of all citizens which, to practical politicians, is more relevant close to election day, when votes count equally, than the realities of governing, when active public opinion is more likely to affect officials' thinking. Together, these reasons explain why opinion research contributes more to responsiveness to the public's policy concerns during election campaigns than in governing.

Why Have Initial Hopes for Polling Not Materialized?

While Gallup and Rae were correct to predict in 1940 that polling would affect the practice of government, we have seen that, in contemporary Canada, their expectations that polls would make a major contribution to policy decisions have not proven accurate. Four assumptions in their analysis help us understand why. These relate to their stress in *The Pulse of Democracy* on media polls, elected officials, and polls with aggregate data, and their view of the sophistication of public opinion.

Gallup and Rae assumed that politicians would refer to polls that appeared in newspapers rather than research initiated by governments. This means that the subjects researched would be decided by the media and pollsters, not by the government. However, the primary source of polling data for the Canadian government today is specially commissioned research. Compared to media polls, this research goes into greater depth, emphasizes policy content less, and even with Access to Information legislation is not nearly as public. The origins and characteristics of contemporary opinion research studies, then, make it more useful for communications than Gallup and Rae anticipated.

Additionally, *The Pulse of Democracy* emphasized the role of elected officials rather than public servants. As noted earlier, public servants generally have fewer incentives to act responsively to public opinion than officials who were elected, and they place more emphasis on technical matters. Related to this, the size and importance of bureaucracy have grown over the last six decades, and public servants have correspondingly become heavy users of the research. Public servants are likelier to employ the research to help with implementation and communications than to guide policy content.

A further explanation is that Gallup and Rae were mainly concerned with aggregate data for the entire population. Ginsberg also assumes that the opinion research that matters covers the whole population, and

Robinson agrees that equal treatment of all citizens' opinions is crucial to the democratic claims for polling. As we saw in chapter 5, however, users of opinion research are often more interested in sub-groups of the population than the population as a whole. And chapter 9 showed that in actual practice, many quantitative studies emphasize specific sub-groups of the population – whether selected demographic groups, people expressing particular opinions, or the clients or potential clients of programs, or involved Canadians. This was illustrated in the GST studies focusing on business owners and the special attention paid to gun users in polling on firearms policy. In both cases, the government hoped to ensure that these groups complied with and accepted the policies. The tendency to stress sub-groups of the population is especially pronounced in qualitative research, another development which Gallup and Rae did not anticipate. The more opinion research stresses sub-groups, the more remote are the chances of it functioning as a sampling referendum.

Finally, from a contemporary vantage point, Gallup and Rae overestimated the sophistication of public opinion. Four implications relevant to this study flow from an assessment of public opinion as relatively volatile, unknowledgable and inattentive. First, if public opinion is understood this way, polls are less likely to provide clear signals about public preferences on policy content. This helps to explain why opinion research did not assist much with the decision on tax-included pricing. Second, the normative argument for following public opinion is less compelling morally than it would be with a conception of stable, informed, and attentive public opinion. This perspective helps to explain why officials in the Mulroney government proceeded with the GST in the face of vigorous public opposition: they were confident that the majority opinion was wrong. Third, to the extent that officials share this impression of mass public opinion, responsiveness to it is also less compelling politically because the incentives are fewer. The likelihood that particular issues will be vote-determining is smaller than Gallup and his contemporaries would have thought, and consequently, on most policies, elected officials have more discretion than many assume to act in spite of public opinion. Fourth, the more limited a conception of public opinion we accept, the more malleable it appears to be; therefore there is a greater probability that it can be shaped and influenced by communications efforts. Specific findings of the public's lack of awareness and knowledge can highlight opportunities for officials to try to educate, lead, change, and perhaps manipulate public opinion without having any effect on policy goals. This applies to some of the findings of low levels of awareness in the government's opinion research on the constitution and gun control.

Together, these factors help to explain why opinion research in government exerts more impact on communications and less on the substance of public policy than Gallup and Rae anticipated. In fairness, of course, they could not have predicted these developments unless they were clairvoyant. What is stranger is that contemporary observers have usually not grasped the implications of these points for understanding the role of opinion research in the policy process.

Should Citizens Be Concerned about Government Opinion Research?

It is important to evaluate the use of opinion research in government. Some have praised it while others are critical. The evidence that polling does not play a major role in guiding policy content should place these views in perspective. Indeed, as the advocates and critics tend to share an assumption that opinion research substantially affects policy content, they risk creating misleading impressions about the functions of opinion research in government. Clearly, many claims about the democratic potential of opinion research or the capacity of polling to undermine leadership by politicians are overstated.

Many of the ways that opinion research influences government communications are innocuous; it is difficult to imagine controversy over some of the technical opinion research about clarifying the language or design of informational brochures or forms. Indeed, the research that helps printed materials become more coherent and useful, or smooths implementation of a policy, may even be praiseworthy. Similarly, before spending substantial sums on a communications campaign, ensuring that a message will be understood as intended is legitimate.[7] Although it seems far removed from the discussions of polling by political scientists and others, this is not inconsistent with notions about making government more responsive. At worst, this type of opinion research may be conducted more often than necessary.

Yet when publicly funded opinion research is used to make government communications more persuasive, it is harder to sweep away the concerns. Angus Reid candidly acknowledges some disturbing implications of using polls to assist with communications:

[Polling can] be used by politicians to manipulate the public, to distort public opinion, to persuade people ... The public is ambivalent on a lot of issues, and so into that ambivalence jumps the politician who learns through polling, the key phrases [and] the key words to be used to take people in directions that really are not based on the public good, [or] the public will, but are based on a narrow ... agenda. You could argue that much of the free trade polling was linked to, not an attempt to listen to what the public was saying, but an attempt to persuade, and some might even say manipulate, the public into believing that free trade was the way to go ... It's not just a question of politicians being recipients of ... the public will, and therefore becoming more noble people as a result of that, and marching off and trying to follow the public will. It is equally the case that politicians want to change the public will.

It is noteworthy that the pollster expresses concerns about communications rather than policy content. Wishing to change public opinion is certainly not unethical in itself, but some uses of opinion research for this purpose may be disturbing. In several of the examples discussed in this book, most clearly in the development of the 'people's package' of constitutional changes, opinion research was drawn upon to try to shape public perceptions of a policy. This applies particularly to the testing of arguments and some of the decisions about language: the government seeks to use its knowledge of public attitudes to be as persuasive as possible. The gauging of target audiences is more complicated and involves a mix of harmless questions, such as who are the clients of a particular program, as well as potentially troubling ones such as which audiences are most likely to be influenced. Similarly, governments may want to raise awareness for straightforward motives such as promoting compliance with a policy, or they may attempt to build approval of the policy and thereby political support. The use of opinion research to justify policies is also problematic because studies of questionable quality are sometimes marshalled for this purpose.

In most cases, it would be too strong to call the communications uses of opinion research manipulative. It is true that increasing legitimacy and support for policies is a primary purpose of government communications – and opinion research helps the government put its best foot forward. However, this is often done without being misleading, and it is often more accurate to speak of persuading, leading, or educating.[8] It should also be kept in mind that in many cases, other actors, such as interest groups, are spending money on advertising and opinion research, and it is unrealistic to expect any government to 'unilaterally disarm' and act without these resources in the public arena. As well, it should be remembered that normally the impact of government communications is small.

Given the evidence that most citizens generally possess limited awareness and knowledge, it would be undesirable for opinion research to figure heavily in policy decisions. Nor does polling offer much promise for improving the quality of citizen participation. However, because polling often seeks to represent all adult citizens equally, it can play an important role, particularly for offsetting the impact of active public opinion. It may even help counter the possible policy consequences of class and other differences in rates of political participation. Polling is often perceived as a 'black art,' a tool employed in secret and mysterious ways, and this impression helps explain why policy-makers are more willing to acknowledge publicly the role of active public opinion in their decisions. Unfortunately, this perception contributes to a situation where opinion research does not receive the credit it deserves for helping to offset active public opinion, especially narrow, private interests. In part because incentives to organize politically differ widely and tend to be strongest for narrow, intense interests, active public opinion is often unrepresentative of the public as a whole. A clear example is that the intense opposition to gun control was not representative of majority opinion – as was demonstrated by polls.

While there are many reasons why majority viewpoints often do not or should not prevail, it is valuable for decision-makers to be exposed to information about mass public opinion. Polls can ensure that they are at least aware of majority opinion. It was healthy and democratic, for instance, for opinion research to help the Trudeau government to anticipate public reactions if it proceeded unilaterally with patriation, or the Mulroney government to learn about public attitudes about the GST, or the Chrétien government to be assured that, despite the opposition from gun users' groups, there was public support for the concept of firearms control. The opinion research potentially served as one of several inputs into government decisions, it improved the governments' understanding of the political environment they would have to act in, and it informed their decisions about how to proceed. This type of input from opinion research modestly enhances democracy and makes a mild contribution to responsiveness of governments, but this should be kept in perspective. Other inputs frequently prevail, and even when policy does correspond with public opinion, opinion research usually makes at most a minor contribution. While the role of polling and focus groups may seem disappointingly small to those who accept the democratic arguments of pollsters, from a perspective that stresses the limited sophistication of mass public opinion, the finding of this book that opinion research guides government communications considerably more than policy content should be a welcome one.

Appendix 1
Excerpts from a Federal Government Poll on the Constitution*

Support for the proposals of constitutional reform, July 1980

1. That Canada have its own constitution, written and adopted by Canadians, by which all changes can be made in Canada rather than continuing to use the present constitution, which can only be changed by the British Parliament.

   81% Do support
   14   Do not support
    5   No opinion

[Other polling indicated that support was not intense, and in some cases lower.]

2. That the constitution guarantee basic human rights such as freedom of speech, freedom of religion, and so on to all Canadian citizens, in such a way that no law, federal or provincial[,] could go against them.

   85% Do support
   11   Do not support
    4   No opinion

3. That, where numbers warrant, language rights be guaranteed, that is, French minorities outside Quebec and English minorities inside of Quebec be guaranteed the right to education in their own language.

---

*Source: Goldfarb Consultants, 'A Research Report for the Canadian Unity Information Office,' July 1980, 10, 8, 17. These question numbers were not in the original report and have been added by the author.

80%   Do support
16   Do not support
4   No opinion

4. That Canadians in all provinces agree to share their economic opportunities by means of the richer provinces helping the poorer ones.

86%   Do support
10   Do not support
4   No opinion

5. That Canadians from every province be allowed to work anywhere in the country, to buy and sell goods and services anywhere in Canada and to invest their money anywhere in the country, without restrictions set by a provincial government.

86%   Do support
10   Do not support
4   No opinion

6. That the Queen continue as the head of state for Canada.

49%   Do support
40   Do not support
11   No opinion

7. What do Canadians want to see happen?

54%   Increase some of the powers of the federal government and some powers of the provinces
22   Give more power to the provinces
11   Give more power to the federal government
10   Change nothing
3   No opinion

8. Who wants more powers?
Canadians were asked whether or not the new constitution should result in their provincial government having more power, less power, or the same amount of power. Overall, 36% feel their province should have more power, and that desire ranked by province is as follows:

62%   Newfoundland
57   Quebec
42   Saskatchewan
41   B.C.

36   Manitoba
34   Alberta
32   Nova Scotia
29   New Brunswick
20   P.E.I.
18   Ontario

N = 2400 (with small provinces oversampled)

Appendices 2.1–2.4
Polling on the Goods and Services Tax

2.1. ENVIRONICS, SELECTED OPINION RESEARCH ON THE GST, 1990*

Focus Canada 902-Q122, March 1990

As you may know the federal government has proposed a seven per-cent tax on most goods and services, known as the Goods and Services Tax, or GST. Do you approve or disapprove of this new tax?

12.0%	approve
82.8	disapprove
5.2	don't know/no answer

N = 2002

Focus Canada 903-Q122, June 1990

Same question as FC902-Q122 above.

16.3%	approve
75.7	disapprove
8.0	don't know/no answer

N = 2029

Focus Canada 904-Q31, October 1990

As you may know, the federal government has proposed a seven per-cent tax on most goods and services, known as the GST. Do you approve or disapprove of this new tax?

21.9%	approve

Source: Queen's University, Centre for the Study of Democracy Archives

71.3   disapprove
6.9   don't know/no answer
N = 2019

2.2. ANGUS REID GROUP, SELECTED OPINION RESEARCH ON THE GST, 1989–90*

January 1989

As you may know, the federal government is considering a major change in the federal sales tax. At present, a federal sales tax of 12 per cent is added to the cost of most manufactured goods like cars and appliances in Canada. There is no federal sales tax right now on services like legal fees and hotel bills. Under the proposed change, the federal sales tax would drop to say 10 per cent, but be applied to a wider range of goods and services. In principle, would you support or oppose this proposed change?
    31% support
    62   oppose
    7   (unsure)
    N = 1503

September 1989

We would like people's opinions on the federal government's proposed new goods and services tax. This tax is scheduled to come into effect on January 1st, 1991. It will be set at 9 per cent and will cover a wide range of goods and services. Overall, based on whatever you might have seen or heard about this, do you support or oppose the federal government's proposed goods and services tax? (Would that be strongly or moderately?)
    5%   strongly support
    13   moderately support
    17   moderately oppose
    59   strongly oppose
    6   (unsure)
    N = 1511

Source: *The Reid Report*, January 1989, 26, September 1989, 3, January 1990, 16, and November/December 1990, 11.

January 1990

Would you be in favour of or opposed to a 7 per cent federal Goods and Services Tax?

27%   in favour
68   opposed
 5   (unsure)
N = 1501

November/December 1990

Overall, do you yourself support or oppose the proposed federal Goods and Services Tax, or GST?

7%   strongly support
21   moderately support
21   moderately oppose
47   strongly oppose
 4   (unsure)
N=1500

2.3. PUBLIC OPINION ON TAX-INCLUDED PRICING IN THE GST, 1989–90*

Angus Reid Group, January 1989

Suppose that the new federal sales tax were introduced. Would you prefer to have this tax as an additional charge calculated at the time that purchases are made, or would you prefer to have this tax already included in the advertised price of goods and services? (The total cost paid would be the same in both cases.)

29%   additional charge at time of purchase
67   included in price
 4   (unsure)
N = 1503

---

*Sources: The Reid Report, November/December 1990, 11; Decima Quarterly, Fall 1989; and Focus Canada, October 1990. These data were previously presented in C. Page, '"Tax Bread – You're Dead": Policymaking at Odds with the Polls,' The Public Perspective (September-October 2001). The Decima and Environics data were also accessed through Queen's University, Centre for the Study of Democracy Archives.

Decima Research, Fall 1989

Some people say that if the new tax is going to be applied, it must be visible – that is, it must be shown separately on the price tags of all products that you purchase. Other people say that it doesn't matter if the tax is visible as long as there is a sign in the store telling you the tax is included in the price and your tax register receipt shows that it has been paid. Thinking of these two points of view, which one is closest to your own?

64%   must be visible
35   doesn't matter
 1   no opinion
N = 1500

Environics Research Group, October 1990

If the GST does come into effect, would you prefer to have the tax included in the ticket price of items or would you prefer the tax calculated and added at the cash register?

49%   included
45   calculated and added at the cash register
 6   (don't know/no answer)
N = 2019

2.4. EXCERPT FROM A STUDY ON THE GST*

Decima Research, November 1989

Arguements [*sic*] in favour of the GST

	Saying Strong Argument	Saying Best Argument
To help products be competitive	46%	23%
To reduce deficit	42	32
To guarantee programs	50	40

Source: Decima Research, 'A Report to the Department of Finance,' November 1989, 25.

Appendices 3.1–3.2
Polling on Gun Control

3.1. SELECTED PUBLIC POLLING ON GUN CONTROL, 1993–4*

Angus Reid Group, October 1993

There are approximately 5 million legally owned rifles and shotguns in Canada, most of which are used for hunting, target shooting and pest control. Federal laws do not currently require the registration of these firearms and therefore there is no record of who owns these weapons. It has been suggested that all firearms used for hunting and other sporting activities be registered with law enforcement authorities. Overall, do you support or oppose requiring all hunting and sporting guns in Canada to be registered?

76% Support strongly
10 Support moderately
5 Oppose moderately
7 Oppose strongly
2 Unsure
N = 1509

Angus Reid Group, October 1994

There's been some discussion and debate recently about Canada's gun control laws. Thinking broadly about this issue, what do you yourself think should be done in terms of Canada's gun control laws? Should

*Source: The Reid Report, October 1993, 32, and October 1994, 27; The Gallup Report (Toronto), 21 November 1994, 2.

our gun control laws be changed so that there are tighter restrictions on gun ownership; should our gun control laws be changed so that there are fewer restrictions on guns and gun ownership; or, should no changes be made to Canada's gun control laws?

70% Tighter restrictions
 5   Fewer restrictions
23   No changes
 2   Unsure
N = 1504

Gallup, November 1994

Would you favour or oppose a law that would require all firearms in Canada to be registered with the federal government?

83% Favour
14   Oppose
 2   No opinion
N = 1011

3.2. EXCERPTS FROM A POLL ON GUN CONTROL FOR THE SASKATCHEWAN GOVERNMENT, 1995*

Canwest Opinion, January 1995

1. Do you think registration of firearms would cause a decrease in crime in your community? IF YES: It has been suggested by some that the cost of a firearms registry, estimated at as much as $100 million, could be better spent on other aspects of crime control, such as increased policing. Do you think a firearms registry would be the best use of this money?

86.4% No
12.2   Yes
 1.4   Don't know

Of the 12.2 per cent who said that a firearms registry would cause a decrease in crime, 45.9 per cent said it would the best use of this money while 39.3 per cent said it would not be.

---

*Source: Canwest Opinion, 'A Survey of Saskatchewan Residents,' January 1995.

2. Canada's Auditor-General has said that our existing firearms control program has not been properly evaluated. Would you support an evaluation to see how current firearms laws are working before any new changes are made?

    73.2%   Yes
    24.3   No
     2.5   Don't know
    N = 1497

Appendix 4
Selected Interview Sources

Interviews were conducted between 1997 and 2000 with ninety-five current and former pollsters, journalists, elected officials, public servants, and partisan officials with government experience. Requests for interviews with government officials were made to those identified as having familiarity with opinion research and/or one of the three policy areas under intensive study.

A majority of these interviews were based on a common script. Questions were prepared seeking general information about how opinion research is employed in the policy process. For the remainder of the interviewees, information was sought about a particular policy area pursued in a case study and questions were geared to the specific experience of each source. Most interviews took between fifty and ninety minutes. Three interviews were conducted by telephone; all the rest were conducted in person, usually in offices. All except five were tape-recorded and then transcribed.

Conditions for the use of the interviews varied according to the wishes of sources: some agreed to have the entire interview for attribution, others participated on a not-for-attribution basis, and still others granted permission later to attribute specific portions of the interview that were presented to them in writing. This flexibility was essential because many sources, especially public servants, would have been unable or unwilling to speak candidly if the interviews had been for attribution. This applies particularly to the interviews on gun control, a policy still being implemented and one so controversial that some officials at the Department of Justice had received death threats.

On the main concerns of this study – especially the extent to which opinion research influences the content of policy and government communications – I examined whether consistent patterns could be found within and across interviews. For the most part, consistency prevailed. In particular, the pattern of responses from pollsters and government officials revealed broad agreement about the nature and extent of the impact of opinion research on policy content and communications.

Following is a partial list of interviewees, including former positions and/or positions held at the time of the interview, and the city in which the interview took place. (Many of the sources have changed jobs since their experience relevant to this research; as well, several have different positions than at the time of the interview.)

Bruce Anderson: principal, Earnscliffe Research and Communications; former president, Decima Research; Ottawa.

Jane Armstrong: vice president, Environics Research Group; Toronto.

Thomas Axworthy: former principal secretary, Prime Minister's Office; Toronto and Kingston.

Chris Baker: vice president, Ottawa, Environics Research Group; former special assistant (Opinion Research), Policy and Research Unit, Prime Minister's Office; Ottawa.

Earl Berger: associate director, Policy, Hay Health Care Consulting Group; Toronto.

Don Blenkarn: former chair, Parliamentary Standing Committee on Finance; Mississauga.

Gary Breen: principal, Gary Breen and Associates; former assistant secretary to cabinet, Communications and Consultations; Ottawa.

Darrell Bricker: president and chief operating officer, Angus Reid Group; Ottawa and Toronto.

John Bryden: MP; Ottawa.

Murray Calder: MP; Ottawa.

Mike Colledge: senior vice president, Angus Reid Group; Ottawa.

David Crapper: chairman, Decima Research; Ottawa.

Rex Crawford: former MP; telephone interview.

Donna Dasko: senior vice president, Environics Research Group; Toronto.

Stan Dromisky: MP; Ottawa.

Hershell Ezrin: former director, Canadian Unity Information Office; Toronto.

Kevin Finnerty: acting manager, corporate issues, Cabinet Office, Ontario; Toronto.

Daniel Gagnier: former deputy secretary to cabinet, Communications

and Consultations; former principal secretary to the Premier of
Ontario; Montreal.
Roger Gallaway: MP; Ottawa.
Martin Goldfarb: chairman, Goldfarb Consultants; Toronto.
Fred Gorbet: former deputy minister, Department of Finance; Toronto.
Grégoire Gollin: president, Créatec+; Montreal.
Ed Greenspon: Ottawa bureau chief, the *Globe and Mail*; Ottawa.
Don Guy: vice president, Public Affairs, Pollara; Toronto.
David Herle: principal, Earnscliffe Strategy Group; Ottawa.
Grant Hill: MP; Ottawa.
Leonard Hopkins: former MP; telephone interview.
Stephen Kiar: senior partner, COMPAS; Ottawa.
Michael Kirby: senator; former deputy clerk of the Privy Council;
    former vice president, Goldfarb Consultants; Ottawa.
Marc Lalonde: former minister of finance; Montreal.
John Laschinger: senior research associate, Northstar Research Part-
    ners; Toronto.
Derek Leebosh: senior analyst, Environics Research Group; Toronto.
Peter Leslie: former assistant secretary to cabinet, policy development,
    Federal-Provincial Relations Office; Kingston.
Marjorie MacPherson: senior vice president, Decima Research;
    Toronto.
Michael Marzolini: chairman, Pollara; Toronto.
Ian McKinnon: principal, Pacific Issues Partners; former president,
    Decima Research; Victoria.
Peter Milliken: MP; Kingston.
Dennis Mills: MP; Ottawa.
Lowell Murray: senator; former minister of state for federal-provincial
    relations; Ottawa and Kingston.
Bob Parkins: former chairman, GST Communications Task Force;
    Ottawa.
Maurice Pinard: professor emeritus, sociology, McGill University;
    opinion research consultant; Montreal.
Bob Plamondon: former special adviser [GST Ministerial Resource
    Group], Department of Finance; Ottawa.
Angus Reid: chairman and chief executive officer, Angus Reid Group;
    Vancouver.
Bob Richardson: senior vice president, Angus Reid Group; Toronto.
Michael Sabia: former director of sales and excise tax, Finance Canada;
    telephone interview.

Hugh Segal: former chief of staff, Prime Minister's Office; former principal secretary to the premier of Ontario; Kingston.

Alex Shepherd: MP; Ottawa.

Paul Steckle: MP; Ottawa.

Andrew Sullivan: senior consultant, Ekos Research Associates; Ottawa.

Michael Sullivan: partner, Gregg, Kelly, Sullivan and Woolstencroft: The Strategic Counsel; former senior vice president, Decima Research; Toronto.

Roger Tassé: former deputy minister of justice; Ottawa.

Tom Wappel: MP; Ottawa.

Michael Wilson: former minister of finance, Toronto.

Conrad Winn: chief executive officer, COMPAS; Ottawa.

Hugh Winsor: national political editor, the *Globe and Mail*; Ottawa.

Notes

Introduction

1 *Globe and Mail*, 3 October 1992, A1, A2.
2 See L.R. Jacobs and R.Y. Shapiro, 'Studying Substantive Democracy,' *PS: Political Science and Politics* (March 1994), esp. 11.
3 See, for example, G. Gallup and S.F. Rae, *The Pulse of Democracy: The Public-Opinion Poll and How It Works* (New York: Simon and Schuster, 1940); and A.M. Crossley, 'Straw Polls in 1936,' *Public Opinion Quarterly* (January 1937).
4 See, for example, F. Newport, *Polling Matters: Why Leaders Must Listen to the Wisdom of the People* (New York: Warner Books, 2004). Other examples of pollsters arguing that opinion polling contributes to democracy include J.M. Stonecash, *Political Polling: Strategic Information in Campaigns* (Lanham, MD: Rowman and Littlefield, 2003), esp. 141–3; K.F. Warren, *In Defense of Public Opinion Polling* (Boulder, CO: Westview Press, 2001); C. Lake and J. Sosin, 'Public Opinion Polling and the Future of Democracy,' *National Civic Review* (Spring 1998); and H. Taylor, 'Polling, Good Government, and Democracy,' *Public Perspective* (July/August 2000), esp. 34.
5 I. Crespi, *The Public Opinion Process: How the People Speak* (Mahwah, NJ: Lawrence Erlbaum Associates, 1997), 157.
6 For example, B. Ginsberg, 'How Polling Transforms Public Opinion' in M. Margolis and G.A. Mauser, eds., *Manipulating Public Opinion: Essays on Public Opinion as a Dependent Variable* (Pacific Grove, CA: Brooks/Cole, 1989).
7 *Wall Street Journal*, 23 March 1994, A16.
8 Appendix 4 explains how the interviews were conducted and lists many of the interviewees. Quotations without endnotes, whether confidential or

attributed, are from the interviews. As well, readers should note that in most cases where I have drawn on confidential interviews for quotations or other material, these have not been given endnotes.

9 Many of the sources have changed positions since the events discussed here or since they were interviewed for this project. For example, Chris Baker left Environics to establish Continuum Research, and Steve Kiar left COMPAS and is now with Phoenix Strategic Perspectives. As well, some of the public servants have left government. The text normally refers to the position relevant to the discussion.

10 See R.Y. Shapiro and L.R. Jacobs, 'Presidents and Polling: Politicians, Pandering, and the Study of Democratic Responsiveness,' *Presidential Studies Quarterly* (March 2001), 156–7. For a description of a study that employs interviews and a case study approach to investigate the agenda-setting phase of the policy process, see J.W. Kingdon, *Agendas, Alternatives, and Public Policies*, 2nd ed. (New York: Harper Collins, 1995), appendix, esp. 232–42.

11 Issue salience in American and British foreign policy is explored in S.N. Soroka, 'Media, Public Opinion, and Foreign Policy,' *Harvard International Journal of Press and Politics* (Winter 2003), esp. 34. The relationship between salience of issues and responsive policy-making is also addressed in A. Monroe, 'Public Opinion and Public Policy, 1980–1993,' *Public Opinion Quarterly* (Spring 1998), 20–2.

1. Public Opinion and Polling

1 G. Gallup and S.F. Rae, *The Pulse of Democracy: The Public-Opinion Poll and How It Works* (New York: Simon and Schuster, 1940), 14.

2 A.M. Crossley, 'Straw Polls in 1936,' *Public Opinion Quarterly* (January 1937), 35. For more on early ideas about the democratic potential of polling, see J.L. Woodward, 'Public Opinion Polls as an Aid to Democracy,' *Political Science Quarterly* (June 1946), 246; S. Ewen, *PR! A Social History of Spin* (New York: Basic Books, 1996), 187; L. Dion, 'Democracy as Perceived by Public Opinion Analysts,' in R.S. Blair and J.T. McLeod, eds., *The Canadian Political Tradition* (Scarborough, ON: Nelson, 1987 [1962]), esp. 200–6; D.J. Robinson, *The Measure of Democracy: Polling, Market Research and Public Life, 1930–1945* (Toronto: University of Toronto Press, 1999), chap. 2; and P.M. Converse, 'Changing Conceptions of Public Opinion in the Political Process,' *Public Opinion Quarterly* (Winter 1987, special supplement), S15.

3 See *Toronto Daily Star*, 29 November 1941, 2; A.A. Porter, 'After Victory, What ...?' *Canadian Business* (December 1942); W. Sanders, 'How Good Is

the Canadian Gallup Poll?' *Public Affairs* (Spring 1943), 138–9; and Robinson, *The Measure of Democracy*, chap. 3.

4 J. Brehm, *The Phantom Respondents: Opinion Surveys and Political Representation* (Ann Arbor: University of Michigan Press, 1993) 6.

5 J.G. Geer, *From Tea Leaves to Opinion Polls: A Theory of Democratic Leadership* (New York: Columbia University Press, 1996); B. Ginsberg, *The Captive Public: How Mass Opinion Promotes State Power* (New York: Basic Books, 1986), and 'How Polling Transforms Public Opinion,' in M. Mar-golis and G.A. Mauser, eds., *Manipulating Public Opinion: Essays on Public Opinion as a Dependent Variable* (Pacific Grove, CA: Brooks/Cole, 1989).

6 R. Dyck, *Canadian Politics: Critical Approaches*, 2nd ed. (Scarborough, ON: Nelson, 1996), 332–3.

7 I. Greene, C. Baar, P. McCormick, G. Szablowski, and M. Thomas, *Final Appeal: Decision-Making in Canadian Courts of Appeal* (Toronto: James Lorimer, 1998), 41.

8 A. Siegel, *Politics and the Media in Canada*, 2nd ed. (Toronto: McGraw-Hill Ryerson, 1996), 27.

9 J. Simpson, 'Pollstruck,' *Policy Options* (March 1987), 4.

10 C. Hoy, *Margin of Error: Pollsters and the Manipulation of Canadian Politics* (Toronto: Key Porter Books, 1989), 8.

11 *Maclean's*, 27 October 1980, 4.

12 See M. Goldfarb, 'Introduction,' in M. Goldfarb and T. Axworthy, *Marching to a Different Drummer: An Essay on the Liberals and Conservatives in Convention* (Toronto: Stoddart, 1988); M. Adams, 'Pro Polling,' *Policy Options* (July 1987); J. Armstrong, 'Plug in Some New Thinking,' *Globe and Mail*, 4 February 2003, A15; A. Turcotte, 'Government by Polling: Do Not Kill the Messenger,' in C. Mowers, ed., *Towards a New Liberalism: Re-creating Canada and the Liberal Party* (Victoria: Orca Book Publishers, 1991); and H. Segal, 'Public Opinion and Public Policy: How Should They Relate?' in C. Cassidy, P. Clark, and W. Petrozzi, eds., *Authority and Influence: Institutions, Issues and Concepts in Canadian Politics* (Oakville, ON: Mosaic, 1985 [1981]).

13 Adams, 'Pro Polling,' 30.

14 Goldfarb, 'Introduction,' xx.

15 F. Newport, *Polling Matters: Why Leaders Must Listen to the Wisdom of the People* (New York: Warner Books, 2004).

16 See R. Weissberg, *Polling, Policy, and Public Opinion: The Case against Heeding the 'Voice of the People'* (New York: Palgrave, 2002).

17 S. Quilliam, 'Government by Polling: The Erosion of Democracy,' in Mowers, ed., *Towards a New Liberalism*, 178.

18 L.J. Sabato, *The Rise of Political Consultants: New Ways of Winning Elections*

(New York: Basic Books, 1981), 314–21. 'Qube' was an experiment with using television to promote participatory democracy through non-random surveys.

19 Ginsberg, 'How Polling Transforms Public Opinion.'

20 Besides Ginsberg's essay, other sources reflecting or discussing this perspective include S. Herbst, 'Surveys in the Public Sphere: Applying Bourdieu's Critique of Opinion Polls,' *International Journal of Public Opinion Research* (Autumn 1992)' and *Numbered Voices: How Opinion Polling Has Shaped American Politics* (Chicago: University of Chicago Press, 1993); and B.I. Page and R.Y. Shapiro, 'Educating and Manipulating the Public,' in Margolis and Mauser, eds., *Manipulating Public Opinion.*

21 D. Easton, *A Systems Analysis of Political Life* (New York: John Wiley, 1965), 363–72.

22 Ibid., 22, 24–5.

23 R. Johnston, *Public Opinion and Public Policy in Canada: Questions of Confidence* (Toronto: University of Toronto Press, 1986).

24 Easton, *A Systems Analysis of Political Life*, 414.

25 K. O'Connor and L.J. Sabato, *American Government: Roots and Reform*, brief ed. (New York: Macmillan, 1994), 346. The main purpose of the present discussion is to show that public opinion can be gauged through means other than opinion research. Although it is beyond the scope of this book, the meaning of public opinion has been extensively if inconclusively debated. See, for example, the five definitions outlined by C.J. Glynn, S. Herbst, G.J. O'Keefe, and R.Y. Shapiro, *Public Opinion* (Boulder, CO: Westview Press, 1999), 16–29.

26 V.O. Key, *Public Opinion and American Democracy* (New York: Alfred A. Knopf, 1961), 421, 552–3.

27 R.S. Erikson, M.B. MacKuen, and J.A. Stimson, *The Macro Polity* (Cambridge: Cambridge University Press, 2002).

28 This distinction is based on the discussion of polls and other methods of expressing public opinion in Ginsberg, *The Captive Public*, esp. chap. 3.

29 A. Fried, *Muffled Echoes: Oliver North and the Politics of Public Opinion* (New York: Columbia University Press), 103.

30 See S. Verba, 'The Citizen as Respondent: Sample Surveys and American Democracy,' *American Political Science Review* (March 1996).

31 J.R. Pennock, *Democratic Political Theory* (Princeton, NJ: Princeton University Press, 1979), 261. See also M. Saward, *The Terms of Democracy* (Cambridge: Polity Press, 1998), esp. 50–3.

32 Pennock, *Democratic Political Theory*, 262.

33 H. Asher, *Polling and the Public: What Every Citizen Should Know* (Washington: CQ Press, 1988), 59; and Gallup and Rae, *The Pulse of Democracy*, 56–7.

34 To simplify somewhat, this means that a reported result with a representative sample of this size would be within three percentage points of the result that would have been achieved if the entire population was surveyed, in 95 per cent of cases. So if a poll indicates that 50 per cent of respondents take a particular position, it might be said that the actual result would be between 47 and 53 per cent, nineteen times out of twenty.

35 M. Sullivan interview.

36 Communication Canada, *Public Opinion Research in the Government of Canada, Annual Report, 2002–2003* (Ottawa: Communication Canada, 2003), 21.

37 B.P. Sigman and S.-K. McDonald, 'The Issues Manager as Public Opinion and Policy Analyst,' in A.A. Marcus, A.M. Kaufman, and D.R. Beam, eds., *Business Strategy and Public Policy: Perspectives from Industry and Academia* (New York: Quorum Books, 1987), 173.

38 See A. Reid, 'Public Affairs Research: Quantitative and Qualitative,' in W.J. Wright and C.J. Du Vernet, eds., *The Canadian Public Affairs Handbook: Maximizing Markets, Protecting Bottom Lines* (Toronto: Carswell, 1988), 123–4.

39 N. Moon, *Opinion Polls: History, Theory and Practice* (Manchester: Manchester University Press, 1999), 178.

2. Public Opinion and Policy-making

1 J.E. Brooks, 'Democratic Frustration in the Anglo-American Polities: A Quantification of Inconsistency between Mass Public Opinion and Public Policy,' *Western Political Quarterly* (June 1985).

2 An example is V.O. Key, *Public Opinion and American Democracy* (New York: Alfred A. Knopf, 1961). See also R. Dyck, *Canadian Politics: Critical Approaches*, 2nd ed. (Scarborough, ON: Nelson, 1996), 335.

3 R.A. Bernstein, *Elections, Representation, and Congressional Voting Behavior: The Myth of Constituency Control* (Englewood Cliffs, NJ: Prentice-Hall, 1989), xiv.

4 Examples include R.A. Dahl, *Dilemmas of Pluralist Democracy: Autonomy vs. Control* (New Haven, CT: Yale University Press, 1982); and C. Lindblom, *Politics and Markets: The World's Political-Economic Systems* (New York: Basic Books, 1977).

5 Brooks cites C.W. Mills, *The Power Elite* (New York: Oxford University Press, 1956) and R. Miliband, *The State in Capitalist Society* (London: Weidenfeld and Nicholson, 1969). Sources which connect polling to elite leadership include B. Ginsberg, 'How Polling Transforms Public Opinion' in M. Margolis and G.A. Mauser, eds., *Manipulating Public Opinion: Essays on Public Opinion as a Dependent Variable* (Pacific Grove, CA: Brooks/Cole, 1989); S. Herbst, *Numbered Voices: How Opinion Polling Has Shaped American*

Politics (Chicago: University of Chicago Press, 1993); and L. Peer, 'The Practice of Opinion Polling as a Disciplinary Mechanism: A Foucauldian Perspective,' *International Journal of Public Opinion Research* (Autumn 1992).

6 See, for example, P.J. Lavrakas and M.W. Traugott, eds., *Election Polls, the News Media and Democracy* (New York: Seven Bridges Press, 2000). Canadian examples include A. Frizzell and A. Westell, *The Canadian General Election of 1984: Politicians, Parties, Press and Polls* (Ottawa: Carleton University Press, 1985), chap. 4; G. Lachapelle, *Polls and the Media in Canadian Elections: Taking the Pulse* (Toronto: Dundurn Press, 1991); P.S. MacIntosh, 'Questions, Questions, Questions: Polls, Politics and the Press in Canada,' in P.W. Fox and G. White, eds., *Politics: Canada,* 8th ed. (Toronto: McGraw-Hill Ryerson, 1995); and D. Taras, *The Newsmakers: The Media's influence on Canadian Politics* (Scarborough, ON: Nelson, 1990), chap. 7.

7 For example, M. Adams, *Sex in the Snow: Canadian Social Values at the End of the Millennium* (Toronto: Viking, 1997), and *Fire and Ice: The United States, Canada and the Myth of Converging Values* (Toronto: Penguin, 2003); and F.L. Graves, 'The Economy through a Public Lens: Shifting Canadian Views of the Economy,' in K. Banting, A. Sharpe, and F. St-Hilaire, eds., *The Review of Economic Performance and Social Progress* (Montreal: Institute for Research on Public Policy, 2001).

8 In addition, a number of sources consider the relationship between legislative voting behaviour and public opinion. The classic source, which reports modest consistency between the two in 1958, is W.E. Miller and D.E. Stokes, 'Constituency Influence in Congress,' in N.R. Luttbeg, ed., *Public Opinion and Public Policy: Models of Political Linkage* (Homewood, IL: Dorsey Press, 1968 [1963]). However, research on the U.S. Congress has limited relevance to Canada as the latter's Parliament is much less powerful than the executive and operates differently.

A further group of sources uses indicators of public opinion other than polls on policy, such as survey data on Americans' self-reported liberalism and conservatism. Examples include R.S. Erikson, G.C. Wright, and J.P. McIver, *Statehouse Democracy: Public Opinion and Policy in the American States* (Cambridge: Cambridge University Press, 1993); and R.S. Erikson, M.B. MacKuen, and J.A. Stimson, *The Macro Polity* (Cambridge: Cambridge University Press, 2002). A critique of this approach can be found in L.R. Jacobs and R.Y. Shapiro, 'Politics and Policymaking in the Real World: Crafted Talk and the Loss of Democratic Responsiveness,' in J. Manza, F. Lomax Cook, and B.I. Page, eds., *Navigating Public Opinion: Polls, Policy and the Future of American Democracy* (New York: Oxford University Press, 2002), 68–73.

9 P. Burstein, 'The Impact of Public Opinion on Public Policy: A Review and an Agenda,' *Political Research Quarterly* (March 2003), esp. 32–4.

10 A similar view is expressed in B.I. Page, 'The Semi-Sovereign Public,' in Manza, Cook, and Page, eds., *Navigating Public Opinion*, 326.

11 Brooks, 'Democratic Frustration in the Anglo-American Polities.'

12 A.D. Monroe, 'Consistency between Public Preferences and National Policy Decisions,' *American Politics Quarterly* (January 1979).

13 A.D. Monroe, 'Public Opinion and Public Policy, 1980–1993,' *Public Opinion Quarterly* (Spring 1998).

14 A.D. Monroe, 'Public Opinion and Public Policy, 1960–1999,' paper presented at the annual meeting of the American Political Science Association, San Francisco, 2001.

15 Monroe, 'Consistency between Public Preferences and National Policy Decisions,' 17, and 'Public Opinion and Public Policy, 1980–1993,' 14–19.

16 F. Pétry, *The Impact of Public Opinion on Public Policy in Canada* (Ste-Foy, QC: Laboratoire d'études politiques de l'Université Laval, 1995), 18. See also F. Pétry, 'The Opinion-Policy Relationship in Canada,' *Journal of Politics* (May 1999), 543.

17 F. Pétry, 'The Opinion Policy Relationship in Canada,' paper presented at the annual meeting of the Canadian Political Science Association, Quebec City, 2001, 12.

18 B.I. Page and R.Y. Shapiro, 'Effects of Public Opinion on Policy,' *American Political Science Review* (March 1983). These authors look at policy outputs two years before the first survey and four years after the final one. They find plausible reasons for excluding 80 per cent of their cases without policy change (for example, based on pre-policy activity as a form of responsiveness, or policies which have hit floors or ceilings), but then they proceed to exclude the other 20 per cent as well.

19 T. Hartley and B. Russett, 'Public Opinion and the Common Defense: Who Governs Military Spending in the United States?' *American Political Science Review* (December 1992).

20 C. Wlezien, 'Dynamics of Representation: The Case of US Spending on Defence,' *British Journal of Political Science* (January 1996), esp. 97, 100. See also R.Y. Shapiro and B.I. Page, 'Foreign Policy and Public Opinion,' in D.A. Deese, ed., *The New Politics of American Foreign Policy* (New York: St. Martin's Press, 1994).

21 See C. Wlezien, 'Patterns of Representation: Dynamics of Public Preferences and Policy,' *Journal of Politics* (February 2004).

22 S.N. Soroka and C. Wlezien, 'Opinion Representation and Policy Feed-

back: Canada in Comparative Perspective,' *Canadian Journal of Political Science*, forthcoming.

23 See R.M. Entman and S. Herbst, 'Reframing Public Opinion as We Have Known It,' in W.L. Bennett and R.M. Entman, eds., *Mediated Politics: Communication in the Future of Democracy* (Cambridge: Cambridge University Press, 2001), 211–19.

24 See Miller and Stokes, 'Constituency Influence in Congress,' 412; L. Powell, 'Issue Representation in Congress,' *Journal of Politics* (August 1982); and J.W. Kingdon, *Congressmen's Voting Decisions*, 3rd ed. (Ann Arbor: University of Michigan Press, 1989), 45–7.

25 See B.I. Page and R.Y. Shapiro, 'Educating and Manipulating the Public,' in M. Margolis and G.A. Mauser, eds., *Manipulating Public Opinion* (Pacific Grove, CA: Brooks/Cole, 1989); and B.I. Page, 'Democratic Responsiveness? Untangling the Links between Public Opinion and Public Policy,' *PS: Political Science and Politics* (March 1994).

26 Kingdon explores factors influencing voting decisions of members of the U.S. House of Representatives, including interest groups, the mass media, and feedback from constituents (*Congressmen's Voting Decisions*, esp. chaps. 2, 5, and 8).

27 General sources include A.H. Cantril, ed., 'The User's Perspective: A Round Table on the Impact of Polls,' in Cantril, ed., *Polling on the Issues* (Cabin John, MD: Seven Locks Press, 1980); and D. Foyle, *Counting the Public In: Presidents, Public Opinion and Foreign Policy* (New York: Columbia University Press, 1999). Sources on uses of polling by Presidents Franklin Roosevelt, Ronald Reagan, and Lyndon Johnson include H. Cantril, *The Human Dimension: Experiences in Policy Research* (New Brunswick, NJ: Rutgers University Press, 1967), esp. 41–2, 71–3; R.S. Beal and R.H. Hinckley, 'Presidential Decision Making and Opinion Polls,' in *Annals of the American Academy of Political and Social Science* (March 1984); L.R. Jacobs and R.Y. Shapiro, 'Lyndon Johnson, Vietnam, and Public Opinion: Rethinking Realist Theory of Leadership,' *Presidential Studies Quarterly* (September 1999); and B.E. Altschuler, *LBJ and the Polls* (Gainesville: University of Florida Press, 1990).

28 R.Y. Shapiro and L.R. Jacobs, 'Public Opinion, Foreign Policy and Democracy,' in Manza, Cook, and Page, eds., *Navigating Public Opinion*, 194–5.

29 *Wall Street Journal*, 23 March 1994, A16.

30 D. Morris, *Behind the Oval Office: Winning the Presidency in the Nineties* (New York: Random House, 1997).

31 Examples include G. Wills, 'The Real Scandal' (Review of Morris, *Behind*

the Oval Office), *New York Review of Books*, 20 February 1997; and J.D. Mayer and L. Kirby, 'The Promise and Peril of Presidential Polling: Between Gallup's Dream and Morris's Nightmare,' in S.J. Wayne, ed., *Is This Any Way to Run a Democratic Government?* (Washington: Georgetown University Press, 2004).

32 J.F. Harris's interview with Ickes, cited in Harris, 'A Clouded Mirror: Bill Clinton, Polls, and the Politics of Survival,' in S.E. Schier, ed., *The Postmodern Presidency: Bill Clinton's Legacy in U.S. Politics* (Pittsburgh: University of Pittsburgh Press, 2000), 94–5.

33 G. Stephanopoulos, *All Too Human: A Political Education* (Boston: Little, Brown, 1999), 329–30, 334.

34 R.B. Reich, *Locked in the Cabinet* (New York: Alfred A. Knopf, 1997), 261.

35 D. Morris, *Behind the Oval Office*, new ed. (Los Angeles: Renaissance Press, 1999), 583.

36 Ibid., 227.

37 L.R. Jacobs and R.Y. Shapiro, 'Public Opinion in President Clinton's First Year: Leadership and Responsiveness,' in S.A. Renshon, ed., *The Clinton Presidency: Campaigning, Governing, and the Psychology of Leadership* (Boulder, CO: Westview Press, 1995), 208.

38 H. Kurtz, *Spin Cycle*, rev. ed. (New York: Simon and Schuster, 1998), 249.

39 This paragraph draws on Reich, *Locked in the Cabinet*, 271–7, 300.

40 See Morris, *Behind the Oval Office*, new ed., 208–9, 389–401; L.R. Jacobs and R.Y. Shapiro, 'The Politicization of Public Opinion: The Fight for the Pulpit,' in M. Weir, ed., *The Social Divide: Political Parties and the Future of Activist Government* (Washington: Brookings Institution, 1998), 95; and E. Drew, *Showdown: The Struggle between the Gingrich Congress and the Clinton White House* (New York: Simon and Schuster, 1996), 226, 287.

41 R.S. Morris, 'Grand Jury Testimony,' 18 August 1998, in communication from the Office of the Independent Counsel, Kenneth W. Starr (documents released 2 October 1998), http://cnn.com/icreport/report2/suppm/suppm114.gif.

42 Stephanopoulos, *All Too Human*, 436.

43 The following discussion stresses the presidency rather than the congressional Republicans, because the latter are less relevant to Canada due to the relative weakness of Parliament.

44 L.R. Jacobs and R.Y. Shapiro, *Politicians Don't Pander: Political Manipulation and the Loss of Democratic Responsiveness* (Chicago: University of Chicago Press, 2000), 279–81.

45 Ibid., 55.

46　Ibid., 323–4.

47　See Morris, *Behind the Oval Office*, 84–6, 93, 183–5, 215–17, 219–220, 281.

48　R.M. Eisinger, *The Evolution of Presidential Polling* (Cambridge: Cambridge University Press, 2003), esp. 187–8.

49　D.J. Heith, *Polling to Govern: The Presidency and Presidential Leadership* (Stanford, CA: Stanford University Press, 2004), esp. 120–1, 137.

50　M.J. Towle, *Out of Touch: The Presidency and Public Opinion* (College Station: Texas A&M University Press, 2004), esp. 113–15.

51　E. Gidengil, 'Bringing Politics Back in: Recent Developments in the Study of Public Opinion in Canada,' in J. Everitt and B. O'Neill, eds., *Citizen Politics: Research and Theory in Canadian Political Behaviour* (Toronto: Oxford University Press, 2002).

52　The following two paragraphs draw on G. Evans, *John Grierson and the National Film Board: The Politics of Wartime Propaganda, 1939–1945* (Toronto: University of Toronto Press, 1984), 90–109, 280–1, 292–4; D. J. Robinson, 'Polling Consumers and Citizens: Opinion Sample Surveys and the Rise of the Canadian Marketing Polity, 1928–1945' (PhD diss., York University, 1996), and *The Measure of Democracy: Polling, Market Research, and Public Life 1930–1945* (Toronto: University of Toronto Press, 1999), chap. 4.

53　Evans, *John Grierson and the National Film Board*, 91. Unfortunately no examples are provided.

54　Robinson, *The Measure of Democracy*, 95.

55　F. Schindeler and C.M. Lanphier, 'Social Science Research and Participatory Democracy in Canada,' *Canadian Public Administration* (Winter 1969).

56　P. Russell, 'A Democratic Approach to Civil Liberties,' *University of Toronto Law Journal* 19 (1969), 119–21.

57　C. Campbell and G.J. Szablowski, *The Superbureaucrats: Structure and Behaviour in Central Agencies* (Toronto: Macmillan, 1979), 199–202.

58　R. Gibbins, 'The Mythical Man in the Street,' *Parliamentary Government* 4, no. 4 (1984), 4. Similar views are expressed in J. Meisel, 'The Decline of Party in Canada,' in H.G. Thorburn, ed., *Party Politics in Canada*, 5th ed. (Scarborough, ON: Prentice-Hall, 1985), 106; and R. Fife and J. Warren, *A Capital Scandal* (Toronto: Key Porter Books, 1991), 249.

59　See N. Pawelek, 'For Whom the Polls Tell: Politics in the Information Age,' *Parliamentary Government* 4, no. 4 (1984); and L. Bozinoff et al., 'Roundtable. Public Opinion: Myths and Realities,' *Canadian Parliamentary Review* (Summer 1991).

60　*Maclean's*, 27 October 1980, 4.

61　Quoted by R.C. Drews, 'Electoral Manipulation and the Influence of Polling on Politicians' (MA thesis, McGill University, 1988), 200.

62 D. McLaughlin, *Poisoned Chalice: The Last Campaign of the Progressive Conservative Party?* (Toronto: Dundurn Press, 1994), 137–8.

63 V. Palmer, *Vancouver Sun*, 27 January 1993, A8.

64 G. Brimmell, 'Paid to Ask: Polling for Government Is Big Business,' *Summit* (December 2002), 12.

65 Quoted in *Montreal Gazette*, 26 August 1995, B1.

66 Drews, 'Electoral Manipulation,' 259.

67 Ibid., 213–14.

68 J.-F. Lisée, *The Trickster: Robert Bourassa and Quebecers, 1990–1992*, abridged English ed., trans. R. Chodos, S. Horn, and W. Taylor (Toronto: James Lorimer, 1994), esp. 44.

69 A. Roberts and J. Rose, 'Selling the Goods and Services Tax: Government Advertising and Public Discourse in Canada,' *Canadian Journal of Political Science* (June 1995).

3. The Practice and Framework of Opinion Research for Government in Canada

1 Treasury Board, 'Government Communications Policy,' 28 November 1996, Appendix D, Annex A, http://www.tbs-sct.gc.ca/Pubs_pol/sipubs/comm/comm_e.html. This definition also appears in Communication Canada, *Public Opinion Research in the Government of Canada: An Orientation Guide* (Ottawa: Communication Canada, 2002), 3, 5.

2 *Globe and Mail*, 20 October 1980, 10. On this point as it applies to the Quebec government, see also *Montreal Gazette*, 6 November 1982, A1, A4.

3 H. Winsor, *Globe and Mail*, 29 October 1997, A4.

4 H. Moroz, 'The Impact of Public Opinion Research on Policy Making with Particular Reference to the Privy Council Office and the Prime Minister's Office' (MA research essay [shortened version], Carleton University, 1987), 46–7; C. Hoy, *Margin of Error: Pollsters and the Manipulation of Canadian Politics* (Toronto: Key Porter Books, 1989), 52, 53; and R. Fife and J. Warren, *A Capital Scandal* (Toronto: Key Porter Books, 1991), 249.

5 *Globe and Mail*, 18 March 1994, A6.

6 *Globe and Mail*, 20 May 1998, A1, A2; Hill interview; and Reform Party, 'Liberal Government Spending on Opinion Polling and Research' (unpublished document, May 1998).

7 Communication Canada, *Public Opinion Research in the Government of Canada, Annual Report, 2002–2003* (Ottawa: Communication Canada, 2003), 19, 15. Custom research refers to studies initiated for the government, in contrast to syndicated studies. As well, public servants occasionally conduct opinion research themselves to save contracting costs.

8 *Globe and Mail*, 12 May 1994, A1, A6.

9 This paragraph draws on 'Liberal Government Spending on Opinion Polling and Research.' See also *Globe and Mail*, 11 February 1995, B7.

10 In 1998, Coopers and Lybrand and Price Waterhouse merged to form Price Waterhouse Coopers.

11 Guy interview; Kirby interview. See D. Walker, 'Pollsters, Consultants, and Party Politics,' in A.-G. Gagnon and A.B. Janguay, eds., *Canadian Parties in Transition* (Scarborough, ON: Nelson, 1989), 388–9.

12 W.T. Stanbury, *Business-Government Relations in Canada: Influencing Public Policy*, 2nd ed. (Scarborough, ON: Nelson, 1993), 310–11.

13 *Globe and Mail*, 15 December 2001, B1, B2.

14 *Globe and Mail*, 1 April 2002, A7.

15 Armstrong interview.

16 *Georgia Straight*, 6 November 1992.

17 This organization is now known as the Canadian Generic Pharmaceutical Association.

18 *Globe and Mail*, 14 November, 1997, A4. See also Hoy, *Margin of Error*, 183–6.

19 Interviews including Dasko interview and Richardson interview.

20 See the reply to Winsor's column by Lawrence Solomon (executive director, Consumer Policy Institute), letter, *Globe and Mail*, 4 December 1997, A24.

21 M. Sullivan interview.

22 Baker interview. Similar comments were made in Kirby interview; Goldfarb interview, and Breen interview. See G.A. Mauser and D.B. Kopel, '"Sorry, Wrong Number": Why Media Polls on Gun Control Are Often Unreliable,' *Political Communication* (January–March 1992).

23 Winsor interview; Greenspon interview; Guy interview; Alan Frizzell, quoted in J.P. Winter, ed., *The Silent Revolution: Media, Democracy, and the Free Trade Debate* (Ottawa: University of Ottawa Press, 1990), 115.

24 *Globe and Mail*, 30 December 2002, A13.

25 Winn interview.

26 Communication Canada, *Public Opinion Research in the Government of Canada, Annual Report, 2002–2003*, 19.

27 Guy interview. See S.D. Ferguson, 'Planning for Issues Management: The Communicator as Environmental Analyst,' *Canadian Journal of Communication* (Winter 1993), 741–2, 746.

28 Although Access to Information legislation helps to contain the practice, occasionally research of a partisan nature is done within publicly funded surveys (Walker, 'Pollsters, Consultants, and Party Politics,' 391). A spe-

cific example involving the Conservative government of 1979–80, before Access to Information legislation existed, is described by Robert Sheppard (*Globe and Mail*, 20 October 1980, 10). More recently, it has been claimed that publicly funded polls helped the Chrétien government decide to call an election in the fall of 2000, and that during the subsequent election campaign they influenced the Liberal party's strategy of attacking the Canadian Alliance's proposal for a flat tax (*Ottawa Citizen*, 8 May 2001, A3; *Globe and Mail*, 8 March 2001, A4).

29 See R.K. Carty, W. Cross, and L. Young, *Rebuilding Canadian Party Politics* (Vancouver: UBC Press, 2000), 191–2.

30 S. Clarkson, 'Yesterday's Man and His Blue Grits: Backward into the Future,' in A. Frizzell, J.H. Pammett, and A. Westell, eds., *The Canadian General Election of 1993* (Ottawa: Carleton University Press, 1994), 33.

31 Goldfarb interview.

32 K. Campbell, *Time and Chance: The Political Memoirs of Canada's First Woman Prime Minister* (Toronto: Doubleday, 1996), 228.

33 McKinnon interview.

34 'Liberal Government Polling and Opinion Research Contracts' (Reform Party Research, unpublished document, May 1998).

35 This responsibility was assigned to Communication Canada between 2002 and 2004 and to the Canada Information Office between 2000 and 2002. Before that, the responsible unit was the Communications Coordination Services Branch within the Public Works and Government Services Department.

36 Baker interview; Guy interview.

37 This paragraph draws on Baker interview; Leebosh interview; and four confidential interviews with civil servants.

38 This paragraph draws on four confidential interviews with public servants; Communication Canada, *Public Opinion Research in the Government of Canada*, 1–12, and 'Government of Canada Enhances Public Opinion Research Contracting Process,' media release, 12 June 2003. See also G. Brimmell, 'Paid to Ask: Polling for Government Is Big Business,' *Summit* (December 2002), 9–10.

39 A standard tendering procedure is still in place for contracts valued at over $400,000.

40 There is also growing use of the internet for government surveys, although questions about sampling remain.

41 Office of the Auditor-General, *Report of the Auditor-General of Canada – November 2003* (Ottawa: Minister of Public Works and Government Services, 2003), chap. 5.

42 M. Goldfarb, 'Introduction,' in M. Goldfarb and T. Axworthy, *Marching to a Different Drummer: An Essay on the Liberals and Conservatives in Convention* (Toronto: Stoddart, 1988).

43 This paragraph draws on 'Sole-sourced Opinion Polling and Research Contracts' (Reform Party Research, unpublished document, May 1998).

44 According to Gaudet, the government failed to provide data on sole-sourcing during 1994–5, although he asked for it in his Access to Information request (K. Gaudet, letter to information commissioner J. Grace, 6 February 1998).

45 The word 'patronage' is used in this context in a story in the *Toronto Star*, 30 June 1995, A11; the latter comment comes from a confidential interview with a pollster.

46 Winn interview.

47 These data appear in 'Government Opinion Polling and Research Contract Distribution' (Reform Party Research, unpublished document, May 1998). HRDC was split into two departments in December, 2003.

48 Guy interview.

49 Baker interview; Gollin interview; Goldfarb interview; McKinnon interview; A. Sullivan interview.

50 Baker interview; M. Sullivan interview; A. Sullivan interview; confidential interviews.

51 Armstrong interview.

52 See K. Kernaghan and D. Siegel, *Public Administration in Canada*, 3rd ed. (Scarborough, ON: Nelson, 1995), 355.

53 For example, Guy interview; Kiar interview; M. Sullivan interview; A. Sullivan interview.

54 Some former government officials warn against overestimating the amount of attention paid to polls by Mulroney (Segal interview) and Chrétien (Baker interview; Breen interview).

55 Goldfarb, 'Introduction,' xii.

56 Kiar interview. The fiscal dividend was a concept used after the Liberal government had achieved a balanced budget in 1997, referring to the situation where the government could contemplate a combination of new spending, tax cuts, and debt reduction.

4. An Overview of the Uses of Opinion Research in the Policy Process

1 This paragraph draws on three confidential interviews.

2 Guy interview; Winsor interview; Leebosh interview; Armstrong interview.

3 *Ottawa Citizen*, 29 May 1998, A1, A2. See also Susan D. Phillips with

Michael Orsini, 'Mapping the Links: Citizen Involvement in the Policy Process,' Canadian Policy Research Networks Discussion Paper F/21 (April 2002), at http://www.cprn.org/documents/11418_en.pdf.

4 A. Sullivan interview. The reference to James Fishkin concerns his studies of deliberative opinion research. See J. Fishkin, *Democracy and Deliberation: New Directions for Democratic Reform* (New Haven, CT: Yale University Press, 1991); and F.L. Graves, 'Towards National Reconciliation through Scientific Public Consultation' (Ottawa: Ekos Research Associates, 8 May 1996).

5 See G.B. Doern and R.W. Phidd, *Canadian Public Policy: Ideas, Structure, Process* (Toronto: Methuen, 1983), 94–106; J.E. Anderson, *Public Policy-Making*, 3rd ed. (New York: Holt, Rinehart and Winston, 1984), 19–21; M. Howlett and M. Ramesh, *Studying Public Policy: Policy Cycles and Policy Subsystems*, 2nd ed. (Toronto: Oxford University Press, 2003), part 3; and Moroz, 'The Impact of Public Opinion Research on Policy Making' (MA research essay, Carleton University, 1987), chap. 4.

6 The concept of agenda-setting is discussed in J.W. Kingdon, *Agendas, Alternatives, and Public Policies* (New York: HarperCollins, 1995), 3–5. Kingdon distinguishes between issues which receive attention and the smaller number of subjects which are 'up for an active decision.' Public opinion, however, plays only a small part in this analysis. For an ambitious study of agenda-setting in Canada that is alert to the significance of the mass media and public opinion, and to variation in the agenda-setting processes for different issues, see S.N. Soroka, *Agenda-Setting Dynamics in Canada* (Vancouver: UBC Press, 2002), esp. chaps. 5 and 6.

7 D. Morris, *Behind the Oval Office* (New York: Random House, 1997), 208–9.

8 A. Sullivan interview.

9 Guy interview.

10 McKinnon interview.

11 A. Sullivan interview.

12 McKinnon's comment may reflect how Decima's work differed from other pollsters. It is important to note that McKinnon considers advising on the development of policy options to be quite different from advising on policy decisions, which he says pollsters should avoid.

13 For example, M. Sullivan interview; McKinnon interview; Armstrong interview; Bricker interview; Marzolini interview.

14 For example, Derek Leebosh says this is done.

15 Bricker interview.

16 Confidential interview with a former public servant in the Department of Foreign Affairs.

17 Segal interview.

18 R.F. Adie and P.G. Thomas, *Canadian Public Administration*, 2nd ed. (Scarborough, ON: Prentice-Hall, 1987), 238; and S. Brooks and L. Miljan, *Public Policy in Canada*, 4th ed. (Toronto: Oxford University Press, 2003), 88.

19 *National Post*, 6 January 2000, A1; Leebosh interview.

20 McKinnon interview.

21 K. Kernaghan and D. Siegel, *Public Administration in Canada*, 3rd ed. (Scarborough, ON: Nelson, 1995), 176.

22 Adie and Thomas, *Canadian Public Administration*, 306–9.

23 Marzolini interview.

24 Kirby interview.

25 Segal interview.

5. Opinion Research and Government Communications

1 See J. Lewis, *Constructing Public Opinion: How Political Elites Do What They Like and Why We Seem to Go Along with It* (New York: Columbia University Press, 2001), 36–7.

2 Department of Justice, 'Firearms Act Now in Force,' media release, 1 December 1998.

3 *Montreal Gazette*, 6 March 1997, A1.

4 See J. Rose, *Making 'Pictures in Our Heads': Government Advertising in Canada* (Westport, CT: Praeger, 2000), esp. 92–4.

5 Sage Research, 'CPP Disability Benefits Program: Evaluation of Print Materials' (Mississauga, 4 March 1998).

6 See A. Roberts and J. Rose, 'Selling the Goods and Services Tax: Government Advertising and Public Discourse in Canada' *Canadian Journal of Political Science* (June 1995), 314.

7 Guy interview.

8 Berger interview.

9 R. Bernier, *Un siècle de propagande? Information, communication et marketing gouvernemental* (Sainte-Foy, QC: Presses de l'Université du Québec, 2001), chap. 9, esp. 184–5.

10 Colledge interview.

11 Reid interview.

12 Decima Research, 'A Decima Research Report to the Department of Finance Regarding the 1993 Budget' (Ottawa, June 1993), 3–5.

13 Insight Canada Research, 'A National Public Opinion Survey of Current Environmental Issues' (Toronto, November 1996), 39.

14 *Globe and Mail*, 4 May 2002, B1, B2.

15 Leebosh interview.

16 Kiar interview.

17 Reid interview.
18 McKinnon interview.
19 See, for example, Earnscliffe Research and Communications, 'Finance Canada Bank Merger Survey' (Ottawa, May 1998); and 'Questionnaire on Pension Issues' (Ottawa, 16 July 1997).
20 Two confidential interviews; and E. Greenspon and A. Wilson-Smith, *Double Vision: The Inside Story of the Liberals in Power* (Toronto: Doubleday, 1996), 275–7.
21 The Longwoods Research Group Limited, 'Print Advertising Test,' [for Revenue Customs and Excise] (Toronto, March 1990), esp. 8–9.
22 *Toronto Star*, 23 February 2000, A6.
23 *Maclean's*, 21 September 1992, 18.
24 Confidential interview. Since this interview in 1999, contradictory evidence has emerged on this question. The Ontario government's own opinion research indicated that one month after it commenced an advertising campaign attacking federal health care policy, Ontarians' support for the federal position had increased from 23 to 29 per cent, while disapproval fell from 71 to 61 per cent. However, the approval rating of the Ontario government's efforts on health also rose from 30 to 40 per cent and the federal government had initiated its own advertising campaign in response to the province's (*Toronto Star*, 8 July 2000, A2). A later federal poll indicated that the Ontario advertising campaign had been more successful than the federal campaign (*Ottawa Citizen*, 24 December 2000, A4).
25 See, for example, *Ottawa Citizen*, 17 August 1999, A3; and Communication Canada, *A Year of Review: Annual Report on the Government of Canada's Advertising, 2002/03* (Ottawa: Communication Canada, 2003), 15–17, 26–37.

6. Opinion Research and Constitutional Renewal, 1980–1

1 A good overview of the efforts to change Canada's constitution is P. Russell, *Constitutional Odyssey: Can Canadians Become a Sovereign People?*, 2nd ed. (Toronto: University of Toronto Press, 1993). More narrowly focused sources providing helpful background on constitutional renewal in 1980–1 include R. Romanow, J. Whyte, and H. Leeson, *Canada ... Notwithstanding: The Making of the Constitution, 1976–1982* (Toronto: Carswell/Methuen, 1984); R. Sheppard and M. Valpy, *The National Deal: The Fight for a Canadian Constitution* (Toronto: Fleet, 1982); and E. McWhinney, *Canada and the Constitution, 1979–1982* (Toronto: University of Toronto Press, 1982).
2 Tassé interview; Kirby interview.

3 G. Jennings, memorandum to N. Mendenhall, 'Survey Research Considerations,' 7 October 1982. National Archives of Canada (hereafter cited as NA), RG Ottawa, 137, Acc. 1984–85/574, vol. 9, file Research and Analysis – Surveys & Polling.

4 G. Anderson, memorandum to P. Tellier, 'CBC–Radio-Canada Poll on National Unity,' 11 April 1979, NA, RG 137, Acc. 1984–85/574, vol. 67, file National Unity – Summary.

5 'Extrait de briefing book de mai 1979,' NA, ibid.

6 Some Quebeckers believed Trudeau was promising increased authority for their province. While the prime minister did not technically promise Quebec additional powers, neither did his speech draw attention to his priority of a Charter to protect rights, his rejection of differential treatment of any province, or his disagreement with the proposals for decentralization by the Pépin-Roberts Task Force on National Unity (see Russell, *Constitutional Odyssey*, 109).

7 S. Clarkson and C. McCall, *Trudeau and Our Times*, vol. 1 (Toronto: McClelland and Stewart, 1990), 179. In general, constitutional reform was not a high priority for Canadians. However, most responded favourably in polls when asked about support for the concept of a Charter of Rights.

8 Axworthy interview.

9 Ezrin interview; Gagnier interview; Axworthy interview; Kirby interview.

10 Axworthy interview; P. Russell, 'The Political Purposes of the Canadian Charter,' *Canadian Bar Review* 61, no. 1 (1983).

11 Kirby interview; Clarkson and McCall, *Trudeau and Our Times*, 292.

12 Axworthy interview.

13 See Sheppard and Valpy, *The National Deal*, 67–8.

14 Axworthy interview.

15 Tassé interview.

16 Goldfarb Consultants, 'A Research Report for the Canadian Unity Information Office,' July 1980, 3, 10, 23–4, NA, RG 137, Acc. 1984–85/585, vol. 10, File Canadians' awareness of, involvement with, attitudes towards and expectations for constitutional reform. Some of the results from this study are presented in Appendix 1.

17 Gagnier interview; Lalonde interview.

18 'Results of public and private surveys done between July 1980 and April 1981 pertaining to the following subjects: I. Patriation of the Constitution [and] II. The inclusion of a Charter of Rights and Freedoms in the Constitution,' 20 May 1981, NA, RG 137, Acc. 1984–85/585, vol. 27, file Surveys on the Constitution.

19 'Briefing Note to Cabinet Ministers on the Constitutional Resolution,' 29

September 1981, Appendix D, 2, 4, NA, RG 137, Acc. 1984–85/574, vol. 23, file 200-2-1 pt. 2.

20 *Globe and Mail*, 6 August 1980, B3.

21 Goldfarb Consultants, 'Consumer Response and Reaction to Constitutional Communications – TV Creatives: A Research Report for Ronalds-Reynolds and Company Limited,' August 1980, 2, 3, 9, NA, RG 137, Acc. 1984–85/585, vol. 10, File Consumer Response and Reaction.

22 J. Rose, 'The Advertising of Politics and the Politics of Advertising,' in C. McKie and B.D. Singer, eds., *Communications in Canadian Society*, 5th ed. (Toronto: Thompson, 2001), 157–8.

23 Goldfarb Consultants, 'Consumer Response and Reaction to Constitutional Communications,' 10, 11.

24 Quoted in Sheppard and Valpy, *The National Deal*, 53.

25 Ezrin interview.

26 Kirby Memorandum, 30 August 1980, in L. Cohen, P. Smith, and P. Warwick, *The Vision and the Game: Making the Canadian Constitution* (Calgary: Detselig Enterprises, 1987), 123. The full title of the memorandum is 'Report to Cabinet on Constitutional Discussions, Summer 1980, and the Outlook for the First Ministers Conference and Beyond.'

27 Ibid., 126. The powers package was also referred to as the powers and institutions package.

28 Russell, *Constitutional Odyssey*, 111–12; Sheppard and Valpy, *The National Deal*, 52; and Kirby Memorandum, in Cohen et al., *The Vision and the Game*, 115–16.

29 Appendix 1 illustrates some of these points. The Goldfarb study of July 1980 found support in the 80–86 per cent range for protecting 'basic human rights,' minority language education rights, fiscal equalization, and mobility rights (questions 2–5). Provincial positions were favoured by fewer respondents. Only 36 per cent said their province should have more power (question 8), and when the question offered four choices about the distribution of powers, only 22 per cent favoured giving more powers to the provinces (question 7).

30 Kirby interview.

31 Axworthy interview.

32 The cabinet was aware in the summer of 1980 that a majority of the public did not support unilateral action, according to a comment by Chrétien late that year (*Globe and Mail*, 11 December 1980, 1, 2, and 12 December 1980, 6).

33 McWhinney, *Canada and the Constitution*, 50.

34 Clarkson and McCall, *Trudeau and Our Times*, 296–7.

35 Tassé interview.

36 P. Doering, memorandum to R. Berger, 'Re: Constitutional Print Campaign,' 26 February 1981, NA, RG 137, Acc. 1984–85/585, vol. 36, file Goldfarb 304-1, January and February 1981.

37 Kirby interview.

38 Doering, memorandum to Berger, 'Re: Constitutional Print Campaign.'

39 C. McKinley, memorandum to P. Myles, 'Re-Testing of Constitutional Ad and Charter of Rights and Freedoms,' 30 March 1981, 1, NA, RG 137, Acc. 1984–85/585, vol. 27, file Constitutional Ad Testing (emphasis in original).

40 P. Myles, memorandum to C. McKinley, 'Re Constitutional Ad Testing,' 1 April 1981, ibid.

41 P.M. Myles, Telecopy to C. McKinley, 1 June 1981, ibid. After reporting that a majority of respondents did not know that the proposed Charter would protect rights which were not currently guaranteed, the document indicates the proportion of respondents saying they 'believe it [a specific right] will be specifically protected or guaranteed in the constitution from now on.' Seventy-four per cent correctly said yes to 'fundamental freedoms such as freedom of religion, thought and expression, and freedom of the press'; for other rights, yes responses ranged from 54 to 65 per cent. Intriguingly, however, 55 per cent also said yes to property rights, an item which was *not* in the proposed Charter.

42 C. McKinley, memorandum to H. Ezrin, 'Benchmark Survey for Tracking the Constitutional Print Ad,' 2 June 1981, 2, NA, RG 137, Acc. 1984–85/585, vol. 39, file Research Findings and Surveys.

   The survey question was 'Do you think that this [recently debated federal motion] provides for the protection of basic rights and freedoms which are not now guaranteed or not?' While 55 per cent of the two hundred Toronto respondents said yes, only a plurality did so in St. John's, Halifax, and French-speaking Montreal. A plurality said no in Vancouver, as did a majority in Calgary. Later in the survey, when asked about the protection of specific rights, majorities said the constitutional proposal would protect each of those rights. Myles, Telecopy to McKinley.

43 McKinley, memorandum to Ezrin, 'Benchmark Survey for Tracking the Constitutional Print Ad.'

44 Ezrin interview.

45 The regional advertising strategy is described in 'Constitutional Communications Strategy,' 7 July 1981, NA, RG 137, Acc. 1984–85/585, vol. 25, file Constitutional Communications Plan – 7 July 1981.

46 Gallup Canada, 'A Study of Attitudes Towards the Canadian Constitution,' July 1981, NA, RG 137, Acc. 1984–85/574, vol. 16, file 2520-1, pt. 1-B.

47 *Montreal Gazette*, 21 August 1981, 1.

48 H.E. Ezrin, memorandum to M. Kirby, 'Gallup Survey,' 20 August 1981, 1, 2, NA, RG 137, Acc. 1984–85/574, vol. 16, file 2520-1, pt. 1-B.

49 Kirby interview.

50 Ezrin interview.

51 'Briefing Note to Cabinet Ministers on the Constitutional Resolution,' 29 September 1981, NA, RG 137, Acc. 1984–85/574, vol. 23, file 200-2-1, pt. 2.

52 Lalonde interview.

53 P.E. Trudeau, *Memoirs* (Toronto: McClelland and Stewart, 1993), 318–19; Clarkson and McCall, *Trudeau and Our Times*, 376; and Sheppard and Valpy, *The National Deal*, 278, 286. The exact form of the proposed referendum was not determined.

54 The threat was not made fully public until the appropriate time, when it could be used to the federal government's advantage (Axworthy interview). This is not to say that the specific use and effect of the tactic were anticipated; the well-prepared prime minister cleverly seized the right moment to employ it. Nor was it a purely political tactic for many federal officials: they genuinely believed that faced with a disagreement between the two levels of government, it was appropriate to ask the public to choose between their positions (Kirby interview). A victory for the federal position would have legitimated its package and thereby made its passage in the British Parliament possible without substantial provincial agreement. A referendum could also have been fought on an uncompromising version of the federal package and therefore excluded features such as the notwithstanding clause, which allowed legislatures to 'override' specified Charter rights for five years (Axworthy interview). Indeed, Trudeau himself was reluctant to compromise his government's package and was tempted to follow the referendum route (Trudeau, *Memoirs*, 322).

55 Kirby interview.

56 P. Lougheed, letter to R. Lévesque, 8 March 1982, in *Constitutional Patriation: The Lougheed-Lévesque Correspondence* (Kingston, ON: Institute of Intergovernmental Relations, 1999), 24–5.

57 Peter Russell, quoted in Cohen et al., *The Vision and the Game*, 71.

58 Cohen et al., *The Vision and the Game*, 61, 81.

59 Goldfarb interview.

60 Kirby interview; Ezrin interview.

61 McWhinney, *Canada and the Constitution*, 112, 114.

62 Goldfarb Consultants, 'A Research Report for the Canadian Unity Information Office,' July 1980, 7. These data should be interpreted cautiously, because respondents may be inclined to overstate their interest in order to avoid appearing uninformed and to appear to be good citizens. See also

McKinley, memorandum to Ezrin, 'Benchmark Survey for Tracking the Constitutional Print Ad,' 2 June 1981, 1.

63 See, for example, T.R. Berger, *Fragile Freedoms: Human Rights and Dissent in Canada* (Toronto: Clarke Irwin, 1981), esp. chap. 4.

64 P.M. Sniderman, J.F. Fletcher, P.H. Russell, and P.E. Tetlock, *The Clash of Rights: Liberty, Equality, and Legitimacy in a Pluralist Democracy* (New Haven, CT: Yale University Press, 1996), 169. See also P. Howe and J.F. Fletcher, 'The Evolution of Charter Values,' in Hamish Telford and Harvey Lazar, eds., *Canada: The State of the Federation 2001, Canadian Political Culture(s) in Transition* (Kingston, ON: Institute of Intergovernmental Relations, 2002), esp. 269.

65 The phrase 'commitment to the spirit of the Charter' is used here because most of the questions analysed by sources such as Sniderman et al.'s *The Clash of Rights* do not precisely measure public opinion on specific Charter rights, which is unfortunate for the present purposes. They do, however, provide some evidence about acceptance of the general values underlying the Charter. (The limitations of such sources result from the finite resources available for this type of survey research.)

66 Decima Quarterly, Spring 1990, R2099 and R2128 (Queen's University, Centre for the Study of Democracy Archives). The question asked in Quebec was 'Would you strongly support, support, oppose or strongly oppose the adoption of a French-only law in your community?' In the other provinces, 'English-only' replaced 'French-only.' The questions were asked during a time of national controversy around the issue.

67 I. Urquhart, 'Infertile Soil? Sowing the Charter in Alberta,' in D. Schneiderman and K. Sutherland, eds., *Charting the Consequences: The Impact of Charter Rights on Canadian Law and Politics* (Toronto: University of Toronto Press, 1997), 46–7.

68 Sniderman et al., *The Clash of Rights*, 22, 41, 38.

69 An implication of this point is that the outcome of a national referendum on the people's package was less certain for the federal government than most of the key actors apparently believed at the time. Moreover, referendums often see a shift in public opinion towards the no side as campaigns unfold (see D.B. Magleby, 'Opinion Formation and Opinion Change in Ballot Proposition Campaigns,' in M. Margolis and G.A. Mauser, eds., *Manipulating Public Opinion: Essays on Public Opinion as a Dependent Variable* [Pacific Grove, CA: Brooks/Cole, 1989], 106–8). A fuller appraisal of the state of public opinion might have led the federal government to act somewhat less confidently with respect to the referendum threat.

7. Opinion Research and the Goods and Services Tax

1 This paragraph draws on V.O. Key, *Public Opinion and American Democracy* (New York: Alfred A. Knopf, 1961), 552–3.

2 The proposition that opinion dikes constrain politicians is endorsed in C.W. Roll and A.H. Cantril, *Polls: Their Use and Misuse in Politics* (New York: Basic Books, 1972), 146–7.

3 For background on the development of the GST, see A.M. Maslove, 'The Goods and Services Tax: Lessons from Tax Reform,' in K.A. Graham, ed., *How Ottawa Spends, 1990–91* (Ottawa: Carleton University Press, 1990); R.M. Campbell and L.A. Pal, *The Real Worlds of Canadian Politics*, 2nd ed. (Peterborough, ON: Broadview Press, 1991), chap. 5; and G. Hale, *The Politics of Taxation in Canada* (Peterborough, ON: Broadview Press, 2002), chap. 8.

4 Campbell and Pal, *The Real Worlds of Canadian Politics*, 392–3.

5 See appendices 2.1 and 2.2.

6 Maslove, 'The Goods and Services Tax,' 30.

7 McKinnon interview; Murray interview; Parkins interview; Wilson interview.

8 Maslove, 'The Goods and Services Tax,' 30.

9 Wilson interview; Gorbet interview.

10 Department of Finance, *Tax Reform 1987: The White Paper* (Ottawa: Department of Finance, 1987).

11 Maslove, 'The Goods and Services Tax,' 31.

12 J. Rose, *Making 'Pictures in Our Heads': Government Advertising in Canada* (Westport, CT: Praeger, 2000), 226. Rose cites a statement by Pierre Vincent, the parliamentary secretary to the minister of Finance (House of Commons *Debates*, 15 May 1992, 10795).

13 The total cost of the twenty-one polls conducted from the 1988–9 fiscal year to the 1991–2 fiscal year was $1.53 million. See Pierre Vincent's response to a question from Peter Milliken in House of Commons *Debates*, 15 May 1992, 10795.

14 Confidential interview. 'Buckley's' refers to the cough syrup which was advertised using the slogan 'It tastes awful. But it works.'

15 Breen interview.

16 Blenkarn interview. The early statements of support from Liberal and NDP spokespeople were also noted by another source, and are referred to in a briefing book supplied to cabinet ministers (Department of Finance, 'Briefing Binder, The Goods and Services Tax' [document prepared for cabinet ministers and their staff], n.d. [1990]).

17 Bricker interview.
18 Sabia interview.
19 Interviews with six government sources including Wilson interview;
    Murray interview; Gorbet interview; Sabia interview.
20 See *Toronto Star*, 27 July 1989, A12, and 26 July 1989, A1, A32.
21 Data provided in *Gallup Report*, 1 November 1990.
22 *Calgary Herald*, 25 November 1989, C2.
23 *Report on Business Magazine*, January 2003, 38.
24 *Gallup Report*, 24 October 1990. In late 1990, 74 per cent of respondents
    disapproved of the government's record (*Gallup Report*, 5 November 1990).
25 Blenkarn interview; Sabia interview.
26 Plamondon interview.
27 *Globe and Mail*, 25 July 1987, A8. This comment may overstate the impact of
    the poll and certainly exaggerates Wilson's role, as Mulroney and the
    cabinet also played a part in the decision.
28 Plamondon interview.
29 Sabia interview.
30 Plamondon interview; Blenkarn interview; Gorbet interview.
31 Five interviewees who were heavily involved with the GST spontaneously
    mentioned the difficulties in determining exactly which food would be
    taxed. One of them said excluding groceries 'opened the door to exemp-
    tions, it caused enormous battles [which have] continued to this day about
    what are groceries, what's a basic food? Is a muffin one? Or six muffins?'
32 *Montreal Gazette*, 18 March 1988, B3.
33 *Globe and Mail*, 25 July 1987, A8; and *Winnipeg Free Press*, 25 July 1987, 13.
34 *Globe and Mail*, 11 December 1987, A1, A2, B1.
35 Gorbet interview.
36 Plamondon interview. Plamondon confirmed the quote with Phillips.
37 McKinnon interview; confidential interview.
38 Plamondon interview.
39 Sabia interview.
40 Blenkarn interview; J. Malloy, 'Reconciling Expectations and Reality in
    House of Commons Committees; The Case of the 1989 GST Inquiry,'
    Canadian Public Administration (Fall 1996), 327.
41 C. Goar, *Toronto Star*, 21 December 1989, A25.
42 Blenkarn interview; Plamondon interview.
43 A. Roberts and J. Rose, 'Selling the Goods and Services Tax: Government
    Advertising and Public Discourse in Canada,' *Canadian Journal of Political
    Science* (June 1995), 319, n. 22.
44 *Calgary Herald*, 20 December 1989, A19.

45 See, for example, *Decima Quarterly*, Fall 1989, 118–19.

46 This paragraph draws on Decima Research, 'A Report to the Department of Finance' (Toronto, November 1989).

47 Gorbet interview.

48 Plamondon interview.

49 Bricker interview.

50 *Calgary Herald*, 20 December 1989, A4.

51 Survey conducted for CFIB December 13–21, 1989 (*The Reid Report*, January 1990, 15). Comparisons of Reid's questions are risky as the wording was changed from survey to survey. As well, after several days of hints, the announcement of the change in rate came on 19 December, part way through the survey period. Therefore, *The Reid Report*'s analysis needs treating cautiously. Still, a similar conclusion is drawn by Roberts and Rose, who cite Decima's data (Roberts and Rose, 'Selling the Goods and Services Tax,' 319, n. 22).

52 Segal interview; Bricker interview; Sabia interview.

53 Plamondon interview; confidential interview.

54 Surprisingly, some media at the time treated this as a broken promise; they assumed that most merchants would include the tax in prices. See *Calgary Herald*, 21 June 1989, A8; 22 June 1989, A4, A20; and 23 June 1989, A4. The same assumption is made by Maslove, 'The Goods and Services Tax,' 36. When the tax took effect, of course, visibility became the norm.

55 Interviews with government officials including Wilson interview; Gorbet interview; Sabia interview. If the legal argument is accepted, then it follows that if the federal and provincial governments had been able to agree to a joint sales tax, it would have been possible to have a fixed rule on whether the tax would be included in purchase prices. After Wilson advanced the constitutional argument at the time, two law professors, Katherine Swinton and Wayne Mackay, separately disputed it, arguing that the federal government had the authority to legislate (*Calgary Herald*, 22 June 1989, A20). However, doubts about the quality of the department's legal advice do not demonstrate the role of political motives or undercut the point that Wilson and other department officials trusted their advice and were influenced by it.

56 Three of these sources readily acknowledged the role of political considerations behind other decisions on the GST.

57 e.g., Segal interview.

58 Four interviews including Bricker interview; Gagnier interview. These sources do not necessarily believe the poll results should have been taken at face value.

59 For details of the following questions, see Appendix 2.3.

60 Gorbet interview.

61 Plamondon interview; Gorbet interview; two confidential interviews.

62 *Globe and Mail*, 25 July 1987, A8.

63 Wilson interview; Plamondon interview.

64 *Report on Business Magazine*, December 1989, 76.

65 Wilson interview; Murray interview; Sabia interview.

66 Plamondon interview.

67 Wilson interview.

68 Gorbet interview; Bricker interview, Plamondon interview. See *The Reid Report*, January 1989, 24.

69 Confidential interview. See *Decima Quarterly*, Fall 1989, 117–18.

70 Decima Research, 'A Report to the Department of Finance,' November 1989, 25. See Appendix 2.4.

71 Gorbet interview.

72 Murray interview.

73 H. Winsor, *Globe and Mail*, 21 December 1989, A15; and C. Goar, *Toronto Star*, 11 November 1990, A14.

74 Maslove, 'The Goods and Services Tax,' 37–8, 41.

75 Gorbet interview; Plamondon interview.

76 Plamondon interview.

77 The revenue-neutral claim and a suggestion that the GST might produce additional revenues which could be used in tackling the deficit appears in Department of Finance, 'Briefing Binder, The Goods and Services Tax,' 6.

78 Confidential interview. Lowell Murray also indicates that the argument that the GST would help the government fight the deficit could not be reconciled with the claim of revenue-neutrality.

79 Gorbet interview. Gorbet is a defender of the decision to present the tax as revenue-neutral in its initial stages.

80 Bricker interview; Crapper interview; confidential interview. The columnist Geoffrey Stevens also judged it a political mistake (*Montreal Gazette*, 24 December 1989, B2).

81 Another confidential source who recognizes the problems the decision caused says that it was necessary in view of the earlier decision to split tax reform into two phases. Had the tax changes been brought in together, people might have been willing to accept a revenue-generating sales tax accompanied by personal income tax cuts.

82 Decima Research, 'August 1990 Omnibus Survey.'

83 Roberts and Rose, 'Selling the Goods and Services Tax,' 320–1.

84 *Report on Business Magazine*, December 1989, 79.

85 Plamondon interview.
86 Breen interview; confidential interview.
87 Confidential interview; Decima Research, 'Preliminary Results of the June 1990 Omnibus Survey,' 6. See also *Globe and Mail*, 5 March 1991, A2.
88 This paragraph draws on Breen interview.
89 Decima Research, 'June 1990 Omnibus Survey Results,' 2. Sixty-six per cent either approved or strongly approved of the Senate delaying or rejecting the GST legislation, with 31 per cent disapproving or strongly disapproving. A public Gallup poll indicated that Canadians favoured the Senate obstructing the GST by a margin of sixty-six to twenty-two (*Gallup Report*, 24 May 1990).
90 Plamondon interview.
91 *Toronto Star*, 11 November 1990, A4.

8. Opinion Research and Gun Control

1 Few secondary sources deal with recent developments in Canada's firearms policy. Two of the most useful are L.A. Pal, 'Between the Sights: Gun Control in Canada and the United States,' in D.M. Thomas, ed., *Canada and the United States: Differences that Count*, 2nd ed. (Peterborough, ON: Broadview Press, 2000); and H. Rathjen and C. Montpetit, *December 6: From the Montreal Massacre to Gun Control* (Toronto: McClelland and Stewart, 1999).
2 *The Reid Report*, October 1994, 27; *Calgary Herald*, 12 October 1994, A3; Environics Research Group, 'Canadian Public Attitudes Towards Gun Control: The Environics Survey,' 8 December 1994, 1; and *The Gallup Poll*, 21 November 1994, 2.
3 Some polls, however, indicated that gun control did not enjoy majority support in every region. See *The Angus Reid Report*, May/June 1995, 35. This survey, taken in May 1995, found 64 per cent support for the legislation nationally, but narrow majorities against in the Atlantic and Manitoba/ Saskatchewan regions. In June 1995, Gallup found that the public favoured a national firearms registry by a margin of 64 to 31 per cent; however, in the prairie provinces a slim plurality opposed the plan, 49 to 47 per cent (*The Gallup Poll*, 6 July 1995).
4 Crawford interview; Steckle interview; *Western Report*, 19 December 1994, 29; G. Breitkreuz, 'Media Easily Suckered by Feds on Bills Numbered C-68,' media release, 8 April 1999; and G. Breitkreuz, 'Government Deceiving Canadians about Gun Registration,' media release, 22 September 1998.
5 Rathjen and Montpetit, *December 6*, for example, 97, 99, 108, 155, 157–8.
6 Ibid., 155.

7 *Toronto Star*, 2 December 1994, A16.
8 K. Campbell, *Time and Chance: The Political Memoirs of Canada's First Woman Prime Minister* (Toronto: Doubleday, 1996), 210.
9 Department of Justice, 'Technical Report: Firearm Ownership in Canada' (report of research by Angus Reid Group), March 1991.
10 Campbell, *Time and Chance*, 147.
11 Rathjen and Montpetit, *December 6*, 108; confidential interview.
12 Registration of *handguns* was already required.
13 *The Reid Report*, October 1994, 25. At the time, this perception appears to have been accurate (although not necessarily well informed). According to Statistics Canada, the rate of police-reported violent crime rose every year from 1978 until 1992. The rate dropped fractionally in 1993 and continued to fall until 2000 when it began to rise again. Absolute numbers peaked in 1993. (See Statistics Canada, *Canadian Crime Statistics 1998* [Ottawa: Minister of Industry, 1999], Catalogue no. 85–205–XPE, table 3.1, 16; and Statistics Canada, 'The Daily,' 17 July 2002, http://www.statcan.ca/Daily/English/020717/d020717b.htm.) The public seems to consistently believe crime rates are rising, even when this is contradicted by official data. (See J. Roberts and L. Stalans, *Public Opinion, Crime, and Criminal Justice* [Boulder, CO: Westview Press, 1997], 26–30, 54–5.)
14 The following four paragraphs draw on confidential interviews with civil servants.
15 Liberal Party of Canada, *Creating Opportunity: The Liberal Plan for Canada* (Ottawa, 1993), 84.
16 *The Reid Report*, October 1993, 32.
17 'Public Opinion Poll: Views of *Gun Owners*,' 1993 (document prepared by Angus Reid Group and supplied to the author by the Coalition for Gun Control). Advocates of gun control did not enjoy majority support from gun owners in all polls. For example, Reid's research in the spring of 1995 indicated that a majority of gun owners were opposed to Bill C-68 (*The Angus Reid Report*, May/June 1995, 32).
18 While the question may have inflated support for gun control somewhat, it is also true that Angus Reid, Gallup, Environics and Insight/Pollara consistently reported support for gun control despite some variation in their question design. The wording of this question on gun registration is provided in Appendix 3.1. The significance of question wording is addressed in the next chapter.
19 Rathjen and Montpetit, *December 6*, 145–6.
20 *Western Report*, 19 December 1994, 29.
21 Government of Saskatchewan, 'Poll says Registering More Guns will not

Decrease Crime,' media release, 5 February 1995; 'A Survey of Saskatchewan Residents,' January 1995 (report of survey by Canwest Opinion), 7,
9–10.

22 The wording of the two questions discussed above is indicated in appendix 3.2.

23 *Alberta Report*, 13 February 1995, 21.

24 *Montreal Gazette*, 31 January 1995, B1.

25 *Globe and Mail*, 1 February 1995, A1, A2.

26 The impact of the Justice Committee should not be overstated. Before
the committee finished its deliberations, Rock stated emphatically to its
Liberal members that he would not accept further amendments (Gallaway
interview; Wappel interview).

27 Wappel interview.

28 Gallaway interview.

29 *Maclean's*, 5 June 1995, 14–18.

30 Environics Research Group, 'Air Guns Ownership in Canada,' July 1995,
6–7.

31 Restricting air guns also remains a concern of the National Safety Council
(E.-J. Therien, letter, *Globe and Mail*, 6 January 2000, A18).

32 While some government officials and eye doctors had thought air guns
should be explicitly included in the legislation, only a small proportion of
the most powerful air guns are covered because their specifications qualify
them.

33 Examples include C.E.S. Franks, *The Parliament of Canada* (Toronto: University of Toronto Press, 1987), esp. 99–115; P.G. Thomas, 'Parties in Parliament: The Role of Party Caucuses,' in A.B. Tanguay and A.-G. Gagnon,
eds., *Canadian Parties in Transition*, 2nd ed. (Scarborough, ON: Nelson,
1996); and D.C. Docherty, *Mr Smith Goes to Ottawa: Life in the House of
Commons* (Vancouver: UBC Press, 1997), esp. 143–51.

34 At about the same time several Reform MPs in urban ridings were trying
to reconcile their general opposition to the legislation with their stated
commitment to reflecting their constituents' wishes. For instance, MPs
from Calgary took sharply contrasting approaches. Reform leader Preston
Manning chose not to poll his constituents and was criticized for this by
pro-gun control Liberal MPs (e.g., House of Commons *Debates*, 12 June
1995, 13591 and 13 June 1995, 13743). Stephen Harper commissioned a poll
with a random sample, which indicated that constituents favoured the
policy. He voted with the government on second reading, but a subsequent mail-in survey he initiated with more information for respondents
showed opposition to the policy; on third reading he voted against the

government (House of Commons *Debates*, 12 June 1995, 13631). Jan Brown's phone-in poll indicated opposition to the bill by a three to one margin and she voted against the government. Finally, Jim Silye commissioned a poll with a random sample, and voted in accordance with the support it showed for the policy. Two other Reform MPs, Ted White of North Vancouver and Ian McClelland of Edmonton, joined Silye in voting with the government, also citing constituency surveys (*Calgary Herald*, 14 June 1995, A2).

35 The estimate of thirty Liberal MPs indicating concerns or opposition appears in the *Montreal Gazette*, 14 June 1995, A13.

36 *Simcoe Reformer*, 6 June 1995, 1.

37 Interviews took place with eleven members of the Ontario federal Liberal caucus of 1993–7. This was not a random sample; several of these MPs earned a reputation in Ottawa for being 'independent-minded' and likelier to criticize or vote against their government than most of their caucus colleagues. They include critics of the policy, reluctant supporters, and strong supporters, and they represent different regions of the province.

38 Shepherd interview; Wappel interview.

39 Dromisky interview.

40 Insight Canada Research, 'Public Attitudes Toward Gun Control' (Toronto, April 1995). Second reading of Bill C-68 was on 5 April 1995, and the Insight poll was taken from April 1 to 6. According to Michael Marzolini, a request from an MP led the director of the party organization to request the poll. Rock had previously referred to polling showing support for gun control in a memorandum to members of the Liberal caucus (A. Rock, Memorandum to Liberal MPs and Senators, 'Re: Firearms Control Program,' 6 December 1994, 2, 3) and in a speech to Parliament (House of Commons *Debates*, 16 February 1995, 9711).

41 The Insight poll has limitations. Urban residents consistently show stronger support for gun control than rural citizens. Dividing Ontario into five regions does not isolate the rural areas of the province. The northern region included the Thunder Bay ridings, Sudbury, and Sault Ste. Marie, where the urban population was probably more supportive of gun control than the surrounding rural communities. For evidence of urban-rural differences on this issue, see Insight Canada Research, *Perspectives Canada*, Spring 1995, cross-tabulations, table 60; and *The Angus Reid Report*, May/June 1995, 35.

42 Insight Canada Research, 'Public Attitudes Toward Gun Control,' 4–5.

43 Ibid., 8–10.

44 Kirby interview.

45 Dromisky interview. This purpose was also suggested by two other MPs, Tom Wappel and Peter Milliken. However, neither used the Insight poll in this way.

46 Milliken interview.

47 Shepherd interview.

48 Crawford interview.

49 *Globe and Mail*, 14 June 1995, A7. Eight of these eleven opponents were from Ontario, as were most of the others who had expressed discontent about the policy. David Docherty's account of Bill C-68 incorrectly claims that twelve Liberal MPs voted against it on third reading. (The same paragraph also states that the entire NDP caucus opposed the bill, when in fact BC MP Svend Robinson voted for it, and confuses Reform MPs Ted White and Randy White [Docherty, *Mr Smith Goes to Ottawa*, 165].)

50 Gallaway interview.

51 Calder interview.

52 Steckle interview.

53 Crawford interview; Shepherd interview.

54 Dromisky interview.

55 Hopkins interview.

56 Calder interview; Wappel interview.

57 Bryden interview; Crawford interview; Dromisky interview; Shepherd interview; Steckle interview; Wappel interview.

58 Wappel interview.

59 Steckle interview.

60 Crawford interview.

61 If the results had not been favourable to the government, of course, they might never have been presented to MPs. However, Marzolini says that he would have presented the data even if they brought bad news for the government.

62 *Globe and Mail*, 9 September 1997, A4. The case eventually reached the Supreme Court, where the federal government successfully defended its authority to legislate in 2000.

63 The results were weighted to reflect the actual provincial distribution of population and the proportion of gun owners in the population (estimated at 13 per cent).

64 Angus Reid Group, 'Canadian *Firearms Act* Quantitative Survey, Final Report,' May 1998, 2, 35, 37.

65 Canadian Facts, 'Report: Firearms Legislation' (Toronto, March 1998).

66 The Ontario government later withdrew its commitments.

67 Environics Research Group, 'Focus Canada 1997–3,' data for omnibus questions for Department of Justice, October 1997, 2.

68 Angus Reid Group, 'Canadian *Firearms Act* Quantitative Survey, Final Report,' 25–28, 39–40.
69 This paragraph draws on confidential interviews with civil servants in the Department of Justice.
70 Confidential interview with a civil servant in the Department of Justice.
71 It has been suggested that standardized questionnaires should not ask hypothetical questions because many people cannot predict their own behaviour well (G. Mason, 'Issues in Designing the Standardized Questionnaire,' in A.J. Love, ed., *Evaluation Methods Sourcebook* [Ottawa: Canadian Evaluation Society, 1991], 31).
72 Angus Reid Group, 'Canadian *Firearms Act* Quantitative Survey, Final Report,' 13–14, 16–17.
73 Confidential interviews with civil servants in the Department of Justice.
74 Angus Reid Group, 'Canadian *Firearms Act* Focus Group Findings: Testing of Radio Ad Concepts, Final Report,' June 29, 1998, 5.
75 Confidential interview; Sage Research Corporation, 'Firearms TV Ad Concept Focus Groups, Final Report' (for Canadian Firearms Centre) (Mississauga, 12 November 1999), 6–7.
76 Angus Reid Group, 'Communications: Overview of Findings' (for Canadian Firearms Centre) (July 7, 1999), 2.
77 Focus group participants were also screened in two other ways. One question excluded those with more than a high school education, as a goal of the research was to ensure that the forms would be understood by those with low education levels. Participants in focus groups were also told 'If you require glasses to read, please bring them, as you will be asked to read over some materials during the group.' This was a polite effort to ensure that all members of the groups had basic reading skills (Angus Reid Group, 'Form Testing: Application for a License and Application to Register a Firearm, Final Report – Phase One & Two,' June 1998, 3).
78 Ibid., 5.
79 This position depends, of course, on placing limited or no weight on intensity of opinion in considering the preferences of the population. J.R. Pennock's analysis of this point was discussed in chapter 1.
80 Herle interview.

9. Constraints on the Use of Opinion Research in Government

1 P.E. Converse, 'Changing Conceptions of Public Opinion in the Political Process,' *Public Opinion Quarterly* (Winter 1987), S18.
2 Breen interview.
3 Herle interview.

4 Crapper interview.

5 Berger interview.

6 The following discussion does not address surveys which have non-random samples such as phone-in or Internet polls. However, some of these may be treated more seriously than they deserve; Brehm suggests that in public debates insufficient attention is paid to the sources of polls (J. Brehm, *The Phantom Respondents* [Ann Arbor; University of Michigan Press, 1993], 7).

7 See Brehm, *The Phantom Respondents*, and S. Althaus, *Collective Preferences in Democratic Politics: Opinion Surveys and the Will of the People* (Cambridge: Cambridge University Press, 2003).

8 J. Mueller, 'American Public Opinion and the Gulf War: Some Polling Issues,' *Public Opinion Quarterly* (Spring 1993), 83–5; and D. Rucinski, 'Rush to Judgement? Fast Reaction Polls in the Anita Hill–Clarence Thomas Controversy,' *Public Opinion Quarterly* (Winter 1993), 585–7.

9 See R.S. Morris, 'Grand Jury Testimony,' 18 August 1998, in communication from the Office of the Independent Counsel, Kenneth W. Starr (documents released Oct. 2, 1998), 23–7, http://cnn.com/icreport/report2/suppm/suppm143.gif.

10 Professional Market Research Society, Ottawa Chapter, panel discussion, 'Trends in Qualitative Research,' 25 February 1999, reported in *Ottawa Research News* (Newsletter, PMRS, Ottawa Chapter), Winter/Spring 1999, 10.

11 P. Walsh, memorandum to H.E. Ezrin, 'Summary of Recent Survey Findings,' 11 September 1981 [?; dated 11 September 1980], 2. National Archives of Canada, RG 137, Acc. 1984–85/574, vol. 68, file 25–10–1, pt. 3. On difficulties with translation of questionnaires, see A. Blais and E. Gidengil, 'Things Are Not Always What They Seem: French-English Differences and the Problem of Measurement Equivalence,' *Canadian Journal of Political Science* (September 1993).

12 G.F. Bishop, R.W. Oldendick, A.J. Tuchfarber, and S.E. Bennett, 'Pseudo-Opinions on Public Affairs,' in E. Singer and S. Presser, eds., *Survey Research Methods: A Reader* (Chicago: University of Chicago Press, 1989 [1980]), 428. The one-third figure occurred when no filter question inquiring whether respondents held an opinion was asked; the use of a filter question reduced the proportion of respondents offering opinions on the Public Affairs Act to less than 10 per cent.

13 G.F. Bishop, A.J. Tuchfarber, and R.W. Oldendick, 'Opinions on Fictitious Issues: The Pressure to Answer Survey Questions,' *Public Opinion Quarterly* (Summer 1986), 248.

14 G. Mason, 'Issues in Designing the Standardized Questionnaire,' in

A.J. Love, ed., *Evaluation Methods Sourcebook* (Ottawa: Canadian Evaluation Society, 1991), 33.

15 Robert B. Hill quoted in 'The User's Perspective: A Round Table on the Impact of the Polls,' in A.H. Cantril, ed., *Polling on the Issues* (Cabin John, MD: Seven Locks Press, 1980), 145.

16 G. Mauser, 'Voter Beware,' *Simon Fraser News*, 22 May 1997, 5.

17 *Los Angeles Times*, 20 May 1993, A5, cited by K.T. Gaubatz, 'Intervention and Intransitivity: Public Opinion, Social Choice, and the Use of Military Force Abroad,' *World Politics* (July 1995), 536.

18 For example, S.M. Lipset and W. Schneider, *The Confidence Gap: Business, Labour, and Government in the Public Mind*, rev. ed. (Baltimore: Johns Hopkins University Press, 1977).

19 Examples include C.J. Glynn, S. Herbst, G.J. O'Keefe, and R.Y. Shapiro, *Public Opinion* (Boulder, CO: Westview Press, 1999), 75; and N. Moon, *Opinion Polls* (Manchester: Manchester University Press, 1999), 40–1.

20 McKinnon interview. See E. Gidengil, 'Bringing Politics Back In: Recent Developments in the Study of Public Opinion in Canada,' in J. Everitt and B. O'Neill, eds., *Citizen Politics: Research and Theory in Canadian Political Behaviour* (Toronto: Oxford University Press, 2002), 78.

21 H. Asher, *Polling and the Public: What Every Citizen Should Know* (Washington: CQ Press, 1988), 49.

22 Quoted in *Vancouver Sun*, 3 May 1997, A3.

23 Asher, *Polling and the Public*, 50.

24 H. Perlstadt and R.E. Holmes, 'The Role of Public Opinion Polling in Health Legislation,' *American Journal of Public Health* (May 1987), 613.

25 Quoted in C. Hoy, *Margin of Error: Pollsters and the Manipulation of Canadian Politics* (Toronto: Key Porter, 1989), 185.

26 W.J. Lanouette, 'Polls and Pols – With a Grain of SALT,' in Cantril, ed., *Polling on the Issues*, 101.

27 Baker interview.

28 COMPAS, 'From Research that Matters to Strategies that Work' [brochure], n.d.

29 Quoted by R. Weissberg, *Public Opinion and Popular Government* (Englewood Cliffs, NJ: Prentice-Hall, 1976), 13.

30 Professional Marketing Research Society, Ottawa Chapter, panel, 'A Behind the Headlines Look at Political Polling,' 28 January 1999.

31 See P. Fournier, 'The Uninformed Canadian Voter,' in Everitt and O'Neill, eds., *Citizen Politics*.

32 E. Greenspon and A. Wilson-Smith, *Double Vision: The Inside Story of the Liberals in Power* (Toronto: Doubleday, 1996), 55.

33 Fournier, 'The Uninformed Canadian Voter,' 95, 104. See also H. Milner, *Civic Literacy in Comparative Context: Why Canadians Should Be Concerned* (Montreal: Institute for Research on Public Policy, 2001), 7–11. Analysis suggesting significant levels of misinformation on certain factual matters is provided in E. Gidengil, A. Blais, N. Nevitte, and R. Nadeau, *Citizens*, Canadian Democratic Audit, vol. 3 (Vancouver: UBC Press, 2004), chap. 4.

34 Breen interview; L.R. Jacobs and R.Y. Shapiro, *Politicians Don't Pander: Political Manipulation and the Loss of Democratic Responsiveness* (Chicago: University of Chicago Press, 2000), 301.

35 James Ramsey, quoted in *Maclean's*, 21 September 1992, 18.

36 P.E. Converse, 'The Nature of Belief Systems in Mass Publics,' in D.E. Apter, ed., *Ideology and Discontent* (New York: Free Press, 1964), esp. 238–45.

37 For example, see D.R. Kinder, 'Belief Systems after Converse,' in M.B. MacKuen and G. Rabinowitz, eds., *Electoral Democracy* (Ann Arbor: University of Michigan Press, 2003), 16.

38 P. McCormick, 'Provision for the Recall of Elected Officials: Parameters and Prospects,' in M. Cassidy, ed., *Democratic Rights and Electoral Reform in Canada* (Toronto: Dundurn Press, 1991), 295. McCormick appears to be thinking of support for political parties, but the observation also applies to opinions on policy issues.

39 D.B. Magleby, 'Opinion Formation and Opinion Change in Ballot Proposition Campaigns,' in M. Margolis and G.A. Mauser, eds., *Manipulating Public Opinion: Essays on Public Opinion as a Dependent Variable* (Pacific Grove, CA: Brooks/Cole, 1989), 106–8.

40 *Saturday Night*, December 1985, 37.

41 Leslie interview.

42 R.A. Young, '"Maybe Yes, Maybe No": The Rest of Canada and a Quebec "Oui,"' in D.M. Brown and J.W. Rose, eds., *Canada: The State of the Federation 1995* (Kingston, ON: Institute of Intergovernmental Relations, 1995), 54.

43 *Globe and Mail*, 15 October 1999, A8.

44 See P. Martin and R. Nadeau, 'Understanding Opinion Formation on Quebec Sovereignty,' in Everitt and O'Neill, eds., *Citizen Politics*, esp. 154–5; and G. Gagné and S. Langlois, 'Is Separatism Dead? Not Quite Yet,' *Policy Options* (June 2000).

45 R.A. Young, *The Struggle for Quebec: From Referendum to Referendum* (Montreal: McGill-Queen's University Press, 1999), 16. Another source adds that 'the initially low levels of support for sovereignty [at the start of the referendum campaign] encouraged Prime Minister Jean Chrétien and

other federal government officials to adopt a "strict silence" strategy'
(H.D. Clarke, A. Kornberg, and P. Wearing, *A Polity on the Edge: Canada and
the Politics of Fragmentation* [Peterborough, ON: Broadview Press, 2000],
159). Further statements about Chrétien and other senior federalists confidently anticipating a comfortable victory are found in C. Campbell, *The
U.S. Presidency in Crisis: A Comparative Perspective* (New York: Oxford
University Press, 1998), 173–4; and L. Martin, *Iron Man: the Defiant Reign
of Jean Chrétien* (Toronto: Viking, 2003), 118, 123.

While some polls in 1995 indicated a near-even split between federalists
and sovereigntists, many analysts anticipated that most of the 'discreet'
respondents who gave 'don't know' or 'no answer' responses would vote
against sovereignty when a referendum took place. The preference of
Quebeckers for the federalist option throughout most of 1995 is documented in M. Pinard, 'Les quatre phases du mouvement indépendantiste
québécois,' in R. Bernier, V. Lemieux, and M. Pinard, *Un combat inachevé*
(Sainte-Foy, QC: Presses de l'Université du Québec, 1997), 47; P. Drouilly,
*Indépendance et démocratie: Sondages, élections et référendums au Quebec, 1992–
1997* (Montreal: Harmattan, 1997), 196–9, 227–8; and Clarke et al., *A Polity
on the Edge*, 160, fig. 6.1.

46 For example, Earnscliffe Research and Communications, 'Final Report to
the Department of Finance, Survey Results,' December 1995 (research
conducted 24 November to 2 December 1995; released 9 August 1996).

47 Asher, *Polling and the Public*, 119.

48 Weissberg, *Public Opinion and Popular Government*, 26. Weissberg is presenting data from the Survey Research Center, University of Michigan.
The sample size was 2,278.

49 *Globe and Mail*, 6 May 1980, 7.

50 This paragraph draws on Winsor interview; Greenspon interview; Breen
interview; Herle interview; and three confidential interviews.

51 D. Herle and E. Alboim, memorandum to P. Daniel, 'Second Mandate
Benchmark Study,' 12 September 1997, 5; and Earnscliffe Research and
Communications, 'Second Mandate Benchmark Study,' 12 September
1997.

52 *Globe and Mail*, 13 November 1997, A27.

53 Professional Market Research Society, Ottawa Chapter, panel discussion,
'Trends in Qualitative Research,' 25 February 1999.

54 This discussion draws primarily on interviews with six current and
former pollsters.

55 The Access to Information Act did not have this effect immediately. The
information commissioner and the courts have generally not acted sympa-

thetically towards government officials who have resisted the release of information. However, from time to time, parts of poll reports are kept secret under provisions of the legislation that, for instance, protect cabinet confidences, advice to ministers, or information which could be harmful to federal-provincial relations. Sometimes, therefore, the copies of reports in the public domain have sections blocked out. In practice, officials frequently make reports publicly available without requiring users to make a formal Access to Information request.

56 For example, see R.F. Adie and P.G. Thomas, *Canadian Public Administration*, 2nd ed. (Scarborough, ON: Prentice-Hall, 1987), 548–9; J. Bryden, 'Reforming the Access to Information Act,' *Canadian Parliamentary Review* (Summer 2001), 5–7; A. Roberts, 'Access: Assessing the Health of Canada's Freedom of Information Laws' (Kingston, ON: School of Policy Studies, Queen's University, 1998); K. Rubin, 'The Pathetic State of Canada's Access to Information Act,' *Hill Times*, 6 July 1998, 6; and J. Reid, 'Transparency, Accountability and Access to Information,' in G. Gibson, ed., *Fixing Canadian Democracy* (Vancouver: Fraser Institute, 2003).

57 Access to Information law has similarly affected other types of information, besides opinion research.

58 Lowell Murray explains, 'We felt that some of the questions we asked would be either resented by premiers or by provinces, or misunderstood, or possibly that it might weaken in some other way our negotiating position. So we resisted the release for quite a while.' Eventually an understanding was reached with the information commissioner that only less recent opinion research from the Meech Lake Accord period would be made public, while research for the Charlottetown Accord period did not have to be released at that time. It is clearer now than in the early 1990s that the government has a limited ability to withhold polling reports, so in this respect research may be more constrained now than in the past.

59 Marzolini interview.

60 Confidential interviews with one current and one former public servant.

61 For example, Laschinger interview; Leebosh interview.

62 The screening questions are included in 'Survey of National Attitudes' (exhibit provided by the witness), Appendix to R.S. Morris, 'Grand Jury Testimony,' 18 August 1998, in communication from the Office of the Independent Counsel, Kenneth W. Starr, 1, http://cnn.com/icreport/report2/suppm/suppm143.gif.

63 D.J. Robinson, *The Measure of Democracy* (Toronto: University of Toronto Press, 1999), 7.

64 Ekos Research Associates, in association with Anderson Strategic Re-

search, 'Final Report: National Opinion Study on Changes to Immigration Policy' (Ottawa: Ekos Research Associates, 21 February 1992).

65 W.T. Stanbury, *Business-Government Relations in Canada: Influencing Public Policy*, 2nd ed. (Scarborough, ON: Nelson, 1993), 310, citing C. Winn in *The Lobby Digest*, January 1991, 1, 9, 10.

66 COMPAS, 'From Research that Matters to Strategies That Work.'

67 Dasko interview; Herle interview. In 2002–3, slightly under half of government opinion research projects dealt with the general population while the others were focused on client groups, civil servants or opinion leaders (Communication Canada, *Public Opinion Research in the Government of Canada, Annual Report 2002–2003*, 22).

68 Mark McCarvill analysed Earnscliffe's polling to compare the views of involved and uninvolved Canadians. He confirmed the existence of demographic differences between the groups, reporting significant differences in their opinions on budget policy. The differences were smaller than he anticipated, however. (M. McCarvill, 'Public Opinion and Federal Budget Policy in Canada, 1995–2001,' MA thesis, Carleton University, 2003, esp. 85–6.)

69 Confidential interview with a civil servant in Finance.

70 Earnscliffe Research and Communications, memorandum to P. Daniels, 'Budget Mail Outs and Phone Survey,' 29 April 1997 (survey of 'Involved Canadians' conducted in February-March 1997).

71 Two confidential interviews with Finance officials. Officials already believed that the involved Canadians read community newspapers heavily.

10. Conclusion

1 Crapper interview.

2 Kirby interview.

3 Segal interview. See G.B. Doern and R.W. Phidd, *Canadian Public Policy: Ideas, Structure, Process*, 2nd ed. (Scarborough, ON: Nelson, 1992), 226.

4 Crapper interview.

5 Breen interview.

6 Kiar interview.

7 Hershell Ezrin expresses this view.

8 See B.I. Page and R.Y. Shapiro, 'Educating and Manipulating the Public,' in M. Margolis and G.A. Mauser, *Manipulating Public Opinion: Essays on Public Opinion as a Dependent Variable* (Pacific Grove, CA: Brooks/Cole, 1989), 307–8, 319.

Index

Abortion rights, 15, 163
Access to Information: effects of
  legislation, 29, 35, 43, 174–7,
  246n55, 247nn57–8; oral reporting
  because of, 51, 174–6; use to obtain
  information about opinion research, 35–6
Accountability of government, 58
Active public opinion, 15–16, 67,
  195; on the constitution, 90; on the
  Goods and Services Tax, 105, 113;
  on gun control, 132, 133, 135,
  139–40, 157
Adams, Michael, 12, 39
Advertising, 5, 30, 33, 68, 227n24;
  and constitutional proposals, 84–
  7, 88–9, 91–4; and federal government communications, 5, 68, 70,
  71–2, 76, 77–9; and the Goods and
  Services Tax, 123–5; and gun
  control, 152–3; in U.S., 28
Agenda-setting, 40, 41 43, 55, 56–9,
  65, 184, 225n6; on gun control,
  134–5
Air Canada, 37
Air guns, 139–41
Alberta government, 137–8

Anderson, Bruce, 109
Angus, Iain, 3
Angus Reid Group, 36, 38, 59;
  opinion research on the Goods
  and Services Tax, 107, 117, 118–19;
  opinion research on gun control,
  131, 133, 136, 146–7, 148–52. See
  also Bricker, Darrell; Colledge,
  Mike; Ipsos-Reid; Reid, Angus
Armstrong, Jane, 53–4, 60
Asher, Herbert, 165, 170
Axworthy, Lloyd, 75
Axworthy, Thomas, 83, 85, 97, 98, 99

Baker, Chris, 39, 44, 48, 62, 71, 212n9
Behind the Oval Office, 24–7, 28
Bennett, Bill, 96
Bernard, Pierre, 95
Bernstein, Robert A., 19
Bias in polling, 37–9, 94–5, 159,
  160–6
Bill C-68. See Gun control
Blakeney, Allan, 98
Blenkarn, Don, 108, 114, 120
Bloc Québécois, 138
Bourque, Christian, 167
Breen, Gary, 59, 126, 173

Brehm, John, 11
Breitkreuz, Gary, 156
Bricker, Darrell, 53, 62, 66, 109, 172
Brooks, Joel E., 19, 21, 23, 185
Buckner, Taylor, 136–7
Budget issues, 71
Bulloch, John, 108, 113
Burstein, Paul, 20–1
Business people, opinion research on, 125–6, 179

Campbell, Colin, 31–2
Campbell government, 32
Campbell, Kim, 42, 133
Canada Pension Plan, 68
Canadian Drug Manufacturers Association, 38
Canadian Facts, 48
Canadian Federation of Independent Business,108, 109, 235n51
Canadian Heritage, Department of, 46
Canadian Information Office, 58, 223n35
Canadian Unity Information Office, 80–1, 84, 85, 93–4, 95
CanWest Opinion, 137
Case studies, 6, 185–7. See also Constitutional proposals; Goods and Services Tax; Gun control
Cassidy, Michael, 112
Charlottetown Accord, 7, 72, 247n58
Charter of Rights and Freedoms, 6, 82–4, 90, 96–9, 100–3. See also Constitutional proposals
Chrétien government, 6, 36, 45, 51, 70, 170, 177, 245n45. See also Gun control
Chrétien, Jean, 36, 50, 80–1, 134, 177, 224n54, 229n32

Citizen engagement, 5, 54
Civil servants. See Public servants and polling
Clark, Joe, 80, 109
Climate change, 73
Clinton, Bill, 5, 24–9, 55, 56, 162, 178; policy issues, 24–6, 55; pollsters as advisers, 24–9, 55
Coalition for Gun Control, 132, 135, 136, 140
Colledge, Mike, 39, 149, 154
Communication Canada, 44, 223n35
Communications, government, 5, 13–14, 34, 47–9, 56, 66–79, 184, 187–94; advertising and policy promotion, 5, 14, 27–8, 30, 33, 68; and assessment of public reactions, 68, 74–8; on constitutional issues, 84–7, 91–4, 100–3; 'feedback loop,' 13–14; on the Goods and Services Tax, 33, 122, 123–5; on gun control issues, 151–5; polling and public relations, 29, 66–7; target audiences, 69–70; tone and language, 71–4; during World War II, 30
Communications, in U.S. politics, 27–9
COMPAS, 36, 40, 166, 172, 179
Conservative party. See Progressive Conservative party
Constitutional proposals (1980–1), 6–7, 80–103, 162, 197–9; active opinion, 90; advertising, 84–7, 91–4; Canadian Unity Information Office, 80–1, 84, 85, 93–4, 95; Charter of Rights and Freedoms, 6, 82, 84, 90, 96–9, 100–3; communications about, 84–7, 91–4, 95, 100–1, 102; People's Package, 87–9, 100; provincial polling, 94–5. See

also Charlottetown Accord; Meech Lake Accord

Contracting process for opinion research, 44–7, 223n39; allocation of contracts to firms, 36; client-firm interaction, 47–51; costs of, 44, 46; patronage, 44, 45–6; sole-sourcing, 44, 45, 46; standing offers, 45; use by different departments, 46–7

Converse, Philip, 159, 168, 169

Conway, Jerry, 171

Copps, Sheila, 7

Costs of government polling: in Canada, 3–4, 35–6, 40, 46, 233n13; in the U.S., 24

Côté, Marcel, 129

Counterfeit consensus model, 19–20, 23, 185

Crafted talk, 28, 29. *See also* Communications

Crapper, David, 43, 49

Crespi, Irving, 5

Crime, public opinion on, 134, 238n13. *See also* Gun control

Criticism of government uses of opinion research, 12–13

Crossley, Archibald, 10

Dasko, Donna, 41

Davey, Keith, 32, 62

Decima Research, 36, 37, 38, 43, 49, 59, 63; opinion research on budget, 71; opinion research on free trade, 70, 188–9, opinion research on Goods and Services Tax, 107–9, 111–13, 114–16, 118–19, 123–6. *See also* MacKinnon, Ian

Deficit, 167, 172

Deliberative polling, 54, 173

Demands and support, 13, 14

Democratic frustration model, 19–20, 185

Democratic linkage model, 19–20, 185, 191–4

Democratic potential of polling, 4, 10–16, 19–20, 31, 60, 100–1, 103, 178–9, 182, 185, 191–6, 211n4

Dingwall, David, 35, 67

Dixon, John, 133

Dodge, David, 109

Drews, Ronald C., 32

Dyck, Rand, 11

Earnscliffe Strategy Group, 36, 46, 47, 172, 179–82, 248n68

Easton, David, 13–14, 185

Economic issues, 61–2, 73. *See also* Free Trade Agreement; Goods and Services Tax

Eisinger, Robert M., 29

Ekos Research Associates, 36–7, 58, 60, 64, 169, 172

Election campaigns, 7, 12, 20, 41–2, 190–1; national (1980), 82; national (1993), 7, 42, 129; national (2000), 222n28; Ontario (1995), 42

Employment issues, 59, 62. *See also* Unemployment Insurance

Environics Research Group, 36, 38; opinion research on the Goods and Services Tax, 118–19; opinion research on gun control, 131, 137, 139–40, 148, 150

Environment, Department of, 58, 72–3

Environmental issues, 37, 58, 62, 72–3

Environmental scanning, 40, 41

Equality of respondents in polling, 15, 177–8, 182, 191–2

Erikson, Robert, 14

Evaluation: communications, 77–8; on constitutional proposals, 91–2; on the Goods and Services Tax, 124, 125

Evaluation, policy and program, 34, 55, 64–5

Evans, Brian, 137

Evans, Gary, 30

Ezrin, Hershell, 85, 87, 95

Feedback loop, 13–14

Finance, Department of, 36, 45, 46–7, 76, 172, 180–1. *See also* Fiscal dividend; Goods and Services Tax; Wilson, Michael

Fiscal dividend, 40, 172, 224n56

Fishkin, James, 54, 173

Focus groups, 5, 16–18, 63–4, 68, 173–9; and communications, 72, 76; and constitutional proposals, 85–7, 91–2; and the Goods and Services Tax, 77, 124–5, 126; and gun control, 152–4; and health care, 171; limitations of, 17, 173–4

Fournier, Patrick, 167

Free Trade Agreement, 70, 106, 188–9, 194

Fulford, Robert, 168

Gallup and Rae theory, 4, 10, 15–16, 25, 31, 35, 43, 60, 100–1, 177–9, 182, 191–3, 196. *See also* Democratic potential of polling; Gallup, George

Gallup (firm), 21; Canada, 11, 30, 94–5, 109, 131; U.S., 12

Gallup, George, 10, 12, 15–16, 43. *See also* Gallup and Rae theory

Gaudet, Kevin, 45–6

Gay and lesbian rights, 42, 102

Geer, John, 11

Gibbins, Roger, 32, 156

Ginsberg, Benjamin, 11, 13, 16, 191

Goldfarb Consultants, 32–3, 36, 37, 171; opinion research related to constitutional proposals, 84, 85–6, 91, 92, 101, 197–9

Goldfarb, Martin, 11, 12, 32, 45, 50, 81–2

Goods and Services Tax, 6, 7, 33, 35, 77, 104–27, 192, 200–3; active opinion, 105, 113; communications, 77, 122, 123–5, 127, 129–30; and groceries, 106, 112–13, 234n31; implementation, 125–6; income tax credit, 106, 120; rate, 113–17; revenue-neutrality, 106–7, 121–3; timing, 106, 110–11, 235n55; visibility, 106, 117–20, 235n54–5

Gorbet, Fred, 110

Government-commissioned polls, 6, 34–7, 44–50

Graves, Frank, 32, 169, 172. *See also* Ekos Research Associates

Greenberg, Stan, 5, 24

Greene, Ian, 11

Gregg, Allan, 43

Grierson, John, 30

Gun control, 6, 7, 131–58, 178, 204–6; active opinion, 132, 133, 135, 139, 140, 157; advertising, 152–3; agenda-setting, 134–5; air guns, 139–41; Coalition for Gun Control, 132, 135, 136, 140; communication, 67, 151–5, 157; compliance, 148–50; federal position, 134–5; focus groups, 152–4; implementation, 7, 147–51, 153, 157; members of Parliament, 141–6; measuring public support, 131–2, 136–7, 146–7, 148; Montreal massacre, 132–3, 134; passive opinion, 131, 132; policy modification, 138–9; provincial polls, 137–8, 205–6; public's fear of crime, 134, 238n13; registration and licensing, 134, 151–4

Guy, Don, 42, 57, 60, 72–3

Hartley, Thomas, 22
Hartt, Stanley, 121
Health, Department of, 46, 51, 63, 69
Health policy: in Canada, 32; in Ontario, 78, 171, 227n24; in the U.S., 27, 28. See also Health, Department of; Tobacco issues
Heith, Diane, 29
Herle, David, 46, 172, 179, 181. See also Earnscliffe Strategy Group
Home insulation, 63
Hoy, Claire, 11
Human Resources Development Canada, Department of, 46, 47, 51, 59, 72
Human Rights Act, 42

Ickes, Harold, 25
Implementation of policy, 63–4; Goods and Services Tax, 125–6; gun control, 7, 147–51, 153, 157
Industry, Department of, 46, 73–4. See also International Trade and Industry
Insight Canada Research (now Pollara), 36, 42, 72–3, 143–6
Interest groups, opinion research for, 37–9. See also Canadian Federation of Independent Business; Coalition for Gun Control

International Trade and Industry, Department of, 73. See also Free Trade Agreement; Industry, Department of
Internet polling, 223n40
Interpretation of data, 20, 50, 170–2; GST 118–19; gun control, 148–51
Involved Canadians (opinion leaders), 179–82, 248n68
Ipsos-Reid, 37, 64. See also Angus Reid Group; Bricker, Darrell; Reid, Angus

Jacobs, Lawrence R., 27–9
Johnson, William, 112
Johnston, Richard, 13–14
Justice, Department of, 134–5, 148, 150, 152, 154–5, 162. See also Constitutional proposals; Gun control
Justification of policy, role of opinion research in, 58–9, 67, 160–1

Key, V.O., 14, 104. See also Opinion dikes
Kiar, Stephen, 40, 47, 212n9
King, William Lyon Mackenzie, 30
Kingdon, John W., 218n26
Kirby Memorandum, 87–8
Kirby, Michael, 47, 50, 60, 63–4, 66, 145; and constitutional proposals, 81, 83, 87–9, 93, 96, 98, 186
Kyoto Protocol, 37

Lachapelle, Guy, 32
Language and bilingual requirements of research, 162
Language and content of communications, 8, 68, 71–4, 76–7
Lanouette, William, 165

Lanphier, C. Michael, 31
Lapointe, Kirk, 35
Laschinger, John, 41, 70
Leading questions, 38, 160. *See also* Bias in polling; Question wording and design
Leebosh, Derek, 132
Lévesque, René, 97–8
Lewis, Robert, 11
Liberal Party of Canada, 7, 36, 42, 82–3, 142–6, 222n28
Longwoods Research Group, 77
Lougheed, Peter, 98
Luntz, Frank, 5

Mail surveys, 180
Manufacturers' Sales Tax, 7, 105–6, 107, 121, 124, 130. *See also* Goods and Services Tax
Map, polling as a, 53–4, 62
Margin of error, 17, 161, 215n34
Market research, 55, 66
Martin, Paul, 35, 36, 46, 47, 76–7, 172
Marzolini, Michael, 42, 143, 145, 166, 240n40, 241n61
Maslove, Allan M., 106
Mass media, 15, 37, 39–40, 90, 181
Mauser, Gary, 163
McCarvill, Mark, 248n68
McCormick, Peter, 168
McKinnon, Ian, 15, 38, 48, 49, 53–4, 56–7, 59, 60–1, 164, 165
McLellan, Anne, 146–7, 151
McWhinney, Edward, 99
Media reports of polls, 37, 39–40
Media-sponsored polls, 39–40, 41, 43
Meech Lake Accord, 7, 178, 247n58
Members of Parliament and public opinion, 32, 42, 81–2; on gun control, 141–6

Methodology of opinion research, 16–18, 38–9, 41, 159–74, 176, 177–83; analysis and interpretation of research, 170–2; bias, 37–9, 161, 163–6; focus groups, 17–18, 173–4; leading questions, 38, 160; margin of error, 17, 161, 215n34; pseudo-opinions, 162–3, 168; questionnaire wording and design, 16, 18, 38, 94–5, 101, 118–19, 131–2, 160–6, 172, 235n51; question order and context, 164–6; sampling, 17, 161, 177–82, 191–2; subjectivity, 170, 173–4; trustworthiness of opinion research, 161, 162, 165–6, 173–4. *See also* Political knowledge
Military spending, U.S., 22
Miller, Warren E., 216n8
Mills, Dennis, 142
Mitchell, Andy, 141
Mitchell, Bob, 137
Monroe, Alan D., 21
Montreal massacre, 132–3, 134
Morin, Claude, 94
Moroz, Helen, 35
Morris, Dick, 24–7, 28, 56, 162, 178; advice on communications, 26; advice on Monica Lewinsky affair, 27, 178; advice on policy, 25–6, 28, 55, 56; advice on strategy, 26, 55
Mulroney, Brian, 50, 121, 224n54
Mulroney government, 3, 6, 35, 36, 43, 105, 132–3, 160–1, 176, 178, 192, 247n58. *See also* Goods and Services Tax
Murray, Lowell, 160–1, 247n58

National Firearms Association, 132
New Democratic Party, 32, 42, 96

New Zealand, sales tax, 110, 129
Newport, Frank, 12
North American Free Trade Agreement, 78
Nowlan, Patrick, 108

Ontario government: economic issues, 61–2; health issues, 78, 171, 227n24; seat belt legislation, 75–6; Ontario Waste Management Corporation, 62
Opinion dikes, 14, 104–5, 127, 128–9, 187
Opinion instability, 159, 168–70
Opinion leaders (involved Canadians), 179–82, 248n68
Opinion-policy relationship, 19–24, 185, 216n8, 217n18
Oral reporting of poll results, 35, 51, 174–6

Page, Benjamin, 21, 217n18
Parti Québécois, 32, 80, 81
Parties' uses of polls: analysis of polls, 41; platforms, 41–2; policy influence, 41, 43; surveys for, 41–4; on gun control, 143–6. *See also* Party-sponsored opinion research
Partisanship in government polling, 222n28
Party caucuses, uses of polls, 42, 143–6
Party discipline, 29, 141
Party platforms, 41–2, 134–5
Party-sponsored opinion research, 37, 40–4, 127, 133, 143–6, 156, 177
Passive public opinion, 15, 16, 18, 131, 155
Patriation of the constitution, 6–7,
80. *See also* Constitutional proposals
Patronage, 45–6
Peacekeeping (Haiti), 61
People's Package (constitutional proposal), 87–9, 97, 99, 100
Penn, Mark, 24
Pennock, J. Roland, 16
Persian Gulf War, 3
Pétry, François, 22
Phillips, Bruce, 112
Pinard, Maurice, 94–5
Policy-making, 3–4, 10–14, 19–33, 34, 48–50, 53–5, 57, 59–65; feedback loop, 13–14. *See also* Constitutional proposals; Goods and Services Tax; Gun control
Policy modification, 8, 60–3; and gun control, 138–9
Policy process, and opinion research, 19–33, 53–64
Political knowledge and awareness, 15, 70–1, 78, 167–8, 188–9, 245n33; on the 1993 budget, 71; on the constitution, 92–3, 101, 230nn41–2; on the Goods and Services Tax, 124; on gun control, 132, 151–2
Political sophistication, 167–8
Political tolerance, 102–3
Politicians Don't Pander, 27–9
Pollara, 37, 42. *See also* Insight Canada Research
Polling, democratic potential of, 4, 10–14, 15–16, 19–20, 31, 60, 100–1, 103, 177–8, 182, 185, 193–6
Polling, history of government, 10, 30
Polling, presidential, 24–9
Polls, types, 16–17

Polls, unscientific, 141–2, 243n6

Polls, uses of, 10, 18; evaluation, 57, 64–5; for implementation, 57, 63–4; to legitimize policy, 14; on policy alternatives, 57, 59–60; as 'road maps,' 53, 62; strategic planning, 53, 56–8

Pollsters as advisers, 45, 50–1, 60–1, 160, 175, 225n12; U.S., 24–9

Populism, 12

Prime Minister's Office, 35, 37, 42, 81, 83, 109

Privy Council Office, 35, 44, 54, 81, 109

Professional Market Research Society, 173–4

Progressive Conservative party: federal, 7, 32, 42, 80, 90, 121, 127, 129 ; Ontario, 42

Propaganda, during World War II, 30

Provincial polling: and constitutional reform 94–5, 98; and gun control, 137–8, 205–6

Public opinion, definitions, 15–16, 104, 214n25

Public opinion research, 13–14, 15–16, 70–1, 74–6, 78, 139, 169–70; federal government definition of, 34–5; influence of, 5, 13, 20; opinion leaders, 179–82; opinion stability, 159, 168–70, 232n69; pseudo-opinions, 162–3; quantity of, 4, 35–6; scope of, 35, 248n67; uses of, 53–64; weakly held opinions, 168–9. See also Costs of government polling; Government-commissioned polls

Public Opinion Research Directorate, 44–5

Public relations: compared with

pollsters' work, 66–7; use of polls, 66–7, 151

Public servants and polling, 31–2, 39–40, 47–50; and communications, 53–64

Public support measurement: and constitutional proposals, 82, 84; and Goods and Services Tax, 105, 108–9; and gun control, 146–7, 148

Pulse of Democracy, 10, 191

Qualitative research, 17–18, 65, 67, 76, 79, 171, 173–4. See also Focus groups

Qube, 12, 213n18

Quebec, 70, 169, 228n6. See also Parti Québécois; Referendum, Quebec (1980); Referendum, Quebec (1995); Sovereignty, Quebec

Question order, 164–5

Questionnaire wording and design, 16, 38–9, 94–5, 101, 118–19, 131–2, 160–6, 172, 235n51

Quilliam, Stephen, 12

Rae, Bob, 42, 86

Rae, Saul, 10, 43, 60. See also Gallup and Rae theory

Ramsey, James, 78

Rathjen, Heidi, 132

Red Book, 42, 134–5

Referendum, proposal for tie-breaking, 96–9, 100, 231n54, 232n69

Referendums, 100–1, 168; Canada (1992), 7, 72; Quebec (1980), 81–2, 98, 228n6; Quebec (1995), 169–70, 245n45. See also Sampling referendum

Reform Party, 7, 35–6, 45, 46, 239n34

Regional variation in public opinion, 131, 237n3; on the constitution, 92, 93–4

Reich, Robert, 25, 26

Reid, Angus, 38, 49, 50, 58, 72, 75, 193–4. *See also* Angus Reid Group; Syndicated polling reports

Reliability of polls, 159, 161, 162, 165

Representation, 12, 15, 16, 31, 32, 161

Republican Party, 27–8

Responsiveness of government to public, 4, 10, 16, 19, 23, 49, 195; U.S., 25, 28

Revenue Canada, Department of, 46, 125

Roberts, Alasdair, 33, 114

Robinson, Daniel, 30, 178, 192

Rock, Allan, 58, 134, 135, 137, 240n40

Rogers, Will, 167

Rose, Jonathan, 33, 114

Russell, Peter, 31

Russett, Bruce, 22

Sabato, Larry, 12

Sage Research Corporation, 68

Salience of issues, 8, 25

Sampling, 17, 69, 161, 177–82, 191–2; challenges in, 161; selective, 17, 69, 177–82

Sampling referendum, 10, 16, 104, 177–8, 185. *See also* Gallup and Rae theory

Saskatchewan government, 137

Schindeler, Fred, 31

Schoen, Doug, 24

Seat belt legislation, 75–6, 148

Segal, Hugh, 37–8, 57–8, 61–2, 69–70, 75–6, 167–8

Shapiro, Robert, 21, 27–9, 217n18

Siegel, Arthur, 11

Simpson, Jeffrey, 11, 12

Soroka, Stuart, 23, 225n6

Sovereignty, Canadian, 163

Sovereignty, Quebec, 7, 33, 81–2, 169–70, 245n45. See also Referendum, Quebec (1980); Referendum, Quebec (1995)

Speller, Bob, 141

Stephanopoulos, George, 25, 28

Stokes, David E., 216n8

Strategic Counsel, 53, 54, 62, 78

Stresses on political system, 13, 185

Subgroups, use of in opinion research, 31, 69–70, 146, 153–4, 170, 178–9, 192, 248n67

Subjectivity in opinion research, 170, 173–4

Sullivan, Andrew, 37, 60, 61, 69. *See also* Ekos Research Associates

Sullivan, Michael, 53, 54, 62, 78

Supreme Court of Canada, 91, 95–6

Syndicated polling reports, 40–1, 65

Szablowski, George J., 31–2

Target audiences, determining, 41, 68, 69–70

Tassé, Roger, 85, 90

Taxation, 60, 167, 170, 172; U.S., 26. *See also* Goods and Services Tax

Technology Partnerships Canada, 73–4

Timing of policy, Goods and Services Tax, 106, 110–11, 235n55

Tobacco issues, 63, 67, 69, 78, 165

Towle, Michael, 29

Trade-offs in policy-making, 53, 115, 169, 170

Translation of poll questions, 162

Treasury Board, 54

Triangulation, 26, 28

Trudeau government, 6, 11, 32, 36, 43. *See also* Charter of Rights and Freedoms; Constitutional proposals
Trudeau, Pierre Elliott, 11–12; and constitutional proposals, 81–3, 89, 90, 96, 97–9, 100, 231n54

Unemployment insurance, 75. *See also* Employment issues
United States, government opinion research compared with Canada, 29
Urban-rural differences, 240n41

Values issues, 26
Veterans Affairs, Department of, 46
Visibility of the Goods and Services Tax, 117–20

Waddell, Christopher, 111
Wappel, Tom, 141–2
Weakly held opinions, 168–9
Weissberg, Robert, 171
White paper on tax reform, 106, 110, 113, 117, 120, 121
Wilson, John, 165
Wilson, Michael, 73, 106, 107, 108, 109, 111, 112, 116, 121, 123, 130, 167. *See also* Goods and Services Tax
Winsor, Hugh, 38, 39, 40, 175
Wlezien, Christopher, 22, 23
World War II, 30

Young, Robert A., 169
Youth unemployment, 59